PRESBY-
TERIAN
CHURCH AT SOUTH
ORANGE
New Jersey
Messrs Rossiter & Wright
Architects
New York.

View showing
PULPIT and
CHOIR GALLERY

EHRICK K. ROSSITER

Designs for Modern Living
1880-1930

Ann Y. Smith

Publisher	Garnet Hill Publishing Company
	www.GarnetHillPublishing.com
Designer	KatArt Graphics, New Milford, Connecticut
Editor	Susan H. Arensberg
Printer	Printed in China by Everbest Printing Co. Ltd. through Four Colour Print Group, Louisville, Kentucky.
ISBN	0-9647769-7-9
	978-0-9647769-7-9

Front cover: Ehrick Rossiter, The Senator Orville Platt House, Washington, Connecticut, 1898.

Back cover: Ehrick Rossiter, The Gunn Memorial Library, Washington, Connecticut, 1908.

Endpapers, front: Rossiter & Wright, Presbyterian Church at South Orange, New Jersey, *American Architect and Building News,* August 5, 1882. Author's collection.

Endpapers, back: Rossiter & Wright, home for Robbins Battell Stoeckel, Norfolk, Connecticut, 1907. Collection of the Norfolk Historical Society.

TABLE OF CONTENTS

FOREWORD

A descendant of the architect told me the drawings had been burned. Deliberately. In the latter part of the twentieth century, legal liability was a looming issue, she explained, one of the anxieties of modern life. For their descendants, the challenges faced by the architects of the late nineteenth century were certainly daunting: the architects had developed then-experimental systems for the structural support of expansive buildings and new and risky systems for powering light and heat in these buildings; in addition, there was a new awareness that faulty ventilation and water systems could transmit disease. The task at hand demanded a masterful response, incorporating new scientific and design standards as an architectural practice found its footing.

For whatever reason, the drawings and office records of the architectural firm Rossiter & Wright and its successor Rossiter & Muller are missing. A stray drawing turns up at in a client's files; the grandson of a partner finds a drawing in his New Jersey attic and sends it to the distant library that commissioned the building; an historically minded granddaughter gathers a file of miscellaneous correspondence and sends it to the Smithsonian; a reprint from an early magazine shows up on eBay. For the most part, however, the drawings and the official records of the practice have vanished.

Nevertheless, a record of the work of Ehrick Rossiter and his partners has survived, even while the drawings and office files have not. Fortunately, the activities of the partners were recorded in contemporary publications and contemporary photographs as the buildings they created attracted the notice of critics and neighbors.

This account was assembled by a careful reading of those contemporary periodicals and early photographs. It would not have been possible to gather this narrative from the fragments of magazine notices, surviving drawings, and local photographs without the diligent sleuthing of fellow travelers, in particular Hugh Goodman, Mary Jo Kenny, Ann Havemeyer and David Kensett Rossiter. The many others who have added valuable insight to the story are listed in the Acknowledgments at the end of this book.

Without the continuing support of my husband, a careful historical writer of award-winning books on motor racing, this work would not have been completed. Joel Finn has been the champion of this project for more than 15 years, traveling to architectural outposts with me and insisting on the highest standards for storytelling and production. I am deeply grateful for his support.

Dating a property can be tricky. Dates might be assigned in a variety of ways—the date a design was published, the date the real estate was purchased or the mortgage taken out, the date on the architect's drawings, the date of the groundbreaking, or the date construction was completed. I have tried to indicate the source of the dates I have used, if I could do so without encumbering the narrative. Otherwise, the reader is reminded that an architectural project is not produced in a single year but evolves over time as it is designed and built and is best understood as a part of an ongoing process.

Hoping for the patience of the general reader, I have included the names of many clients drawn from contemporary publications for the benefit of local historians and preservationists researching the many towns where the architects worked. Although it wasn't necessary, or practical, to research the local records for each of these hundreds of projects, readers interested in the buildings may find that the client names here will help them construct a richer account of town histories by identifying these locally relevant projects through city directories, land records, and local histories.

Logically enough, the book begins with an overview of Rossiter's youthful preparation for his life's work in Chapter One and then proceeds to a fairly straightforward account of his architectural projects, organized chronologically, in Chapters Two and Three. I have taken liberties within the decades, recognizing the fluid nature of assigned design dates, in order to group projects in geographic clusters and to make regional relationships more apparent. In Chapter Four, I consider Rossiter's clients in greater detail, identifying their shared characteristics and discussing the working relationship between the architect and his clients. In Chapter Five, I review the architectural styles that exemplify Rossiter's projects and the implication of these design choices for the self-image and aspirations of both client and architect. In Chapter Six, I turn to the organization of spaces in these buildings as a reflection of changing relationships among family members, servants, guests, and strangers at the turn of the twentieth century and review the challenges of changing technologies in domestic interiors. Finally, I consider the role the surviving buildings continue to play in our communities today.

I believe that architecture shapes our image of our families and our communities, that the buildings of our past play a role in defining our current neighborhoods. I hope that our future will be served by projects as gracious as those designed by Ehrick Rossiter and his peers, enriching our lives at home, at work, and at leisure.

Ann Y. Smith
Roxbury, Connecticut, 2012

PREFACE

At the turn of the twentieth century, architects and their clients created the buildings that shape the America we know today. While the star-quality architects of the nineteenth century and the landmark buildings they designed in major cities during the Gilded Age have been well studied, the actual building of our communities—one block at a time—was the creation of less celebrated designers. More than 10,000 architects were in practice in the United States by 1910, creating the homes, commercial buildings, schools, churches, and clubs that shape our lives today.

Ehrick Rossiter was in the vanguard of this rising profession, then in its infancy. Bred to the task, Rossiter was the son of a prominent painter and a New York City heiress and was raised in a household devoted to aesthetics, culture, and stylish living. His father was an artist of note, and his maternal grandfather was a wealthy real estate developer in New York City, connected to some of the city's most prosperous families.

As an architect, Ehrick Rossiter embodied the priorities of American society at the end of the nineteenth century. Stylistically, his designs reflected the aspirations of his affluent clients, who expected sophisticated homes in the city and in their rural retreats. Programmatically, Rossiter adapted new technologies to accommodate the density of urban life while promoting social and healthful living through architecture. Professionally, Rossiter, a graduate of the first four-year architectural program at an American university,[1] built a successful career in this new profession, capitalizing on the burgeoning consumer economy of the late nineteenth century.

Early in his career, Rossiter, a painter's son, wrote a book recognized today as one of the leading authorities on color for Victorian houses. As his practice grew, he designed houses that reflected the evolving relationships among family members, guests, and servants, mirroring a domestic society in rapid change.

The lovely county estates that Rossiter designed in the village of Washington, Connecticut, have been featured in books, magazines, tours, and exhibits. Less well known are the gracious country houses and churches he designed in nearby New Milford, Litchfield, Ridgefield, and Norfolk; the mansions in Hartford, New Haven, and Southport; and the buildings for The Hotchkiss School in Lakeville (a village in the town of Salisbury), the Ingleside School (later the campus of the Canterbury School) in New Milford, and The Gunnery School in Washington.

From his offices in New York City, Rossiter designed projects for clients across the eastern United States. With his partners Frank A. Wright and, later, John Muller he designed low-cost housing and country estates, as well as suburban developments and co-op apartments in New York City. They designed libraries, town halls, clubs, resorts, park facilities, and churches in communities of all sizes throughout the northeast— more than 350 projects over a career that spanned 45 years.

Rossiter's designs reflect the aspirations of middle-class Americans at the turn of the twentieth century in the homes and the communities they created for modern living.

EHRICK K. ROSSITER 1854-1941

Joseph West photograph. Collection of the Gunn Memorial Library and Museum, Washington, Connecticut.

Rossiter on a drive in Steep Rock park in Washington, Connecticut, in the early years of the 20th century. He had purchased the land to prevent it from being acquired by a lumber company and later set up a land trust to protect it in perpetuity. Remembering the land as it was during his school days, Rossiter was opposed to allowing automobiles in the park.

"The beauty of architectural form is one of the contributing factors in human happiness."

Ehrick Kensett Rossiter, *The Hartford Courant,* 2/26/1910.

CHAPTER ONE: THE EDUCATION OF AN ARCHITECT

Ehrick Rossiter built a successful career in architecture through conservative designs and a cultivated network of social and artistic connections. In the decades spanning the turn of the twentieth century, he designed buildings in traditional styles, reassuring structures in a rapidly changing world. His clients were drawn from a circle of associates that included his extended family, his schools, and his clubs. As his practice grew, existing clients commissioned additional projects and introduced Rossiter to their friends, extending the architect's network of clients. Rossiter's early prominence in the profession and his social connections brought his success in the clubby Gilded Age.

Family and Education

Thomas Pritchard Rossiter (1818-1871), the architect's father, was a painter of landscapes and allegories and a colleague of the first artists to develop a distinctly American style of painting. A native of New Haven, Connecticut, Thomas Rossiter moved to New York in 1839. Within a year, he set off to Europe, beginning a six-year sojourn to study painting and architecture in the company of fellow artists, including Thomas Cole and John Frederick Kensett, who would become the acknowledged leaders of the new American painting style.

Returning to New York in 1846, Thomas Rossiter established himself as a prominent member of the so-called Hudson River School of painters. These artists depicted the American landscape as the revelation of the divine in American nature, as did their contemporaries, the Transcendentalist writers Emerson and Thoreau, who believed that "nature is the symbol of the spirit."[1] Although painting tour de force landscapes remained the focus of many Hudson River School painters, Rossiter also pursued the underlying spiritual and moral lessons of the American experience in paintings that depicted inspirational topics in American history and Biblical epics.[2] He was elected a member of the National Academy of Design in 1849 and was a founding member of the Century Association, New York's leading men's club organized to promote fine arts and literature.

Refined as a result of his European experience and dashing as a result of his natural good looks, Thomas Rossiter successfully wooed Anna Parmly (1830-1856), the young daughter of the wealthy New York real estate developer and pioneer in dental medicine, Dr. Eleazer Parmly. The couple wed in 1851 and traveled to Paris for an extended honeymoon, anticipating a life immersed in European culture. Their son, Ehrick Kensett (the first name honoring his mother's twin brother and the second honoring his father's great friend, the painter John Kensett), and his twin sister, Charlotte Evangeline, were born in Paris on September 14, 1854. Two and a half years later, a second daughter, Anna Rosalie, was born in Paris. Rossiter's wife died a short time later, on April 30, 1856.

Heartbroken, Thomas Rossiter and his three young children returned to New York to live in a house built by his father-in-law, Eleazar Parmly, at 11 West 38th St. The house had been designed with Rossiter's input by his friend the architect Richard Morris Hunt (1827-1895) while they were together in Paris. When Hunt returned to New York, the original design for a three-story house was altered at Parmly's insistence, making the house taller and thinner. Dr. Parmly, whose wife died in 1857, while the house was under construction, added a fourth floor to the house and determined to live in the house with the young Rossiters. The façade of the building, as designed by Hunt, was notable as the first Neo-Greek building in New York, reflecting the designer's study at the École des Beaux Arts in Paris.[3] Dr. Parmly took a strong hand in the construction of the house, acting as general contractor. When the building was completed in 1857, Rossiter worked in a studio on the fourth floor and opened an art gallery on the first floor that showcased his own paintings as well as the work of several of his colleagues in the Hudson River School.[4]

Things did not go well in the new home. In 1860, Thomas Rossiter married his first cousin, Mary Sterling (1829-1907) of Cleveland,

Thomas Rossiter painted this image
of his family shortly after their move to
the new home he designed along the
Hudson River at Cold Spring, New York.
Ehrick Rossiter is on the left, riding a
tricycle. His sisters and half brother are
in the center of the group and his father
and stepmother are standing at the back.
Thomas Rossiter's father is seated next
to Ehrick, and various Sterling relations
are also depicted.

who had traveled to Paris with Thomas and Anna Rossiter on their
honeymoon and accompanied Thomas when he brought the children
home following Anna's death. After their marriage, Thomas and Mary
and his three children moved to a new home in Cold Spring, New York,
60 miles north of the city along the Hudson River. A year later, Sterling
Rossiter, Thomas and Mary's son, was born. A painting by Thomas
Rossiter shows the extended family outside the house, which Thomas
is believed to have designed as a fashionable Italian villa, with a broad
piazza overlooking the river.[5]

Dr. Parmly put the ambitious West 38th St. house on the market, but it
did not sell. Hunt, the architect, had sued Parmly when he refused to
pay the design bill, the first American lawsuit over an architect's fees.
Parmly disputed his responsibility for the contract as well as the extent
of Hunt's involvement in supervising the project and refused to pay.
The court determined that Hunt was owed his fees, but awarded him
only 2.5% of the project's costs, rather than the customary 5%.[6]

Ehrick Rossiter was six years old when his grandfather went to court with the architect Hunt and his father remarried and moved the new family up the Hudson River. Within a year, the Civil War erupted. As the war drew to a close, Ehrick was sent to Washington, Connecticut, to attend the progressive new school there founded by Frederick Gunn in 1850. The school was recommended to Thomas Rossiter by his friend the prominent Brooklyn Heights minister Henry Ward Beecher, who was born in Litchfield, Connecticut, and had sent his own son to The Gunnery. Beecher's sister Harriet was the author of *Uncle Tom's Cabin*, the pivotal anti-slavery novel, and Beecher, Gunn, and Rossiter were committed abolitionists; indeed, Gunn's anti-slavery views were so unpopular in his native Connecticut that he left Washington in the 1840s and moved to Pennsylvania for several years before returning home to open his school. [7]

During the time Ehrick Rossiter was a student at The Gunnery, from 1865 to 1871,[8] the school was conducted in the Gunns' home on the hillside southeast of the Washington green. Classrooms, housing for students, and the Gunn family quarters were contained in the single two-story house. Ehrick's sisters Charlotte and Anna Rosalie also attended the school until 1869, when an expansion program was undertaken. A third floor was added and a hexagonal tower was built at the side of the house. Ehrick, who stayed at the school during the expansion, experienced the construction process, a sort of school of applied arts.

Gunn taught a classical curriculum in a relaxed environment that also encouraged an appreciation of the natural environment, moral values, and athletic competition. The students read aloud from Homer, Virgil, Shakespeare, and Scott, and Rossiter later recalled that city boys, like him, were "made to join in active sports [and to] lead a hearty out-door life to teach manliness, fortitude and self-reliance."[9] School life also included weekly receptions with townspeople, the Judea Lyceum where current affairs were debated, and theatrical events put on by a lively Drama Association promoted by the school. Ehrick Rossiter thrived in the progressive educational setting and was deeply influenced by the charismatic Frederick Gunn, who encouraged the students to tramp the rugged land around the school grounds and at the school's camp at nearby Lake Waramaug in order to experience nature first hand. Rossiter also may have joined the students in the summer of 1865, when Gunn led

Thomas Rossiter was a confirmed abolitionist and celebrated the Emancipation Proclamation by painting this image, completed the year the Proclamation was issued. Rossiter's abolitionist convictions were shared by the prominent Brooklyn minister Henry Ward Beecher and Frederick Gunn, who operated a school in Washington, Connecticut. Beecher advised Rossiter to send his older children, including Ehrick and his two sisters, to Mr. Gunn's school in 1866, beginning Ehrick Rossiter's lifelong passion for the town.

them on a 40-mile hike to Long Island Sound at Milford, Connecticut, for ten days of overnight camping and camaraderie. Rossiter retained a deep affection for the school and the countryside around it for the rest of his life.

Ehrick's world fell apart in the spring of 1871. His father died in May and was buried in Grove Street Cemetery in New Haven with his first wife; they were joined in the burial plot by his second wife upon her death in 1907.[10] Ehrick contracted typhoid fever, and his grandfather sent the young graduate on a "sea cure" across the Atlantic. The boy recovered by the time he arrived in England, and he soon returned home.

Back in the United States, Ehrick Rossiter enrolled in the first class in the new architectural program at Cornell College. His admission records report that he prepared for Cornell at Mr. McKinney's School in Ithaca, sometime during 1871. There were 21 students in this class, but four years later Rossiter was one of only two students from that first class to receive a degree from the program, in a tiny class of only four graduates.

Professor Charles Babcock organized the new architectural program at Cornell, emphasizing the practical considerations of building. Babcock, who had a degree in classics and was also an Episcopal priest, had apprenticed with the architect Richard Upjohn and married Upjohn's daughter. Upjohn, best known for his romantic gothic design of Trinity Church in New York City, was a proponent of the Gothic Revival style in architecture and the theories of John Ruskin, which celebrated the gothic over the classical as an expression of craft and community. True to Ruskinian precepts, the courses Babcock created at Cornell focused on the science of structures and building materials, the work of the craftsman rather than the geometric theorist. Building technology, mechanics, and architectural theory formed the course of study in the first two years, with design work beginning only in the third year.

The architectural drafting classes were conducted in unheated wooden barracks, recalled by a later graduate as "so cold that students and faculty work[ed] in overcoats and gloves while watercolors froze" in the long winters in upstate New York.[11] Nevertheless, Rossiter enjoyed his time on campus. He was active in a prominent Cornell fraternity, Psi Upsilon, and an editor of a campus yearbook. For a short time he sponsored the "Rossiter Prize" for the best student architectural drawing—$30 and an exhibition of the drawing on the drafting room walls.[12]

He may have been feeling particularly prosperous in 1875, the year the prize was first awarded. His grandfather Dr. Parmly died that year, providing that a share of his considerable estate, valued at $1.5 million, should be divided among Ehrick and his sisters, an amount equal to the bequests made for Anna Parmly's surviving siblings.

After his graduation from Cornell in 1875, Rossiter followed Babcock's recommendation that classroom studies should be augmented with two or three years of training in an established architectural practice before an architect opened an independent office. His daughter Edith recalled that Rossiter served as a draughtsman in the office of Henry Hobson Richardson, one of the most influential American architects of the nineteenth century. Although no documentation has been located to confirm this association, Rossiter may have worked in the Staten Island offices of Gambrill and Richardson from 1875 to 1877. Richardson had moved to Brookline, Massachusetts, in 1874 to supervise the construction of his competition-winning design for Trinity Church in Boston, but his New York partnership with Gambrill continued until 1878. During these years, Richardson prepared preliminary sketches each week at his home in Brookline, Massachusetts, and sent them down to the office in Staten Island to be transformed into construction documents.[13] Rossiter's family was acquainted with Richardson, making Ehrick's daughter's memories of this apprenticeship plausible.[14]

At the time, Gambrill and Richardson were working on several projects that Rossiter would echo in the work he did when he opened his own practice. In addition to the influential designs for Trinity Church in Boston, the Ames Free Library in North Easton, Massachusetts, and the Watts Sherman house in Newport, Rhode Island, the Gambrill and Richardson office was then preparing drawings for commercial buildings (the Hayden Building in Boston) and for renovations to churches (All Soul's Church in New York City) and city mansions (the Joseph Choate house in New York City). The office also designed a commercial building for the B. Austin Cheney family in Hartford. During this apprenticeship, Rossiter would have been exposed to a variety of building types, from commercial and ecclesiastic to residential; a variety of building materials and structural systems, including wood and masonry; and a variety of fashionable styles, including the new Shingle style and what would later be known as Richardsonian Romanesque, characterized by heavy masonry and oversized round-headed arches.

In June 1877, Ehrick Rossiter married Mary E. Heath (1855-1948), the daughter of a successful lumber merchant. The Heaths lived in Allegheny City, a rapidly growing town across the Allegheny River from downtown Pittsburgh, Pennsylvania. Though not as wealthy as other families in Allegheny City and Pittsburgh, including the Cassatts, the Carnegies, and the Heinzes, the Heaths were affluent, with a substantial house valued in 1870 at $50,000—more than ten times the cost of middle-class houses described in the contemporary architectural press. The Heaths, including John (1827-1895), his wife, Henriette Gaskill

FRANK WRIGHT (1854-1949), Rossiter's architectural partner from 1880 to 1910. Wright was responsible for much of the work in New Jersey. Courtesy of Mary Jo (Burke) Kenny, Monmouth Hills, Highlands, New Jersey.

(1826-1909), and Mary's older brother, Frank, were attended by two servants in residence. The newlyweds Ehrick and Mary Rossiter applied for a joint passport in June, 1877, and probably traveled to Europe for an extended honeymoon. On the passport application, Rossiter reported that he was 5 feet 7 inches tall and weighed 150 pounds.

The couple returned to New York City, perhaps in anticipation of the birth of their first child, Frank Heath Rossiter (1879-1941), named in honor of Mary's older brother. The family moved into the Rembrandt Apartments, next door to Carnegie Hall. Rossiter opened his architectural practice in a Parmly property at 658 Broadway and within a year formed a partnership with Frank Ayers Wright (1854-1949). The partners' office was at 160 Fulton St., but it moved to 149 Broadway in 1882 and remained there until 1888.

Like Rossiter, Frank Wright was a graduate of the Cornell architectural program, graduating with the class of 1879. A native of Liberty, New York, he studied at the Newburgh Academy in Newburgh, New York, along the Hudson River, before enrolling at Cornell. While he was a student at Cornell, he taught the program's architectural drawing classes and operated an independent architectural practice. As early as 1877, he published the design for a cottage in West Virginia in the leading architectural periodical of the era, *American Architect and Building News.*[15] Although they were not on campus at the same time, Rossiter and Wright were members of the same fraternity, Psi Upsilon, and were likely to have had friends in common. Theirs was a partnership with practical advantages. Each man was a college-educated architect with several years of experience and some standing in the field. Based in New York City, they attracted a variety of urban clients, and Rossiter cultivated clients east and north of the city in Connecticut while Wright concentrated on business west and south of the city in New Jersey, insuring a wide net in the search for clients.

CHAPTER TWO: BUILDING A PRACTICE: 1880-1890

Together, Rossiter and Wright developed strategies to market their partnership, promoting and then exploiting the new publications and clubs founded as the architectural profession was taking shape. Between 1870 and 1910, the number of self-identified architects in the U.S. census records increased from 2,000 to 16,613.[1] As the profession grew, so did organizations and publications serving the field.

Publications and Professional Recognition

Rossiter and Wright were adept at positioning themselves at the forefront of these activities. They were members of the National Arts Club in New York, the American Institute of Architects, and, later, when the AIA moved to Washington, the New York Chapter of the AIA. They were among the early members of the Architectural League of New York, joining in 1885, and took an active role in the League's annual exhibitions, beginning in the first year of these events, 1886.[2] They submitted designs for competitions sponsored by the new architectural publications and provided additional illustrations for specialized building periodicals, including *American Architect and Building News* and *Scientific American*. Nearly 200 Rossiter & Wright projects received notice in the architectural press between 1879 and 1910, with another dozen Rossiter projects published in the next two decades. Between 1882 and 1886, Wright also wrote a series of illustrated essays on how to draw buildings in perspective and other architectural studies, which were published as a handbook and serialized in periodicals.[3]

Architectural books found ready publishers and avid readers in the 1870s and 1880s, and Rossiter and Wright capitalized on this opportunity to promote the partnership as well. Architectural books published before the Civil War provided theories of style or served as carpenters' guides. After the war, profusely illustrated books with elevations, floorplans, and the details of construction and decoration dominated the architectural literature. Some were intended to be pattern books; others offered to sell homeowners sets of the plans illustrated, a sort of mail order design service. Advertising was included in these books featuring tiles, plumbing fixtures, and paints, which a builder could purchase to finish the house. Architectural publishing flourished, with dozens of books of the sort released between 1868 and 1882.[4]

Rossiter and Wright wrote one of these books, on the aesthetics of house painting, an appropriate topic for Rossiter, an artist's son. The book recommended schemes for the arrangement of color on the exterior and the interior of houses, along with remarks on color theory and architectural style and practical advice on the application of paint. One thousand copies were printed in the first edition of the book in 1882, and a second edition, also limited to 1,000 copies, was published the following year.

Rossiter and Wright's book, *Modern House Painting,* was well reviewed in the July 8, 1882, issue of *American Architect and Building News,* although a critic complained that Rossiter suggested fugitive colors like black and recommended too many different colors to be used on the houses in some of the illustrations. The book was hailed as a pioneering resource for color selection in *Building* magazine in January 1884. Rossiter and Wright, however, were disappointed with the quality of the color printing in the first edition, a key feature of a book on color. The second edition was intended to correct the color plates, with several new plates substituted for faulty illustrations in the first edition and several new color schemes added. Intended for homeowners, the book proposed to assist them in instructing the painters they hired to finish their new homes. The publisher, William Comstock, a specialist in architectural books and periodicals, included 20 color lithographs in the book, showing the proper use of color in exterior and interior applications. The handsomely printed plates indicated the texture of each surface on the house elevations that suggested the effects of sunlight and shadow. Protective paper was laid on top of the plates to shield them from wear. The book was a high-quality production, aimed at middle-market homeowners during a boom in residential building.

Rossiter wrote an introductory essay on the principles of color and the suitability of multiple-hued palettes for the new Queen Anne architectural designs. A separate chapter was devoted to the practical aspects of preparing the surfaces to be painted and mixing the paint itself. Each of the 20 color plates was discussed in detail, describing the purpose of the color selection and its arrangement on the house. Rossiter may have again been dissatisfied with the color plates printed for the second edition since he suggested in the text, printed separately from the plates, various ways to correct the colors when the paint was being mixed. Several of the plates suggested "modern" colors for older homes in the classical styles popular before the Civil War. The back pages were filled with advertising from suppliers of paints and varnishes, sash chains, glass and other domestic building materials.

In the text, Rossiter welcomed the new "modern" house designs. He asserted that these houses, unlike the classical houses popular in the earlier years of the 19th century, were designed from the inside out, allowing the form of the house to be determined by a floor plan suitable for modern living rather than being confined to the classical, symmetrical box as was the case in the earlier houses. Rossiter claimed that designing the plan before the exterior derived from gothic precedent, when the arrangement of the rooms was functional (and usually asymmetric) rather than formal (symmetric). At the same time, he applauded the eclectic nature of the modern style, which permitted finish details to be designed in a more classical style regardless of the purportedly "gothic" nature of the floor plan. "The tendency is to substitute for the heavy and clumsy Gothic [finish] detail, the more delicate, graceful, and refined features which characterize the renaissance of the Grecian and Roman styles...Our houses are, in consequence, gradually assuming a more homelike and picturesque character much to be preferred to the...style so monotonously prevalent [in the earlier, classical] period."[5]

Rossiter recognized that these varied and picturesque elevations provided an opportunity for a greater variety of color than had been used earlier in the century. However, he cautioned that color could be misused, pointing out that there had been "repeated failures and absurdities" and that some combinations of colors were "miserable in the extreme." He called for "real, positive colors" to replace the gray, neutral tints previously recommended for stylish houses in northern climates. "Positive colors, if not too harsh, but mellowed and softened down in hue or dulled in tone, will be found to harmonize with natural objects as well as anything distinctly artificial can, or ought."[6]

Rossiter's chapter on color reviewed the differences between primary colors (red, yellow, blue), secondary colors (made by combining two of the primary colors, resulting in green, orange, and purple), and tertiary colors (made by mixing two of the secondary colors, resulting in russet, olive, and citrine). "Tones" of color could be achieved by mixing the color with white (for a reduced tone), black (for a darkened tone) or gray (for a dulled tone). Complementary colors were those that combined the color's opposite; for example, red is the complementary color of green (blue plus yellow). Rossiter described the theories of contrasts and harmonies in color and tone, laying the groundwork for his discussion of the color recommendations illustrated in the plates.

Applying these basic tenants of color theory to the selection of color combinations for the modern house, he declared that primary colors should not be used at all in the tasteful home. Rather, secondary colors, modified by "tones," were more suitable. Tones derived from the mixture of a secondary color with gray or black were preferred over those mixed with white. "These rich and sometimes somber, colors give a house a certain character and dignity, which the washed-out looking light drabs and lavenders generally fail to produce. Modern taste of the best kind does not seek for exciting effect, for decided hues, for glare, and for obtrusiveness; but for results which will be restful; for softness of color, and for that subdued and quiet expression which should characterize the exterior of every house in which refinement is supposed to lodge."[7]

He admonished the reader to use only combinations of colors that were in harmony, perhaps by adding some of the first color to the second color. He also recommended that the scheme incorporate colors that were comparable in tone (similarly positioned along the gray scale), alluding to the harmony of musical notes. He concluded the chapter on color by reviewing the difference between cool colors and warm colors, pointing out that the contrast between cool colors, such as blue, and warm colors, such as yellow, could strengthen a palette combination, or defeat it.

Throughout the discussion of color, Rossiter reminded the reader that his guidelines were flexible and that the proper selection of colors was really a matter of good taste. Although he suggested additional readings

ROSSITER & WRIGHT, *Modern House Painting,* New York: William T. Comstock, Second edition, 1883. Author's Collection.

Rossiter & Wright promoted their new partnership by publishing their designs in contemporary architectural magazines and books. *Modern House Painting,* first issued in 1882, two years after the partnership was established, was widely recognized as an authoritative guide to the use of color for the multi-patterned houses in the Queen Anne Revival style.

on color theory and the mechanics of paint application, in the end it was clear that the careful homeowner would want to consult an expert—maybe the son of a painter?—on the important matters of tasteful color selection. "The colorings that with some designs would be very effective, on others would be out of keeping. The fact is that a house should be painted so that its salient features of form and detail will be enhanced. The coloring should be subordinated to the design."[8]

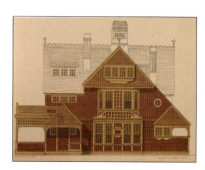

In the notes that accompanied the color plates, specific principles emerged. In a shingle style house, Rossiter recommended that the lower floors be painted with a rich, "heavy" shade that continued through a "middle harmony to the lighter tones of the gable peaks." The trim should be painted in a cooler color, "giving great strength of contrast, emphasizing the body colors [on the clapboards and shingles]." Shutters were inappropriate for more substantial houses, like the one illustrated in the particular example: "A building of this class ought not to have outside blinds." The shutters would interfere with the appearance of the window arrangement. Many of the notes for the plates also describe the color of the wood shingled roofs, which were to be painted in a manner consistent with the overall color scheme. Rossiter also cautioned against the use of bright colors to pick out details of the trim. "The authors

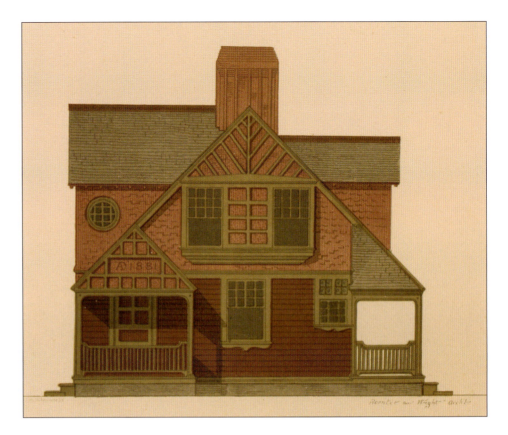

do not believe in the practice, which obtains to a great extent lately, of picking out small members in a brighter color than the rest, in order to enliven the whole. This gives a building a choppy and mincing effect, and instead of bringing out and helping the architectural design in a subordinate way as color should, it is apt to result in undue emphasis of features which ought to be kept back, and to give other parts a relative importance that is far from desirable. Let it be bourne [sic] in mind that color is chiefly important in architecture as an adjunct of form and that it can never quite take the place of form."[9]

He reminded readers that color applied to different materials on the house elevations would take to the various materials differently. "The effect of a stain and a paint is quite different, even though precisely the same colors be employed. Hence the shingles, which are shown in the plate as the same as [the] body color of the first story, would not really appear the same [as the clapboards of the first story]. The surface of the material has a great deal to do with color effect."[10]

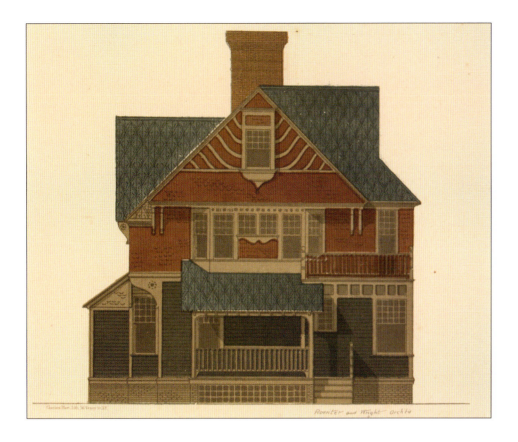

Interior color schemes raised a new set of issues for Rossiter. He reminded readers that, of course, the color selection of interior finishes needed to be done in concert with the furnishings. In addition, "The various rooms of a house should be painted, papered or kalsomined [a mixture of lime and pigment] in such a way as to give each a distinctive character. The scheme of color used for the living-room should differ essentially from that of the bed chambers, boudoirs, etc. and while a richness and quietness of effect should be sought in one, a cheerful and sunny appearance should be aimed at in the other." [11]

As with the exterior, there was a balance to be sought from the base to the ceiling. "Darker colors should prevail at the bottom, lighter ones at the top." Wallpapers needed to conform to the system, using the dominant color in the paper as a guide. "The color [of wallpapers] should represent the background of the paper and not the figure." [12]

Rossiter loved the front hall. For him, it was more a matter of status than a means of circulation among the rooms in the houses of the

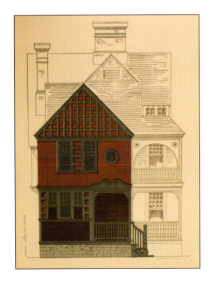

1880s. "It is the part that one sees first upon entering a house and the last to be seen as one leaves it, therefore the importance of creating a favorable impression." Even in an inexpensive house, the hall could be made impressive with tasteful paint colors to achieve a "richness of effect," using colors of "considerable body and brilliancy" and a few well-designed strips of pine for the wainscoting.[13]

He concluded the book with a discussion of ceiling painting, which he recognized was a specialized skill in house painting, requiring different materials—very likely a watercolor fresco—and consequently requiring different colors. He recommended light, airy colors for the ceilings, with the dark colors reserved for the recessed coves in the perimeter cornices. If the centerpiece, a decorative relief at the middle of the ceiling, repeated the cornice colors, it should be done in a way that was lighter and more refined, so as to be less conspicuous.

The book is a vivid window into the aesthetics of the Queen Anne Revival style and the efforts of Rossiter and Wright to establish their firm among the architectural "players" of the 1880s. As their practice evolved in the subsequent decades, their ideas about color and design changed, but the book was a valuable distillation of color for domestic architecture in the 1880s and helped the firm establish a place in the profession.

The publication of the book and the designs of the firm that were illustrated in various architectural publications helped attract clients. Over the next 30 years, Rossiter & Wright completed at least 350 projects in New York, Connecticut, and New Jersey, as well as projects in more distant locations, including Missouri, Texas, and New Hampshire.

The Early Years: Working the Connections
During the early years of the partnership, Rossiter & Wright prepared designs for competitions, for friends, and for projects in their respective hometowns. Some of the designs for architectural competitions, sponsored by the contemporary press, focused on the problems of building homes for the burgeoning working class. The firm submitted designs for competitions and won third place in one sponsored in 1881 by *Carpentry & Building* for a $3,500 house. In 1883, at least six houses were designed for publication rather than clients. With the projected

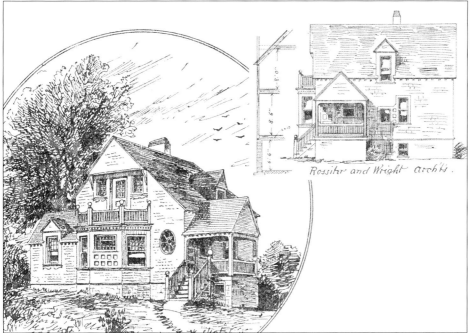

ROSSITER & WRIGHT, *Design for a Small House, costing from $500 to $800,* **1883.**

Rossiter & Wright entered competitions sponsored by architectural magazines and published and exhibited a variety of designs for homes, schools and churches as a method of promoting their practice in the early years.

LEFT ROSSITER & WRIGHT, *Design for a Side hill Cottage, costing from $1,000 to $1,500,* **1883.**

Even modest homes such as this one, without plumbing or other utilities, were designed with porches, a balcony, a bay window and ornamental siding. As an option, the kitchen could be put in the basement enabling the owner to have a dining room or another bedroom on the first floor.

TOP ROSSITER & WRIGHT, *Design for a Cottage costing $1,800 to $2,000,* **1883.**

With a larger budget, a builder could have larger rooms and more of them, a fancier entrance hall with a landing on the stairway and the opportunity for an indoor bathroom, although installing the bathroom came at an additional cost. More elaborate masonry was suggested, with roof top cresting and a decorative clustered chimney.

American Cottages. New York: William T. Comstock, 1883. Reprinted in William T. Comstock, *Country Houses and Seaside Cottages of the Victorian Era,* Mineola, N.Y.: Dover Publications, Inc., 1989.

ABOVE ROSSITER & WRIGHT, *Small house for the sum of $2,500,* 1883.

For a little more money, the owner could have an entrance hallway with a fireplace, and indoor plumbing. The architects recommended painting the roof shingles Indian red, the elevations a brownish yellow and the trim in dark green.

ABOVE RIGHT ROSSITER & WRIGHT, *$3,500 cottage,* 1883.

For $3,500, the builder could have a larger house with more rooms, a finished third floor and separate stairs for servants, as well as indoor plumbing and a portable hot air furnace.

RIGHT ROSSITER & WRIGHT, Suburban Cottage for $4,000, 1883.

Characteristic of the houses the architects were designing for clients in New Jersey and Long Island, a suburban house in this price range was large enough to include five large rooms on the first floor and a full compliment of plumbing and heating fixtures. Like many of their suburban homes in this market, the entrance hall was on the side of the house, facilitating circulation from the hall to each of the first floor rooms and retaining the front of the house for the more public rooms.

American Cottages. New York; Reprinted in William T. Comstock, *Country Houses and Seaside Cottages of the Victorian Era,* Mineola, N.Y.: Dover Publications, Inc., 1989.

houses estimated to cost between $500 and $4,000, these published designs were provided with extensive notes about the construction details and utilities. Other drawings for homes, schools, and churches were published and were exhibited at the Architectural League in New York City without client attribution; these may have been intended to promote the firm to prospective clients.

In addition, the firm designed projects for clients who intended to build. In the early years of the practice, many of these clients were recruited from family and friends in the towns where Rossiter and Wright had connections.

The Early Projects: Family and Friends in the 1880s
In 1880, Rossiter designed a schoolhouse for Cold Spring, New York, where his father's home had been. A three-story structure, it was topped by a belfry but otherwise looked like a Queen Anne-style house.[14] In 1883, the partners designed a $7,000 extension to a home in Cold Spring.[15] Rossiter designed modest seaside summer homes and studios for artists, building on his father's connections with painters. In 1880, he designed a masonry studio for the painter R. Swain Gifford's summer home at Nonquitt, Massachusetts, that was 18 by 24 feet, and covered with a steep hip roof and a cupola over a cluster of gables and Tudor-inspired windows.[16] In 1887, in nearby South Dartmouth, Massachusetts, he designed a shingled, gambrel-roofed cottage and adjacent studio with a skylight in the gambrel roof for the landscape painter and art teacher Dwight Tryon. The Tryon commission led to a Rossiter & Wright-designed home at nearby Quisett for Tryon's friend Dr. Milton Yale. The partners also designed a shingle-covered two-family house for William L. Van Kirk in Pittsburgh in 1885[17] and a church for the nearby town of Tyrone in 1887; these clients were probably introduced to the architects through the connections of Rossiter's father-in-law in western Pennsylvania.[18] In 1893, Rossiter designed a brick home in St. Louis, Missouri, for G. E. Sterling, undoubtedly a relative of his stepmother.[19] The houses in Pittsburgh and St. Louis featured large Richardsonian arches, asymmetric façades, multi-paned Queen Anne windows, and half-timbering in the prominent gables.

ROSSITER & WRIGHT, School house in Cold Spring on Hudson, N.Y., 1880. *American Architect and Building News* 12/4/1880

In the first decade of their practice, the architects relied on family and friends for commissions. This school house in the Queen Anne style was designed for Cold Spring, where Rossiter's father had a house.

ROSSITER & WRIGHT, Studio for R. Swain Gifford, 1880. *American Architect and Building News,* 4/24/1880.

A painter's son, Rossiter designed homes and studios for artists. It's not certain that this studio, with large windows and a separate room for making etchings, was actually constructed since photos of Gifford's studio as built are somewhat different from this image.

ROSSITER & WRIGHT, Homes for William Van Kirk, Pittsburgh, Pennsylvania, 1885. *American Architect and Building News* 12/4/1880

Probably designed for a friend of Rossiter's in-laws in Pittsburgh, this pair of houses, each costing $7,000, was designed side by side with a unified façade, to look like one house.

ROSSITER & WRIGHT, Proposal for a Y.M.C.A. in Newburgh, New York, 1881. *The Builder and Wood-Worker*, 8/1882.

Frank A. Wright had connections in Newburgh where he had gone to school, but this proposal was passed over in favor of a design by the brilliant New York architect, Stanford White.

Frank Wright had well-established connections in Newburgh, New York, where he had studied before attending Cornell. In 1881, Rossiter & Wright submitted a proposal to the competition for a YMCA building there, which was rejected in favor of a design by the highly regarded New York architect Stanford White. In 1886, Rossiter & Wright submitted a proposal for the Newburgh Academy, Wright's alma mater, which was accepted.[20] Both designs were conceived in an eclectic Revival style, with round-headed masonry arches inspired by the Richardsonian Romanesque. Rossiter & Wright's unsuccessful design for the YMCA, which would have been positioned at the intersection of Smith and 3rd St., had a fanciful two-story Dutch gable on the smaller end of the building, facing the side street. The design accepted for the Newburgh Academy was the architects' most impressive project in the first years of their partnership: it was a three-story building with a hip roof and large central gable crowned by a belfry and clustered chimneys, and it cost the significant sum of $53,933. Horizontal masonry banding extended across the symmetrical façade, and large hexagonal towers were positioned at each end. A few years later, in 1892, the firm designed Riverside Flats in Newburgh, intended to offer modern housing at a "rental within the reach of people in moderate circumstances."[21] In 1883 Rossiter & Wright designed a private chapel in nearby Irvington-on-Hudson, a compact cross-form building with a cone-topped tower, buttressed walls, and round-headed windows, again in the Richardsonian Romanesque style. The chapel was built as a memorial to the engineer and inventor Henry Rossiter Worthington, who may have been a Rossiter relation.[22]

In the first decade of their practice, the partners submitted proposals for two large design competitions: one at Cornell College, where they had trained, and the other at the University of Vermont, for a library being given to the school by Rossiter's uncle Frederick Billings. In spite of having an insider's advantage, the young partners were not able to secure either commission.

The project at the University of Vermont was a library to house the books collected by conservationist George Perkins Marsh and acquired for the college in 1882 by Frederick Billings. Billings, who was married to Anna Parmly's younger sister and was therefore Rossiter's uncle, made a fortune as the president of the Northern Pacific Railroad

ROSSITER & WRIGHT, Newburgh Academy, Newburgh, New York, 1886. *American Architect and Building News*, 4/10/1886. Author's collection.

The partners were successful in securing this commission in Newburgh for Wright's alma mater. With a budget of $54,000, it was one of the largest projects of their first decade in practice.

ROSSITER & WRIGHT, Worthington Memorial Chapel, Irvington-on-Hudson, 1882. *American Architect and Building News*, 4/22/82. Author's collection.

This memorial chapel, seating 160 people, was commissioned by the widow of inventor Henry Rossiter Worthington, who may have been related to the architect. It survives, with later additions, as the chapel of St. Joseph of Arimathea in Westchester County.

before retiring to his native Vermont. He purchased George Perkins Marsh's childhood home in Woodstock to serve as his country estate. Billings determined to build a library at the college to house the Marsh collection, initially committing $75,000 to the building. Rossiter & Wright were among the firms submitting designs. They proposed a compact two-story masonry building centered on a reading room with a large arched window flanked by a square clock tower that accommodated the stairs. An arcaded entrance and loggia with a hipped roof was tucked alongside the tower. Behind the reading room on its far side, steep hip roofs covered offices and book storage.[23]

Billings was not happy with any of the initial submissions for the library, including one from H. H. Richardson, but since Richardson had designed a library at Woburn, Massachusetts, that Billings liked, he selected Richardson as architect for the Vermont library. The resulting building is a masterful design in heavy stone with a central pavilion and flanking wings lined with a band of windows high on the walls under the cornice. It was a simpler and more powerful design than Rossiter & Wright's. The Rossiter & Wright firm was only three years old, and Billings may have thought that his nephew was not yet up to the task of designing the important project. In 1884, Billings hired Rossiter to make "repairs and improvements" to his country estate in Woodstock,

Vermont. According to a historic structures report prepared for the National Park Service, which now owns the Woodstock property,[24] Rossiter submitted plans for enlarging the stable in June 1884. However, the following year, Billings hired architect Henry Hudson Holley of New York to remodel his Woodstock house, certainly the more prestigious project.

Some years after Billings died in 1890, his widow hired Rossiter to demolish the old stable in Woodstock and design a new building to house horses, carriages, and sleighs. In 1895, Rossiter provided preliminary designs, which survive, although the family apparently made a number of changes in the placement of the windows, which were stylish but small in Rossiter's drawings, and modified the door placement. A persistent family legend claims that Rossiter's design for the building was four feet smaller than the existing foundation in both directions. While the architectural relations may have had their disappointments, family relations remained cordial. Rossiter's children visited in the Billings home regularly between 1897 and 1911. Frederick Billings, Jr., Frederick's son and Rossiter's cousin, hired the architect to design the Royalton residential hotel in New York in 1897. (On the other hand, Frederick, Jr.'s sister Laura hired the architect Charles Platt to design her home in Manhattan in 1904 and her summer home in Woodstock, Vermont, in 1906.) Some years later, Richard Billings, another of Frederick Sr.'s sons, who lived in Minneapolis most of the year, hired Rossiter to design his summer home in Woodstock, a brick Colonial Revival house with a projecting two-story columned portico, which was begun in 1910 and completed in 1913.

Another prestigious commission that the firm sought and lost in these early years was for a building on the Cornell campus. Alfred Barnes, a New York textbook publisher and a trustee of Cornell College, offered to provide $40,000 to supplement funds raised by students led by John R. Mott (later the winner of the 1946 Nobel Peace Prize) to build a YMCA building on campus. College president Andrew Dickson White telegraphed Frank Wright in 1887 to come to Ithaca to discuss the plans for the new building. However, the chairman of the college board of trustees, Henry Sage, had other ideas. A big supporter of the college, Sage had already donated endowments and many buildings to the school, including a residence for women, a chapel, an infirmary,

ROSSITER & WRIGHT, competition proposal, Billings Hall-Marsh Library, University of Vermont, 1883. *American Architects and Building News*, 10/27/1883.

The partners' competition proposal for the library, in the Richardsonian style, was rejected by the library's benefactor, Rossiter's uncle, who instead hired H. H. Richardson himself to design the building for the Marsh library collection that he was donating to the college.

and a library. He talked to architect William Henry Miller about the YMCA project and switched the site for the project to one preferred by Miller. Wright complained that he did not have enough time to change his design to accommodate the change in site, and Miller got the job. Wright threatened to sue the college for 1% of the $40,000 project budget if Rossiter & Wright were not reimbursed for its expenses in preparing the design for the first site. The college paid the firm $323.45 for these costs. Wright, disgusted, wrote that there was "[no] competition where the designer works upon different data."[25] The partners must have been particularly surprised by the turn of events because they had just completed the design for a summer house in Washington, Connecticut, for Alfred Barnes's son Richard, across the street from the summer home Rossiter was building for himself.[26]

Whether through strategy or personal taste, Rossiter and Wright staked out homes for themselves in the suburban regions surrounding New York that contributed greatly to the firm's success over the next 20 years. Wright was attracted to the residential developments in northern New Jersey, where he built his own residence in South Orange in 1884 and where he took an active role in several significant suburban developments. His wife was from Newark, and her family connections may have attracted the couple to the area. A competitive golfer and avid clubman, Wright thrived in the emerging and affluent suburbs of northern New Jersey. Rossiter, on the other hand, remained a resident of New York City but cultivated a circle of sophisticated clients at his summer home in northwestern Connecticut. By 1883, Rossiter staked his claim in Washington, across the street from his former school The Gunnery, and over the next several decades he transformed the town with his architecture and conservation efforts. These country outposts of the firm led to significant business on both fronts, west and northeast of New York City, and reinforced the architects' business activities in the city when their suburban clients commissioned work at their homes or businesses there.

In spite of their differing social, recreational, and geographic orientations, the partners remained close. The work of the firm, whether in New Jersey or Connecticut, was consistently signed "Rossiter & Wright," although it seems likely that the actual responsibility for projects within the office would have been assumed by the partner

ROSSITER & WRIGHT, Schoolhouse for The Gunnery, Connecticut, 1882. Archives of The Gunnery School.

Rossiter's first commission in Washington was the 1882 schoolhouse for his alma mater, The Gunnery, a hip-roofed building covered in shingles and clapboards.

side of the green in New Milford for a new Episcopalian congregation. The All Saints Memorial Church was a gift to the congregation from Sarah Sanford, of New Milford, and her husband William Black, for a short time a member of a jewelry firm in New York, who moved to New Milford after their marriage in 1871. The gothic stone church was finished with a square crenellated and buttressed tower. A half-timbered parish house, probably designed by the firm, was built behind the church.

Rossiter began to plan a summer home for his family in 1883 on property he purchased in the autumn of 1882. The land was across the street from The Gunnery School, on the crest of the hill at the Washington green with long westerly views across the Shepaug valley. The six-acre site, purchased from John Brinsmade and George Brown, included Sampson's Rock, a geologic anomaly that was a fixture in Gunnery lore. The young Rossiter family had been spending summers at Thomas Rossiter's former home in Cold Spring, New York, but found the heat oppressive and worried about the threat of insect-carried infection. After the birth of their second son, Kensett, in 1881, they spent two summers in a rental property belonging to the Brinsmade

All Saints Memorial Church and Rectory, New Milford, Conn.

1912

ROSSITER & WRIGHT, All Saints Episcopal Church, New Milford, Connecticut, 1882. Post card, Author's collection.

family in Washington while Rossiter designed his dream house, a large home with a three-story bay overlooking the western valley, on their newly purchased land. An adjacent carriage house was to include staff quarters on the second floor.

There was a change in plans. Beginning the estate's construction in 1884 with the carriage house rather than the main house, the Rossiters decided to alter the floor plan of the carriage house to accommodate their family residence. In the redesigned carriage house, a larger room intended for carriages was converted to a dining room and general sitting room for the family. A smaller carriage room "was turned over to the servants." The stable became the kitchen, and the grain room above became a small bedroom for guests. The harness closet became a pantry. The second story, intended originally as a gardener's apartment, was adapted to three bedrooms for the family, and the hayloft was divided into storage and a room for the children. The 35- by 54-foot building, thus modified, was built at a cost of $3,600, Rossiter reported to the press. Both the redesigned carriage house and the main "House to be Built" were published in architectural periodicals in 1883.[44]

Construction of the main house was delayed and modified before it was finally begun in 1887 and completed in 1889. Some years later, Rossiter told a young visitor that he postponed building the main house because he wanted to purchase forested land in the Shepaug valley—the view from the site of his proposed house—to protect it from being sold to a lumber company.[45] In October and December 1886 he purchased nearly 90 acres in the valley and over the next three years bought another 48 acres, including a prominent geological feature, Steep Rock, a dramatic curved cliff overlooking the Clam Shell, a circular contour in the Shepaug River. In 1925, Rossiter organized a local land trust to preserve land in the area and to receive his donation of 100 acres at Steep Rock, ensuring the preservation of this section of the rocky river valley into the future.[46] At about the same time, the trust purchased additional land in the area from Rossiter.

By the time the Rossiter's primary summer home, The Rocks, was completed in 1889, it had been modified somewhat from the design published in 1883. The earlier sketch showed the western elevation and the first- and second-floor plans. In that sketch, a hall and stairwell

LEFT ROSSITER & WRIGHT, carriage house conversion, Washington, Connecticut, 1883. Copy of a scrapbook clipping, courtesy of Chris Woods, a subsequent owner of Rossiter's summer home in Washington.

Rossiter's first domestic project in Washington, Connecticut, was the conversion of a design he'd done for a carriage house to be used instead as a temporary summer quarters for his family. The carriage room was converted to his family's sitting room and the stable became the kitchen.

RIGHT EHRICK ROSSITER, The Rocks, his summer home in Washington, Connecticut; as designed, in 1883. *(western elevation). American Architect and Building News, 6/9/1883.*

EHRICK ROSSITER, The Rocks, his summer home in Washington, Connecticut; as built, in 1889. *(eastern elevation)*. Joseph West photo, Collection of the Gunn Memorial Library and Museum, Washington, Connecticut.

Built on property across the street from The Gunnery School, Rossiter's summer home became the base for his projects in northwest Connecticut, eventually including more than 35 projects in Washington alone.

dominated the first floor, with a bow-shaped parlor at the south end of the house projecting out into a western bay; a dining room and a kitchen were on the north side of the house. As completed in 1889, the house was larger. The western bay was expanded and tucked under a long sweeping roofline. Open porch pavilions were positioned to take advantage of the views on the north and south ends of the western elevation. The formal entrance on the eastern elevation, oriented to the road, included a covered porch, a circular cone-topped tower, and a large three-story gable-roofed wing on the north side of the tower.[47] While Rossiter was building The Rocks, another Washington client began a project across the street. Richard Barnes, the son of the Cornell trustee, had been Rossiter's classmate at The Gunnery. He bought the high meadow southwest of Rossiter's summer home, assembling the property in several transactions between 1884 and 1887, and built the summer house Westlawn; the Rossiter designs for the house were published in 1885. The home was a profusion of blocky gables and porches covered with shingles and half-timbering, perched above a long lawn and oriented toward the views to the west.

ROSSITER & WRIGHT, Westlawn, the summer home of Richard S. Barnes, Washington, Connecticut, 1885. *(above, southwestern elevation); American Architect and Building News, 6/27/85; (below, northeastern elevation);* Joseph West photo, Collection of the Gunn Memorial Library and Museum, Washington, Connecticut.

The first domestic design commissioned in Washington was for Richard Barnes, a former classmate at The Gunnery School, whose summer home was built across the street from Rossiter's.

ROSSITER & WRIGHT, Rock Gate, summer home
for Lucius A. Barbour, Washington, Connecticut,
1885. *(left, northern façade, as designed)* American
Architect and Building News, 11/21/85, Author's
collection; (*right, as built*) George William Sheldon,
Artistic Country-Seats, New York: D. Appleton and
Co., 1886-87. Reprinted in Arnold Lewis, *American
Country Houses of the Gilded Age,* New York:
Dover Publications, 1982.

Rossiter designed a home in the more fashionable Shingle style in
1885 for Mrs. Richard Barnes's brother Col. Lucius A. Barbour, a
Hartford-based wool merchant. Barbour may also have known Edward
Van Ingen, who was a woolens importer and merchant in New York and
who owned a substantial property on the south side of The Gunnery,
across the street from the Barbour site. Barbour was then president of
the Willimantic Linen Company, believed to operate the largest cotton
thread factory in the world.[48] Barbour's summer house was built on the
west side of the hilltop, just south of the Barnes and Van Ingen homes.
The Barbour house, Rock Gate, built for $22,000 and published in
several contemporary periodicals,[49] was an ambitious undertaking.
Tucked into the rocks at the crest of the hill, it was sited to take advantage
of the glorious view across the Shepaug River valley shared by the
Rossiter and Barnes houses. A large Richardsonian arch sheltered the
entrance porch on the northwestern façade. The long sweeping roof
(altered through a later addition), shingle cladding, and wide bands
of windows recalled the best of the contemporary summer houses in
the Shingle style. A profusion of circular porches and turrets opened
to the southwesterly views. The adjacent carriage house, complete with
shingles and a cone-topped tower, was a vision of the Shingle style in
miniature.

Rock Gate was designed for Richard Barnes' brother-in-law on the same ridge overlooking the Shepaug valley. At twice the budget, the Barbour project was a stylish house in the Shingle style, with a long sweeping roof, shingle-covered walls and horizontal bands of windows.

Across the street and just south of The Gunnery property, Edward Van Ingen's house was probably enlarged and embellished by Rossiter while the Barnes and Barbour houses were under construction. Van Ingen's primary residence was a substantial house on East 71st Street in Manhattan, where he lived with his wife, three children, and 12 servants. One of the country's largest importers of woolens, he was also a real estate developer in the city, purchasing property for $1.75 million in one deal at Herald Square. Van Ingen's great wealth was well known; two night watchmen on his household staff apprehended burglars breaking into his Manhattan house in 1905. He built the summer home in Washington to please his wife, who was a close friend of two women associated with The Gunnery.[50] Van Ingen first may have built a "starter" house on the property designed by the New York architects Potter and Robertson; that design was published in 1879.[51] The house was soon enlarged by Van Ingen, probably with designs by Rossiter. The renovations included rusticated stone cladding on the first-floor elevations, a porte-cochère for the ceremonial arrival of visitors, a servants' wing, enclosed porches on the west wing, and bold half-timbering, similar to the half-timbering Rossiter used in the Village Hall in South Orange, New Jersey, in 1894 and the Emma S. Clark Library in Setauket, New York, in 1892. A half-timbered gatehouse

ROSSITER & WRIGHT, District School for Washington, Connecticut, 1887. *Yearbook* of the Architectural League, 1887.

His neighbor Edward Van Ingen commissioned Rossiter to design a new public school in Washington so that Van Ingen could remove an existing District School that interfered with the view from his house.

ROSSITER, Swedish church, Washington, Connecticut. 1889. Joseph West photo, Collection of the Gunn Memorial Library and Museum, Washington, Connecticut.

Rossiter donated his services to the new Swedish congregation, designing a small church with a Stick Style frieze on the bell tower.

and large carriage house may have been built during this expansion of the Washington house, also designed by Rossiter.[52] Van Ingen paid to replace a Washington public schoolhouse that was in the way of the view from his property in 1888, with Rossiter as the architect for the newly sited school building. The expansion and remodeling of his estate were probably done at the same time. Rossiter also provided designs for a charitable project sponsored by Van Ingen's wife in 1893, the "Holiday House," a country hotel near Steep Rock, where respectable working girls from New York City, who were members of a social club associated with St. Bartholomew's Church, came for wholesome vacations in the out-of-doors.

In 1889, Rossiter provided the design for a small Swedish church on the Shepaug River in Washington Depot. Modest and plain, the wooden building was outfitted with a belfry ornamented with a Stick style frieze, a pent roof on the front gable, and a side entrance porch on the high side of the steep site.

Rossiter's reputation in Washington spread to nearby towns. In 1887-88, he remodeled a venerated 18th century house in nearby Litchfield. The house, an icon of the early years of the Colonial Revival movement because of its association with the celebrated 18th century builder William Sprats and its prominent 18th century owner Julius Deming, was made even "more colonial" through the Rossiter renovations. Rossiter duplicated the original, west-facing Palladian façade on a new projecting porch on the south elevation overlooking the garden. "Colonial" dormers were added to the roof, along with bay windows on the first floor of the southern elevation and an expansive rear wing. The alterations were commissioned by Julius Deming Perkins, who had recently inherited the house from his aunt.

In Greenwich, along the coast in southwest Connecticut, Rossiter designed a home for Miss Jennie Kent in 1889. It was one of the first homes in a new development at Belle Haven, a former farm purchased from Augustus Mead, the son of a Gunnery graduate who would build a Rossiter-designed cottage at Lake Waramaug in Washington in 1894. Rossiter also designed a house in Ridgefield, Connecticut, for W. A. Jenner in 1889.[53]

Rossiter's Connecticut clients brought business to the partners in New York, while New York clients commissioned projects in the regions surrounding the city. Richard Barnes, the Gunnery classmate who commissioned a summer home in Washington in 1885, also hired the architects to design a stable extension at his city residence in 1887. Dr. Safford G. Perry, a dentist and inventor of dental equipment at the end of the nineteenth century,[54] hired Rossiter to renovate his house at 46 West 37th St. in New York in 1884 and later to design a house near his second office in Yonkers in 1892 and his $10,000 summer house in Washington, Connecticut, in 1908. In addition, between 1896 and 1901 Rossiter prepared two designs for a modest school and library in Homer, New York, where Mrs. Perry served on the Building Committee.

ROSSITER & WRIGHT, Alterations to the Julius Deming house, Litchfield, Connecticut, 1888. Collection of the Litchfield Historical Society, Litchfield, Connecticut.

In order to expand an 18th century house to suit the 19th century lifestyle of the original owner's grandson, Rossiter added a wing to the back of the house, seen here to the right, to accommodate a larger kitchen and service spaces. He added dormers for new bedrooms on the third floor. The slightly projecting portico on the western façade of the house was adapted and expanded as an extension to the south side of the house, shown above, with bay windows to either side, overlooking the garden. This was Rossiter's first in-depth study of an 18th century house, and was the foundation of his subsequent designs in the Colonial Revival.

ROSSITER & WRIGHT, Telfair house, Flatbush, Brooklyn, New York, 1885. (left) *The Builder and Wood-Worker*, 6/1884, (right) Photo by C. D. Arnold.

This Brooklyn house was characteristic of the high quality of Rossiter & Wright's suburban houses in the 1880s, with well-designed Queen Anne Revival variety on the exterior and a "convenient interior" organized around a side entrance hall.

Other projects were commissioned by clients elsewhere in New England and New York. In Worcester, Massachusetts, Rossiter & Wright designed a $40,000 brick home for Charles Washburn in 1885. A successful manufacturer of steel and iron wire, Washburn and his wife raised their daughter and four sons in the house, located near the family's factory.[55] In Brooklyn, New York, Rossiter & Wright designed a handsome shingle-clad home for a doctor, J. H. Telfair, in the Flatbush neighborhood, which was professionally photographed and illustrated in *The Builder and Wood-Worker* magazine in June 1884. In addition, the partners designed renovations in 1886 for a barn and stable in Brooklyn for William Butler, who was a real estate agent and took in boarders, young men working as clerks in real estate, dry goods, produce, and banking. The architects also designed a similar stable in Brooklyn for their Washington client Richard Barnes in 1887.[56]

Rossiter & Wright designed a block of four row houses on the Upper West Side in 1886, an addition to a six-story brick commercial building on Mulberry St. in 1889,[57] and a home in Far Rockaway, Long Island, in 1888.[58]

STABLE FOR
W. L BUTLER ESQ
BROOKLYN. L.I.
ROSSITER & WRIGHT Architects
149. B'way. N.Y.C

ROSSITER & WRIGHT, Stable for W. L. Butler, Brooklyn, New York, 1884. *American Architect and Building News,* 1/16/1886. Author's collection.

The client for this stylish Brooklyn stable was in the real estate business and also ran a boarding house for up-and-coming young men. In real estate, appearances matter.

ROSSITER & WRIGHT, Row houses at 137-143 W. 81st Street, New York City. 1886. Levi Collection, Avery Architectural and Fine Arts Library, Columbia University, New York.

The firm designed four row houses in the rapidly developing Upper West Side that balanced a variety of Queen Anne Revival motifs to create harmony across the facades, while retaining the distinctive identity of each unit.

The block of four row houses was commissioned by Louis Frankenheimer in 1886 and was located at 137-143 West 81st St., between Columbus and Amsterdam Ave.[59] Clients for two of the four row houses were Albert Levi and Herman Rosenblatt. Built during the first decade of speculative development on the Upper West Side, following the opening of the Ninth Ave. El in 1879, these single-family houses were similar to hundreds being constructed in this area over the next 20 years. The façades of the four Rossiter & Wright houses were related in massing and materials but sufficiently varied to retain the individuality of the separate units. Typical of the decade, the façades featured rounded two-story bays and Tudor gables on three of the four units. Recent critics have singled out this group for particular ridicule: Christopher Gray described them in the *New York Times* as "a circus sideshow of architectural forms: stumpy little columns, strangely placed keystones and angled bays alongside traditional decoration like the egg-and-dart motif."[60] Others have viewed the row more kindly, with architect Robert A. M. Stern calling the group "exceptionally vivacious."[61]

In 1889 the firm designed a six-story brick extension on a commercial building owned by Thomas Hays at 145 Mulberry St. The large addition, 27 by 31 feet, costing $12,000, helped the firm establish its credentials in the commercial markets in the city.

Rossiter & Wright's prospects were bright. The firm was well established in New York as a result of the partners' participation in the organizations serving the new profession, the publication of their designs in respected architectural periodicals, and their effective cultivation of affluent clients through a network of friends in the suburbs.

The Rossiter & Wright houses on W 81st Street. A.Y. Smith photo.

ROSSITER & WRIGHT, *Modern House Painting,*
New York: William T. Comstock. Second edition,
1883. Author's Collection.

CHAPTER THREE: BUILDING COMMUNITIES: 1890-1930

Rossiter and Wright remained partners for 30 years, with an increasing number of clients and increasingly complex projects, including city apartment buildings and hotels, churches, schools, libraries, and park buildings. Many of these projects addressed the new demands of an urban clientele, who were just figuring out what they wanted and needed in both a city environment and in their country retreats. Rossiter & Wright also expanded the architectural vocabulary of its designs, reaching beyond the Queen Anne and Shingle styles that characterized the work of its first decade, designing buildings in the Colonial Revival, Dutch Revival, and Tudor Revival styles. In addition, the architects worked with a greater variety of building materials, including those developed for safer structures and those with more advanced technologies promoted for the health and convenience of the owners.

Expanding the Office

As established architects with a greater variety of projects, the partners expanded their offices and took on apprentices of their own. In 1888, the firm moved its offices to 47-49 Liberty St. in New York, moved again in 1895 to larger offices at 92-96 Liberty, and in 1900 went to 95 Liberty St., an office building filled with builders and engineers, including the Association of Electrical Engineers, shipbuilding engineers, and mining engineers. Among the associates working with the firm in these years were C. A. Hutchings, Robert Wakeman Gardner, Francis Bent, and Luther Birdsall. Others whose names are associated with published projects of Rossiter & Wright included D. A. Gregg, C. G. Walter, J. M. Kerr, and one known only by his last name, Coleman.

Charles A. Platt was the most prominent architect to work with Rossiter & Wright, although his effort with the firm was limited to a single project, a co-operative apartment building in New York City in 1907. Well-known as a painter, etcher, and garden designer, Platt had only recently turned to architecture, designing country estates for friends in New York and New Hampshire and several projects for Rossiter's cousin Laura Billings in Vermont and New York. The joint effort between Platt and Rossiter & Wright was sponsored by William Taylor, who initially built a co-op at the northeast corner of 66th and Lexington in 1906 designed by the architects Pollard & Steinan. Taylor hired Rossiter & Wright to design a second cooperative apartment building adjacent to his first, the second one at the southeast corner of 67th and Lexington. Even though the Pollard & Steinan building was Platt's first apartment design, Rossiter & Wright invited Platt to draw the façade of its building next door, creating a visually balanced block.[1]

Hutchings worked with Rossiter & Wright on the Royalton Hotel in 1897, although he had his own office at 27 East 20th St. in New York and designed independent projects, including a substantial $12,000 house in Montclair, New Jersey. Gardner, who also worked with Rossiter & Wright on the Royalton Hotel, was known as an archaeologist and author as well as an architect. He was working independently as an architect by 1906, when he designed windows for a Manhattan shop at 911 Broadway, between 20th St. and 21st St., a block east of 6th Ave.'s "Ladies Mile," a prominent shopping district. Frances Bent, sometimes described as the head draftsman for Rossiter & Wright, learned the profession as an apprentice in the office. He was working for the partners by 1890 and may have continued in this role until he was appointed Associate Architect for the State of New Jersey in 1905. He was appointed State Architect for New Jersey in 1917. Luther Birdsall was probably associated with the office of Rossiter & Wright, as well: His business address was 95 Liberty St. beginning in 1896, and he signed drawings for a project in Washington, Connecticut, for Rossiter's brother-in-law. Birdsall set up an independent office at 150 Nassau St. in 1901 and went into partnership there the following year as Birdsall and Sturges. On his own, he designed residences on Long Island as well as a railroad station in Huntington and the town hall in North Manhasset before he retired in poor health in 1906.

The practice of architecture was becoming more complex, as contemporary professional periodicals made clear in the variety of topics they addressed. Successful firms were expected to provide the services of draftsmen, engineers, construction supervisors, and contracts supervisors as well as designers. This increasing complexity is reflected in a comparison of the specifications issued by Rossiter & Wright for the construction of a summer home. The specifications issued by the firm for a project in 1896 were six pages long; those issued in 1911 were 26 pages long, with an additional 10 pages of specifications for the client's dairy barn.

Rossiter & Wright hired architectural and engineering specialists as outside contractors for its more complicated projects. For example, in the first decade of the twentieth century, the firm used Pattison Bros. Consulting Engineers of New York to do the foundation plans for the headmaster's house at The Hotchkiss School in Lakeville, Connecticut, and Ernest Bowditch, a Boston engineer, to do the plumbing plan, although this was not a particularly complicated project. A Mr. Young, probably of New York, did the watercolor renderings for project proposals during this period.

As the firm grew, the partners prospered. The Wrights, whose three daughters and a son were born between 1886 and 1896, moved to an expansive and stylish home of Wright's design in Short Hills, New Jersey, in 1900.[2] They spent the summers at the Water Witch Club in Highlands, later known as Monmouth Hills, on the Atlantic shore. Near his Short Hills residence, Wright cultivated potential clients while he pursued the new national rage for golf—he was a charter member of the Canoe Brook Country Club in Summit and a member of the prestigious Baltusrol Golf Club in nearby Springfield. He cut quite a figure; his family remembered that he dressed like an artist, with a flowing cravat.

The Rossiters and their four children—including a daughter, Edith, born in 1889, and their third son, Ehrick Winthrop, born in 1895—continued to live in Manhattan but spent their summers in Washington, Connecticut. In 1905, the family moved into an apartment in the prominent new cooperative building at Central Park Studios, 15 West 67th St., home to many painters and writers, where Rossiter was managing director. Studio apartments featured double-height "studio" spaces intended for artists, which also appealed to those who liked the look of the dramatic "salon." In 1910 they were living in another studio building at 27 West 67th St., and four years later they were living at 33 West 67th St. By 1918 they were renting an apartment at 15 Central Park West. Reflecting their status in society, they were listed in the Social Register. Rossiter's clubs were artistic: Since 1890, he'd been a member of the Century Association, the premier cultural club of writers, artists, and their supporters, where his father had been a founding member. He was also a trustee of the American Fine Arts Society; a member of the McDowell Club, an artists' club in New York; and a member of the University Club in Litchfield County. He was the president of the Village Improvement Society in Washington, Connecticut,[3] formed, like others across New England, to retain or enhance the charm of colonial villages through architectural and landscape enhancements. He sent his sons to Harvard and his daughter to Smith College. Three Irish servants were part of the household in New York, and the Coll family, with their 10 children, served as caretakers at the Washington property.

Rossiter & Wright in New Jersey: 1890-1910
In New Jersey during its heyday, the firm continued to provide designs for the new suburban neighborhoods west of New York City and the seaside communities in Monmouth County.

Business was brisk in the towns around Newark. Five new homes were designed in South Orange between 1890 and 1892, along with an addition for a billiard room for another client. At least seven more Rossiter & Wright houses were built in South Orange by 1905.[4] These homes were more elaborate than the firm's earlier work, as the billiard room addition suggests. The surviving examples are wood frame houses with brownstone foundations and a variety of octagonal towers and bay and oriel windows. Household utilities had advanced—one two-story frame house had electric bells, gas lights, bath and laundry fittings, and hot water heating; there were various interior finishes such as mantels and hardwood trim. Such a house cost $15,000 in 1894. The picturesque South Orange Village Hall was designed by the partners in 1894.[5] A design for a school for "Orange Valley," announced in 1894, may also have been intended for South Orange.[6]

ALL. SO. ORANGE, N.J.

The partners took an active role in the developing suburbs west of Newark, with more than 30 projects designed in the Oranges, including the Village Hall in South Orange.

In the town of Orange, designs for the Hillside Presbyterian Church were drawn in 1891 and drawings prepared two years later for the Orange Mountain Club House, a hotel formerly famous for its water cure that had recently burned. Between 1891 and 1893, Rossiter & Wright designed at least two homes in town and in 1905 prepared designs there for a large English timber house with a 35-foot library.[7] In 1910, the partners designed several houses in a new development at Mountain Station, near the Orange Mountain Club House, addressing the developer's requirement that the buildings be "fireproof."[8] They designed another "fireproof" house in Oakland, Bergen County, in northern New Jersey.[9]

In East Orange, Rossiter & Wright designed a three-story brick commercial building containing stores and apartment flats.[10] In West Orange, in the now-legendary planned garden community of Llewelyn Park, which had been laid out before the Civil War, the partners designed a two-story frame house with a slate roof, costing $20,000, in 1895.[11] Between 1890 and 1905, the firm built eight houses in Short Hills and

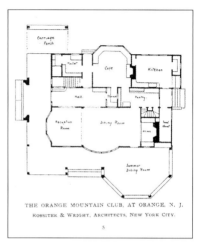

ROSSITER & WRIGHT, Orange Mountain Club, Orange, New Jersey, 1893. *Yearbook,* The Architectural League of New York, 1893-1894.

Country hotels appealed to urban residents in the late 19th century. Earlier sanatoriums for the popular "water cure" were converted to fashionable hotels and clubs like this one in Orange, New Jersey, which had a café, a dining room and a summer dining room filling the first floor. Like many of their commissions in Orange and South Orange, the architects designed the Orange Mountain Club in the Queen Anne Revival style, with half timbering that was beginning to look old fashioned by 1893.

Summit, including several at the Brantwood Club, where the architects have been credited as developers.[12] Bishop Hill was designed there for Charles W. L. Roche, a real estate developer, who commissioned the commercial building in East Orange. Several of the houses in Short Hills were on Hobart St., including Goodview, at 407 Hobart St., another home for Frank A. Wright.[13]

West of Short Hills, the firm designed a house in Bernardsville in 1893[14] and a house in Upper Montclair in 1900.[15] In 1914, Wright designed structures for Montclair's Glenfield Park, including a bridge, a shelter, a sand court, and a field house.[16] In Morristown, northwest of Newark, the firm designed four houses between 1889 and 1891.[17]

Back in Plainfield, the partners designed at least six homes between 1890 and 1903.[18] Typical of this stage in their careers, these houses were larger and better finished than the work Rossiter & Wright previously designed in Plainfield—one house was a two-story frame house on a large foundation, 66 by 79 feet, with steam heat, hardwood trim, and a slate roof; it was valued at $35,000.

In 1897, the firm was busy with new buildings at Middlebrook Heights in Bound Brook, west of Plainfield, including a clubhouse for the Middlebrook Country Club, a stone memorial tower, and four houses, including one for George Lamont, president of the club.[19] These houses, like the clubhouse, were generally two and a half-story frame houses valued between $3,500 and $8,000. Wright built a house there for himself, valued at $12,000, and Frances Bent, the firm's draughtsman, built himself a house there for $6,000. The following year, the firm designed three more houses at the Country Club, a school, and a three-story brick bank building with lodge rooms for local club meetings and apartments.[20]

North of Newark, Rossiter & Wright worked in the town of Englewood, designing their typical suburban homes, a two and a half-story frame house, roughly 35 by 45 feet, priced at $6,000.[21] In Ridgewood, they designed homes in this manner and also alterations to the Union Church Society building in Ridgewood Park.[22] In Rutherford, they designed a brick commercial building, The Franklin, in 1899.[23]

"GOODVIEW," RESIDENCE FOR MR. F. A. WRIGHT.
Rossiter & Wright, Architects.

ROSSITER & WRIGHT, Goodview, the home of Frank A. Wright, Short Hills, New Jersey, 1900. *Yearbook,* The Architectural League of New York, 1900.

Wright continued to build houses in the suburban New Jersey towns where the firm was active, moving westward as the New York suburbs expanded. As built at 407 Hobart Street, this house was more closely related to the partners' earlier designs in New Jersey than this watercolor suggests, with its plain white walls implying a single story cottage in the style of the English Arts and Crafts revival.

At the turn of the century, the partners designed several projects in Hackensack, north of Newark, including a stone library, a gift to the town from Senator William M. Johnson. The library was planned to house 20,000 books as well as a local history museum and was expected to cost $30,000 to $40,000. The senator, who was a lawyer and had been president of the New Jersey Senate and Assistant U.S. Postmaster General, also commissioned the firm to design homes for himself and for his son.[24] Other projects dating to the turn of the century in Hackensack included alterations to a two and a half-story frame home for E. E. Poor (whose brother was Rossiter's client in Shelter Island, New York, at the same time), a clubhouse for the golf club, and at least one of their standard two and a half-story frame homes, this one 42 by 50 feet.[25]

In Newark, the firm demonstrated its versatility, designing smaller homes in urban neighborhoods, commercial buildings, two-family houses, and recreational facilities for public parks. For a client in the Homestead Park development, the partners designed a house in 1895

New Jersey Senator and lawyer William Johnson donated the Rossiter & Wright-designed library to his hometown, providing sufficient funds for a building to house 20,000 books. The architects also designed homes in town for Johnson and his son, along with a clubhouse for the local golf club and several other residences.

that was, at one and a half stories and 31 by 38 feet, smaller than their customary New Jersey houses. Still, it cost $5,000.[26] Several years later they designed two properties for a client at Spruce and Washington St., including a three-story brick commercial building, 46 by 65 feet, perhaps an apartment building, and stable.[27] In 1901 in Jersey City, the transit hub between Newark and New York City, they designed four two-family houses, each one a two and a half-story frame house valued at $4,000, at Webster and Reservoir Ave.[28]

The firm's most important projects in Newark were buildings for Branch Brook Park on the city's north side. In 1905, the partners designed a boat and field house and two new shelters, one measuring 35 by 35 feet and the other 30 by 60 feet. The structures were described as "picturesque shelters for boys and girls…(adjoining) the young people's athletic field and the wading pool. [One of the buildings] is finished on the outside with cement stucco and coated with Lafarge cement. Inside and out it is built with a view to the roughest useage [sic] and small cost of maintenance."[29] In 1914, Frank Wright designed a bandstand and pavilion for the park.

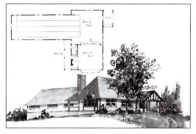

FRANK A. WRIGHT, *Treetops*, Wright house at the Water Witch Club, Monmouth County, New Jersey, 1896. Collection of Mary Jo (Burke) Kenny, Monmouth Hills, Highlands, New Jersey.

FRANK A. WRIGHT, The Rumble, the Stalls and the Railroad Station at Water Witch Club, Monmouth County, New Jersey. Collection of Mary Jo (Burke) Kenny, Monmouth Hills, Highlands, New Jersey.

While Rossiter & Wright were building middle-class homes and churches, club houses and parks in the suburbs of northern New Jersey, the firm was also designing summer homes in the seaside developments of Monmouth County. The partners had designed projects in the area early in their career, between 1881 and 1883, including a cottage at Spring Lake, churches in Atlantic Highlands and Long Branch, and a house in Fairview. Between 1892 and 1898, they designed several houses in Rumson,[30] and in 1893 they designed a school in Oceanic, now part of Rumson.

In Highlands, on the peninsula north of Rumson, Rossiter & Wright were active at the Water Witch Club, a private residential and social club established in 1895 by a group of New York businessmen and architects, led by the New York real estate developer Ferdinand Fish. Among the attractions of the high rocky site, 265 feet above the water, were spectacular vistas across the Raritan Bay to Manhattan to the north, the Atlantic Ocean to the east, and the Navasink River to the south. Ferries carried residents across the bay into the city. The Water Witch Club, the most exclusive of several summer residential communities developed in the region at the end of the nineteenth century, grew within several

Frank Wright designed six houses for clients in the new summer development at the Water Witch Club in Highlands, Monmouth County, New Jersey, including one for his own family. Covered in shingles and perched on the steep site, many of the houses were ringed with porches on the first and second floors that were supported with double height columns and arches.

"We are a family club with no ambition except to guard our membership and keep to unconventionality and informality."

Frank A. Wright, at the Water Witch Club in 1898.

years to include 40 seasonal cottages clustered around a club house on the high bluff. Among the founders were several architects who had worked with the prestigious firms McKim Mead & White and Carrère and Hastings in New York. Wright was a founder and an officer of the club, and the earliest houses constructed there were designed by Rossiter & Wright. Completed by June 1896, these included a summer home for Wright, as well as the seasonal homes for William B. Taber, an insurance executive, and Livingston Middleditch, a publisher. The following year, homes were built for Lemuel Skidmore, a New York lawyer, and Edward S. Atwood, who was listed in the census simply as a "capitalist." A home for Dr. S. Seabury Jones was completed in 1898.[31] Livingston Middleditch, who published law reports, also commissioned Rossiter and Wright to design his winter home in South Orange; his son Lyman later married one of Wright's daughters. Rossiter & Wright also designed a cottage in Water Witch for Cornelius Poillon, a ship builder, whose son married another of Wright's daughters.

Set upon steep and twisting roadways, the Water Witch lots were deliberately small and clustered to encourage congeniality among the residents. These summer homes were more compact than many of the summer homes designed then by the firm in northwest Connecticut,[32]

RESIDENCE OF LEMUEL SKIDMORE.
"SEABLINK."

but they were carefully sited on the crest of the Water Witch Club cliffs to afford privacy while sharing a series of common stone walls and landscaping that emphasized the shared community. Several of the houses were perched on the steep hillsides so that more than one floor opened onto ground level. Open porches wrapped around the upper floors facing the water views in three directions. Covered in shingles, the houses featured a variety of Colonial Revival details, including columns, gambrel roofs, bay windows, dormers, and balustrades. The firm also prepared designs for a train station for the Water Witch Club, and for stables and a combination bowling alley and billiard room. The designs were published in a promotional brochure for the club, but the bowling alley and stables were not built.[33]

In addition, Rossiter & Wright designed a dozen homes elsewhere in Monmouth County. These included in Allenhurst in 1897, a two-story frame dwelling for $30,000, and a shore cottage for the Downer family in Mantoloking in 1900, and others in Long Branch, Deal, Sea Bright and Belmar.[34] The firm also designed a frame house for W. B. Law in 1899 in Lawson Station, which was probably in New Jersey; like Brigadoon, it seems to have vanished from modern maps, a developer's dream not realized.

RESIDENCE OF CORNELIUS POILLON.

Rossiter & Wright in Connecticut, 1890-1910

In Connecticut, Rossiter continued to transform the south side of the Washington green with new residences. In 1892, Rossiter designed a Shingle-style summer home, The Sumacs, east of the Barbour house, for William Hamilton Gibson, a celebrated artist and naturalist and fellow Centurion in New York. In 1894, Rossiter designed Heathcote for his wife's parents, John and Henrietta Heath, just south of The Rocks on land that the Heaths' son Frank had acquired. That house burned just after the turn of the century. Heathcote was replaced by another house, surely of Rossiter's design, although the 1902 drawings were signed by Luthar Birdsall, who was probably affiliated with Rossiter's office before opening his own practice that same year. Since John Heath died in 1895, it's likely that Frank Heath lived in Heathcote with his mother until the fire and was the client for the house that replaced the one that burned. It was one of Rossiter's first Washington houses with elements in a more modern "colonial" style.

In 1894 Rossiter also designed a summer home in the then old-fashioned Queen Anne Revival style, for William and Amy Spencer Church on the ridge just east of the Washington green. The same year he began work on a new campus for The Ridge School, just south of Willamy, the Church house. The Ridge School was established by William Gold Brinsmade, the younger brother of John Chapin Brinsmade, who had taken over The Gunnery from his father-in-law, Frederick Gunn. John and William were also the nephews of Gunn's wife, Abigail, and the grandsons of the long-time colonial minister of the Washington Congregational Church, the Reverend Daniel Brinsmade. William taught Classics at The Gunnery after he graduated from Harvard in 1881. When he opened The Ridge School, he advertised that it was to be a small residential school for only 20 students, all boys (The Gunnery was then coed) and emphasized that The Ridge School would be conducted in a "cottage" atmosphere. The campus consisted of a main building and two smaller dormitory cottages, with a riverside building for recreation. The school building and residential buildings were designed in gambrel-roofed cottage style, echoing the founder's goals, and perched on the steep hillside.[35] After the turn of the century, as the school campus was being completed, Rossiter designed another house, The Gables, in the then out-of-date Queen Anne Revival style, just south of the school for the serial Rossiter client Dr. Safford Goodwin Perry.

ROSSITER & WRIGHT, The Sumacs, the home of William Hamilton Gibson, Washington, Connecticut, 1892. Joseph West photo, Collection of the Gunn Memorial Library and Museum, Washington, Connecticut.

Gibson's home was a graceful combination of the Shingle style, with its rusticated stone foundation and smooth bands of shingles, and the emerging Colonial Revival style, with its gambrel roofs and Palladian window. Gibson was then a renowned illustrator and naturalist and at the height of his career.

ROSSITER & WRIGHT, The Gables, summer home for Dr. and Mrs. Safford G. Perry, Washington, Connecticut, 1908. Joseph West photo, Collection of the Gunn Memorial Library and Museum, Washington, Connecticut.

This was the third home the architects designed for Dr. Perry over 25 years, including earlier projects in New York City and Yonkers. With its bold half timbering and clustered chimneys, it was the last of their work in the Queen Anne Revival style. In addition, Rossiter designed a small library in upstate New York for a civic project sponsored by Mrs. Perry in 1897.

ROSSITER & WRIGHT, The Gate House for Hickory Hearth, New Milford, Connecticut, 1904. Collection of Robert and Jennifer Manouse, New Milford.

The wind-powered water tower, with an observation deck, probably supplied water to Mrs. Black's home and her nearby Ingleside School.

In 1895, Rossiter designed a home in New Milford for Mrs. William Black, the widow of the benefactor of All Saints Church, her husband having died in 1889. William Black had encouraged economic activity in New Milford in the 1880s, investing in the local Electric Light Company, the Agricultural Society, and the New Milford Wannopee Pottery company. Sarah Sanford Black, a New Milford native, may have commissioned Rossiter to design several cottages on Terrace Place, behind the church they commissioned from Rossiter in 1882, for a School for Young Ladies, a residential school she operated there after 1892. The house Mrs. Black built, Hickory Hearth, was sited just north of the New Milford green on what was reputed to be the site of New Milford's first home. The well on the property was a revered town relic. The shingled house Rossiter designed for Mrs. Black was a large cottage with a long sweeping roof over a deeply recessed front porch. A picturesque gatehouse and a large carriage house, both in a half-timbered Queen Anne Revival style, were also built on the property.

Mrs. Black moved her cottage-based Terrace Avenue school to a former hotel across the street from her home in 1897. The Ingleside School attracted the daughters of affluent New Yorkers including Mamie Van Ingen, Edward Van Ingen's daughter, who had been a student there in 1894.[36] Mrs. Black hired Rossiter to design a school for boys north of her new home in 1899, a stucco and half timbered building named Weantinaug Hall, which became a post graduate classroom for the Ingleside School in 1904 when the boys' school floundered. After the Ingleside School's main building, the former hotel, burned in 1902, Black hired Rossiter to design a replacement building in 1903, Foundation Hall, a shingle-covered Colonial Revival classroom and dormitory attached to a brick Federal-era home that survived the fire. In 1906, Mrs. Black commissioned Rossiter to design The Bungalow, a gambrel-roofed retreat on the grounds north of her house for alumnae of the Ingleside School. Meanwhile, on Treadwell Avenue, a block to the east of the school's main campus, Rossiter designed at least one gambrel-roofed cottage for the Hine family in 1898 and may have designed others.

At the end of the nineteenth century, Rossiter provided designs for two final Queen Anne Revival homes in Connecticut before taking up the Colonial Revival style in earnest. The first commission in the old style was a small Shingle style house in Washington, Orchard Terrace, just

Smaller homes were also designed for city residents seeking a stylish retreat in the country. The house for choral director and Washington native Arthur Woodruff combined elements of the Queen Anne Revival, the Shingle style and the Colonial Revival.

One of their final designs in the Queen Anne Revival style with multiple steep gables and diamond pane casement windows, this home was created for an engineer who would go on to work on the electricification of the London Underground.

north of the green, for another Gunnery graduate, Arthur Woodruff, a Washington native who had made his reputation as an orchestral and choral director in New York City. The grander house, The Alders was designed in 1898 for the Charles Spofford family in cultured and stylish Norfolk, on the northern border of Litchfield County.

The Colonial Revival took hold in the residential work of Rossiter & Wright. In 1900, the Trowbridge family asked Rossiter to convert their large Victorian house on Washington's green into the newer style by replacing the mansard roof with a high gambrel roof to create a colonial look for the house, which they then named Dunover. In 1904 The Gunnery commissioned a design for a dormitory, named Bartlett Hall for the headmaster's father, which Rossiter designed as a symmetrical colonial-style house with dormers in the gambrel roof and a balustrade over the columned porch. In 1907 he designed a colonial-style building for the Washington Club north of Bartlett Hall, complete with a cupola, corner quoins, and classical portico. In the same year, he designed a library, the Gunn Memorial Library, just north of the Washington

ROSSITER & WRIGHT, The Gunn Memorial Library, Washington, Connecticut, 1907. Joseph West photo. Collection of The Gunn Memorial Library and Museum, Washington, Connecticut.

The Colonial Revival was in full force in Washington in the first decade of the 20th century, characterized by symmetry, cupolas, classical columns, and fan-lights. These neighboring buildings, shown opposite and above, were constructed of Rossiter's favorite materials for rural buildings at the turn of the century: shingles, rough cast and field stone.

ROSSITER & WRIGHT, La Tourelle, home of Henry Siddons Mowbray. Washington, Connecticut, 1901, 1907. Joseph West photos, Collection of the Gunn Memorial Library and Museum, Washington, Connecticut.

ROSSITER & WRIGHT, the home and studio of Louis Vaillant, Washington, Connecticut, 1904. Joseph West photos, Collection of the Gunn Memorial Library and Museum, Washington, Connecticut.

The homes and studios for artists Mowbray and his former student Vaillant were designed in a classical style influenced by architecture of the Italian countryside. Mowbray, a founder of the American Academy in Rome, was a proponent of Italian classicism in American mural painting. His ceiling murals are preserved in the Gunn Memorial Library in Washington, and in many Beaux Arts buildings throughout the United States.

Club, with a façade constructed of Richardsonian rusticated stone, gathered locally, and Colonial Revival details on the doorway, cupola, and pediment. Rossiter's designs now encircled the Washington green. In 1910, he remodeled the Federal-era church on the green, replacing a mid-century Victorian porch with a classical pedimented veranda embellished with paired ionic columns, and sheathing the belfry under the steeple in an elegant colonnade.

Many of the new houses designed and constructed in Washington at the turn of the twentieth century, Colonial Revival and otherwise, were sited on the few roads that ran like fingers pointing north from the green into former farmland, accommodating the New Yorkers who arrived on the train in search of a rural retreat for the summers. Rossiter designed a summer home and studio there for the prominent muralist H. Siddons Mowbray (1858-1928), and a nearby summer home and studio for Mowbray's student Louis Vaillant (1876-1944). Mowbray was a well-traveled artist of considerable reputation in the United States and Europe. At the turn of the century, he was at the height of his career, completing murals for high-profile projects designed by McKim Mead and White, such as the Vanderbilt house at Hyde Park and the University Club and Morgan Library, both in New York City. He was a member of the Century Club, among many other clubs, and a founder of the American Academy in Rome. William Hamilton Gibson introduced Mowbray to Washington, and the muralist built a summer home designed by Rossiter there in 1900. Within a few years, Mowbray converted the house into a year-round residence, adding a studio wing, also designed by Rossiter, in 1907. In 1913 Mowbray provided the ceiling murals for the Rossiter-designed library in Washington as a memorial to his first wife, who died in 1912. Mowbray, who later married his wife's sister, was active in the village, serving as president of the library in 1921. Vaillant was Mowbray's student in the life drawing class at the Art Students League in New York. After visiting Mowbray in Washington, Vaillant persuaded his mother to build a Rossiter-designed house there in 1904, where he painted classical allegories in the adjacent studio for the remainder of his life.

Rossiter's projects for Mowbray and Vaillant were conceived in the newly respected classical style, although these projects were inspired more by Italian precedent than the American colonial, having low hip roofs with

The most fully developed Washington houses in the Colonial Revival style were designed for some of the town's most prominent summer residents including a U. S. Senator, a wealthy investor and property speculator, and a wealthy widow with a proud lineage.

exposed roof rafters along with the typical classical symmetry. Rossiter also designed colonial-influenced projects in Washington during this period. Modest but stylish cottages with gambrel roofs, shed dormers, and deep porches, draped in shingles, were built for the families of Brooklyn insurance broker William Van Sinderen and his wife, the former Mary Brinsmade, in 1905;[37] for Dr. Frederick Wersebe, in 1908; and for the artist and former Gunnery student Herbert Faulkner, in 1908. Faulkner, who studied painting in Venice, turned to wood carving and book illustration when he returned to Washington, working in a studio, also designed by Rossiter, that was next door to Mowbray's property.

Meanwhile, Rossiter designed a colonial farmhouse, plain and symmetric, for the Mairs family of Irvington-on-Hudson on land between the Barnes carriage house and the Barbour house on Ferry Bridge Road. In 1910 Rossiter designed a home and studio for the artist Walter Russell on the road to Roxbury, south of the houses on Ferry Bridge Road, a sprawling two-story house with a $10,000 mortgage. He also designed a modest colonial home for the Isaac Hebbard family next door to the Barbour house in 1913, and a hybrid craftsman/colonial house, Muwagha Lodge, for Arthur Shipman of Hartford, sometime after 1913, on one of the roads north of the green.

The trophy houses in the Colonial Revival style in Washington were the homes Rossiter designed for Senator Orville Platt, Cornelius Gold, and Ruth Standish Baldwin. Designed for affluent clients in a patriotic age, they presented Rossiter's most fully realized vision of the Colonial Revival. The first of these homes, for Senator Orville Platt (1827-1905), was built on Ferry Bridge Road, on land purchased in 1898 from Edward Van Ingen. Platt, a Washington native and Gunnery graduate, had been active in Connecticut state politics before serving as U.S. Senator for 26 years, from 1879 until his death in 1905. An enormously influential senator, he was involved with legislation on all of the critical national issues of the turn of the twentieth century: patent protection, Indian affairs, currency reform, Cuba, Panama, and the Philippines. He was appointed a regent of the Smithsonian in 1899. His second wife, Jennie Smith Hoyt, a long-time friend and a widow whom he married in 1897, was an advocate for child labor reform, prison reform, and women's education and was the first curator of Washington's historical collections. She commissioned the house as a gift to her new husband, creating one of Rossiter's most accomplished Colonial Revival homes. Sited next door to the Gibson home on Ferry Bridge Road, the Platt house, Kirby Corner, was a showplace of the best of American traditional style.

Cornelius Gold, a Wall Street banker who actively traded in Washington real estate between 1886 and 1911, was the heir to a fortune based on his father and uncle's invention of a steam heat apparatus and a successful investor in railroads in the Midwest. Another of the many Brinsmade descendants, Gold built a home in Washington, Prospect Hill, designed by Rossiter just after the turn of the twentieth century. It was a country house solidly conceived in the Colonial Revival style, festooned with dormers and porches overlooking the Shepaug River valley to the northwest of the Washington green.

Edgewood, the home Rossiter designed for Mrs. William Baldwin, was perhaps his archetypical American colonial monument, deliberately recalling the home of George Washington himself, with a double-height, columned Mt. Vernon style porch running the full length of the south side of the home, overlooking extensive gardens and, beyond them, the Washington green. Mrs. Baldwin, who bought her land from Cornelius Gold in 1910, was a proud descendant of Miles

Standish of the Mayflower legend, the widow of the president of the Long Island Railroad, and a trustee of Smith College. Pedigree, wealth, and education were distilled in this house, which Rossiter published in the Architectural League's Yearbook in 1912. Rossiter must have particularly admired this house, for after he retired in 1920, he sold The Rocks and purchased Edgewood, and a decade later sold it to his youngest son, Winthrop.

The stylish Washington projects encouraged others in northwest Connecticut to hire the cultured architect to design projects for their country retreats.

Rossiter was a member of the Litchfield County University Club, founded in 1896, and through the club was introduced to future clients in Norfolk, Lakeville, and Litchfield. The club, limited to 175 members, met twice a year in towns around the county. Among the illustrious guests and honorary members were the presidents of Yale and Trinity colleges. The meetings included presentations of timely and academic topics followed by entertainment, including musical performances and dinners brought in from Delmonico's restaurant in New York.

ROSSITER & WRIGHT, Standish (later Edgewood), home for Ruth Standish Baldwin, Washington, Connecticut, 1910. Joseph West photos, Collection of the Gunn Memorial Library and Museum, Washington, Connecticut.

Mrs. Baldwin commissioned a residence based on George Washington's home, Mount Vernon, with a double height porch running the full width of the house. Ten years later, this quintessential American design became Rossiter's home in retirement.

ROSSITER & WRIGHT, renovations to the home of Mr. and Mrs. Carl Stoeckel, Norfolk, Connecticut, 1900-1906. Photo Frank H. DeMars. DeMarsImages.com.

Between 1900 and 1906, the Stoeckels added a larger service wing (to the right) and a circular porch around the music room (to the left), along with an impressive double height circular entrance porch and a roof line balustrade, transforming an Italianate design into a Classical Revival design and expanding the house for ambitious musical events and entertainments.

The undisputed leader of the club was Carl Stoeckel, who, though not a college graduate, was made an honorary member of the club he founded because of his generous support of the club's meetings and projects. At the turn of the century, Stoeckel and his wife, Ellen Battell Terry, who were married in 1895 a few months after the death of her father Robbins Battell, hired Rossiter to remodel the historic family home on the green in Norfolk.[38] Over the next 15 years, they transformed a prominent Italianate house into an even grander home in a loosely defined Colonial Revival style, suitable for the kind of entertaining they intended. The colonial house had been updated in an Italianate style in the 1850s by Robbins Battell, who also added a wing to the south of the main house to accommodate a combination music room and library in 1880. The alterations commissioned by the Stoeckels at the turn of the twentieth century, probably designed by Rossiter, included a colonnade around the south wing and an addition to the north side of the house for a larger dining room, related service rooms, and verandas overlooking the village and the long views to the west. A third floor was added to accommodate important guests from New York and abroad. The Italianate pediments over the windows of the main house were removed, and a rooftop balustrade in the Georgian style was added,

contributing to the colonial appearance of the house. A columned entrance doorway was set within a grand circular double-height porch. Inside, the house was updated with modern bathrooms and electricity as well as classical detailing in several of the main entertaining rooms and the central hallway.

Although the Battells had long hosted musical events in their house and other locations in Norfolk, the Stoeckels undertook a more ambitious venue to serve the growing choral societies in the region. Carl Stoeckel, whose father, Gustave, was the first music and singing instructor at Yale (a position sponsored by the Battell family), was committed to choral and orchestral music, believing that the phenomenally popular opera music had been overwhelmed with tinsel and trapdoors. Choral and orchestral music, on the other hand, was the epitome of truth in the musical arts, he believed. The Stoeckels commissioned Rossiter to design a freestanding auditorium on their property for larger choral and, soon, orchestral concerts. In 1902 the Stoeckels built an "experimental" concert hall behind Whitehouse, to test the acoustics for the new hall. The temporary structure, made of wood and covered in tar paper, was based on the proportions of Steinway Hall in New York.

ROSSITER & WRIGHT, Music Shed, Norfolk, Connecticut, 1906. Photo Frank H. DeMars. DeMarsImages.com.

The Music Shed, built by the Stoeckels in the valley behind their house, was designed in the Colonial Revival style, with detailing similar to the contemporary, but much smaller, Washington Club.

ROSSITER & WRIGHT, Greycote, home for Richmond Paine, Norfolk, Connecticut, 1906. Photo: Frank H. DeMars. DeMarsImages.com

ROSSITER & WRIGHT, Huttlein, home for Robbins Stoeckel, Norfolk, Connecticut, 1907. Photo: Frank H. DeMars. DeMarsImages.com

EHRICK ROSSITER, School for Norfolk, Connecticut, 1913. Post card courtesy of the Norfolk Historical Society.

In 1906, the permanent Rossiter-designed Music Shed of splendidly resonating wood was built in the valley behind Whitehouse. The Music Shed, a name Stoeckel intended to conjure the power of music to "shed light," was expanded during its construction and again in the years that followed, so that by 1910 it could accommodate a choir of 425 on stage and an audience of 1,500.[39]

Rossiter's designs for the Stoeckels were much more "modern" than the 1898 half-timbered house he created a few years earlier for the Spoffords around the corner from Whitehouse in Norfolk. Several other commissions in Norfolk followed in the first decade of the twentieth century, more modest homes in the Colonial Revival style, including houses for Richmond Paine (1906), director of the Litchfield County Choral Union (founded by the Stoeckels), and New York lawyer Robbins Stoeckel (1907), Carl Stoeckel's younger brother. Rossiter designed a school for Norfolk in 1913, an office building for Robbins Stoeckel (not built), two homes and a gardener's cottage for Mrs. Helen H. Jenkins (1916-1917), and alterations to houses for E. H. Fallows, William Moseley, George Case, Edmund Brown, and the Norfolk Inn. Later, in 1929, Mrs. Stoeckel commissioned Rossiter's firm to design a stone observation tower at Haystack Mountain honoring her father.[40] The firm also submitted a design for a town hall in 1908, which was not built, and renovations to the Church of Christ and to Battell Chapel in 1927.

The Stoeckels and Rossiters were friends, trading visits to their homes in Washington and New York City. According to Rossiter's daughter, Edith, the Stoeckels purchased the Rossiter's New York City apartment in the Central Park Studio building in 1914.

Through the Litchfield County University Club, and perhaps with the endorsement of the Stoeckels, Rossiter was introduced to the headmaster of The Hotchkiss School in Lakeville. Headmaster Edward G. Coy was a member of the club, along with several other faculty members at the school, including Huber Gray Buehler, who became the new headmaster in 1904.

Buehler had grand ambitions for the school, which prospered and was greatly expanded during his 20-year tenure. Rossiter served as the school's architect during these years, designing and supervising

ROSSITER & WRIGHT, Headmaster's House, The Hotchkiss School, Lakeville, Connecticut, 1910. Courtesy of The Hotchkiss School Archives.

Rossiter designed an addition to the Master's house, more than doubling its size and refining its Colonial appearance to make it more suitable for the school's image, aspirations and fund-raising efforts.

$180,000 in capital projects there.[41] These projects included new construction as well as the modernization and expansion of the existing buildings, which had been designed by the New York architect Bruce Price in 1892. Rossiter's new buildings included a servants' hall, an infirmary (both 1905-1906), a field house (1908-1909), a boathouse (1911), and a barn (1912-1913). Between 1905 and 1908, Rossiter prepared designs to upgrade the utilities in the school's existing buildings and directed the expansions of the existing facilities as the school grew. In the kitchen, Rossiter installed refrigeration rooms, a lift, and a dumb waiter; he upgraded the boiler that generated electricity for the main building and installed electric lights there; he installed showers in the Bissell residential hall; and he added a fire escape for the boys' rooms on the upper floors of the main building. He also expanded the dining room, the recitation room, the classrooms, and the gym. In the gym, he added a new running track and two squash courts as well as a slide from the running track to the swimming pool, which must have been a delight for the boys. Over the next two years, Rossiter designed extensions for the chapel, including an organ alcove and a cupola to

ROSSITER & WRIGHT, Connecticut State Building, Jamestown Exposition, 1907. Post card. Author's collection.

Benjamin Tallmadge House, Litchfield, Connecticut. Collection of the Litchfield Historical Society, Litchfield, Connecticut.

improve ventilation during religious services; he also expanded the classrooms and the recitation hall, and made further modifications to the headmaster's office, the gym, and the pool. Rossiter designed an enclosed walkway joining the Bissell residential building with the main school building, a decided advantage in the blustery winters in Connecticut's northwest hills. Much of the work was mundane, but the campus experience must have reminded Rossiter of his happy and formative years at The Gunnery, and the work introduced him to potential clients among the trustees of the school.[42]

Buehler, a legendary promoter of the school and successful fund-raiser, cultivated prospective and established donors, as well as alumni, in his home, which was enlarged by Rossiter in 1910 to provide a more suitable environment for Buehlers' entertaining. The newly expanded headmaster's house included 18 bedrooms and seven bathrooms. An important feature in the addition was an impressive oak-paneled study, where Buehler received faculty and students, as well as a stylish white dining room and large verandas overlooking formal gardens and the lake beyond. Buehler's nephew recalled that meals at the Buehlers were like those in world-famed restaurants: "There were seldom fewer than twelve around the table, with more at the frequent parties."[43] Although the school hired Cass Gilbert to prepare a campus plan in 1915, Rossiter continued to work for The Hotchkiss School on mundane but necessary projects, providing the designs to move the kitchen from the basement of the headmaster's house to the main floor, adjacent to the dining room, in 1921, making life easier for the servants and eliminating a noisy dumb waiter that had been used to bring the food to the dining room from the basement kitchen. Rossiter drew plans to expand the school's dining room, yet again, in 1925. [44]

Meanwhile, Rossiter was at work designing homes for the affluent in other Connecticut towns, including Litchfield, Ridgefield, New Milford, and Bridgeport.

Rossiter was already known in Litchfield because of his renovation of the Deming house in 1887, and he remained socially and professionally associated with the town as he conducted his study of the Tallmadge house in Litchfield for adaptation to the Connecticut State Building at the Jamestown Exposition in 1907. Several new commissions were secured in Litchfield during the first decade of the twentieth century, the height of the town's Colonial Revival fervor.[45] Charles Deming, a grandson of Litchfield's 18th century leader Julius Deming, hired the architect to design his retirement home on a lot he purchased on North St. in 1899.[46] A symmetric two-story house with a hip roof and double-height columned porch, it was a classical design for the middle class. In 1903, Seymour Cunningham, a Washington, D.C. businessman with family ties to Litchfield,[47] hired Rossiter to design a summer home for his family on South St. Cunningham, later the president of Litchfield's Village Improvement Society, was attuned to the Colonial Revival and worked with the Olmsted landscape designers to reimagine the Litchfield green in a colonial style. The hip-roofed house Rossiter designed for the Cunninghams had a double-height circular porch, bolder than the one for the Charles Deming house; the design displeased Cunningham's wife. She recalled, "It wasn't a pretty house...Some wit said it reminded him of the front of a ferry boat, and we have laughed so often at the thought."[48] Rossiter may also have designed a gambrel-roofed dairy barn for the summer home of Yale Medical School physician B. Austin Cheney, for whom he would design a home in New Haven in 1918.[49]

Closer to New York City, Rossiter was commissioned to design a summer estate, in Ridgefield, Connecticut, for A. Barton Hepburn, chairman of New York's Chase National Bank. Hepburn was an influential figure in New York and in national politics and finance. He was a member of the New York legislative committee that investigated railroad rate discrimination leading to state legislation that served as the model for the Interstate Commerce Act. He served as U. S. Comptroller of the Currency under President Harrison and was a founder of the Graduate School of Business at Columbia University. A native of the tiny farming village of Colton in upstate New York who remained loyal to his country origins, he twice married women from northern Vermont. The grand country home Hepburn commissioned from Rossiter to be built in Ridgefield in 1902 satisfied both Hepburn's nostalgia for his rural roots and his status as a nationally prominent business leader. The Colonial Revival home, with double-height paired columns and pedimented porticos, corner quoins, and roofline dormers, was set on a high ridge. A small farm, with chickens, cows, and horses, was tucked in back, with elaborate gardens and a pool placed between the mini-

ROSSITER & WRIGHT, the Charles Deming house, Litchfield, Connecticut. Collection of the Litchfield Historical Society, Litchfield, Connecticut.

ROSSITER & WRIGHT, Seymour Cunningham house, Litchfield, Connecticut. Collection of the Litchfield Historical Society, Litchfield, Connecticut.

The emphatically Colonial Revival country home for the New York banker A. Barton Hepburn had the litany of colonial references stuffed onto each façade: front, back and both sides. A working farm was established behind the formal gardens at the back of the house, and soon Hepburn acquired a larger farm in the countryside nearby. Later, he commissioned Rossiter to design seven libraries near his childhood home in upstate New York and a dormitory at his alma mater, Middlebury College, in Vermont.

farm and the house. A few years later, Hepburn bought a 150-acre farm nearby, expanding his rural empire in suburban Connecticut. Within a decade he and Rossiter would undertake a series of projects to build libraries in upstate New York and to support Hepburn's alma mater, Middlebury College, in Vermont.[50]

Elsewhere in Connecticut, Rossiter added a double-height classical pediment to the Charles Beach house on the south end of the green in New Milford in 1910 and designed houses for clients in Danbury and Bridgeport.[51] He designed a building for the Bridgeport City Savings Bank in 1910, one of many local institutions expanding to support the city's prospering manufacturers.[52]

THE PRESIDENT'S HOUSE, VASSAR COLLEGE.
ROSSITER & WRIGHT, ARCHITECTS, NEW YORK CITY.

ROSSITER & WRIGHT, President's House, Vassar College, Poughkeepsie, New York, **1895**. *Inland Architect and News Record*, Vol. XXXIL, No. 8 (1898). Ryerson and Burnham Libraries Book Collection, The Art Institute of Chicago. Digital File # 1A3205_2651 © The Art Institute of Chicago.

Rossiter & Wright designed a formal Tudor Revival brick home for the official campus residence of the President of Vassar College.

Rossiter & Wright in Suburban New York

Between 1890 and 1910, the firm designed a cluster of estate properties and campus buildings in Westchester County. In 1896, it designed the president's house at Vassar College, a stone Tudor Revival home that was published in the annual Yearbook of the Architectural League, and a recitation hall, apparently not built, that was published in the yearbook in 1897. The firm also designed houses and additions to homes in Ardsley-on-Hudson, Brewster, Bedford, Mt. Vernon, White Plains, and Yonkers, as well as a house at Spuyten Duyvil in Riverdale.[53] The 1898 home in White Plains was for J. J. Brown, later the president of the village, who operated a branch of the Keeley Institute, a treatment center for alcoholics and addicts, perhaps in the Rossiter & Wright building.[54] In 1900, the firm designed a two-story stone-and-cement addition to the Millbrook home of Daniel Lamont, the Secretary of War from 1893 to 1897 during Grover Cleveland's administration and later the vice president of the Northern Pacific Railroad.[55] The addition contained a billiard room, ballroom, and bowling alley. The firm also designed a 25- by 30-foot gardener's cottage for the estate.[56] Rossiter

In one of the partners' first domestic designs in the Colonial Revival style, this symmetric design was made more dramatic with the double-height entrance porch, not to mention the flags and the side porches projecting at 45 degrees from the house.

& Wright proposed a hotel in Tarrytown, published in the Architectural League's Yearbook in 1900, which may or may not have been built.

On Long Island, the architects designed estates and mid-market housing developments as well as schools and libraries for the suburbs developing in the region. They expanded their reach in Brooklyn, building at least 10 additional houses there, many described as two-and-a half-story frame houses, roughly 30 by 60 or 30 by 40 feet and priced between $5,000 and $8,000. Most of these were built in the Seagate neighborhood, at the southwestern end of Brooklyn, overlooking the ocean.[57]

Rossiter & Wright also designed substantial homes in exclusive developments, including Port Washington, Mill Neck, Oyster Bay, Lloyd's Neck, and Old Field Point, all along the north shore; Shelter Island, East Hampton, and Quogue on the eastern end of Long Island; and Islip on the south shore.[58] Several of these houses, while less imposing than the more celebrated Long Island estates, were valued between $50,000 and $80,000, making them the most costly of the Rossiter & Wright country houses. The 1909 house at Old Field Point, which burned to the ground shortly after completion, was for Mrs. Howard Gibb. Her brother was Clinton Rossiter, an officer of the Long Island rail lines and a developer of exclusive real estate communities in northern Long Island. Clinton and his sister may have been related to the architect. The 1898 home on Shelter Island was for Charles Lane Poor, whose brother hired the architects for a project in Hackensack the same year.[59]

Rail lines ran to the south shore of Long Island by 1869, and Rossiter & Wright were busy designing homes in the new developments that grew up near the stations there. They designed homes in Cedarhurst and Woodmere, two of the Five Towns region later known for its gracious neighborhoods. They designed three homes in Cedarhurst between 1899 and 1903, of which two were two-and-a-half-story frame houses, 72 by 40 feet, valued at $15,000; the third was smaller, at 40 by 35 feet.[60] Between 1901 and 1903, one of the Cedarhurst clients, Robert L. Burton, also commissioned at least half a dozen projects from Rossiter & Wright in nearby Woodmere. Burton, a real estate developer with offices in New York City, owned Woodmere. Literally. He took majority control of the property there in 1878 and built a new village center for his 400-acre residential community on a peninsula between Jamaica Bay and Hempstead Bay. Envisioning a private residential estate, he built a railroad station, and commercial buildings including a market and other stores in a development with every city convenience except sewers, according to the *New York Times*.[61] He built 40 new houses there costing $8,000 to $50,000, modeled on upscale suburban developments at Germantown, Pennsylvania, and Brookline, Massachusetts. Burton hired a number of architects to design the suburban estates. The Rossiter & Wright projects were described in contemporary publications as renovations to frame houses (at least six, at roughly $6,000 per project) and renovations to a frame-and-stone stable.[62] Burton did not sell his houses, renting them instead on an annual contract. When the Long Island Railroad was electrified and connected to New York City through the subway, which the *Times* suggested Burton anticipated, he sold the entire project for around $3 million. Twenty years later, in the 1930s, Burton's son and Rossiter were spending the winters at the same small inn in Florida—another client's family having bonded with the architect.

In addition to houses, the firm designed community facilities and workplaces on Long Island. In 1891, it designed the Emma Clark Library in Setauket, a lovely little building with corner quoins on the brick-surfaced first story and whimsical half-timbers in the gables. In Dutch Kills, a section of Long Island City in Queens, the firm designed a concrete paper mill for the Central Paper Company in 1903.

ROSSITER & WRIGHT, Emma S. Clark Library, Setauket, New York, 1891. Collection of Beverly Tyler, Courtesy of the Three Villages Historical Society, East Setauket, New York.

Elements of the Tudor Revival, notably the half timbering, were playfully applied to this small library on Long Island.

The first design for the small library
was essentially a colonial cottage,
the simplest of the cottage designs
that Rossiter & Wright began to use
for summer homes in northwest
Connecticut and New Jersey at the
turn of the century.

Elsewhere in New York State, Rossiter designed a small, shingled
building for the Glen Haven library in the Finger Lakes region of New
York and then redesigned the building to house both the town library
and a one-room school, at a cost of only $2,300. Located on the south
side of Skaneateles Lake, the area initially attracted New Yorkers for
the "water cure," but by the end of the nineteenth century, many New
Yorkers, as well as a group of professors from the Pennsylvania Dental
College, came to the resort and built summer homes nearby. Rossiter
may have stayed in the Glen Haven resort on the picturesque lake, and
he was persuaded to take an interest in the library project by the wife
of his frequent client, Mrs. Safford G. Perry, whose family summered
in the town. In Liberty, New York, Wright's birthplace, the architects
designed alterations to a small church in 1891.[63]

Rossiter & Wright in New York City

Even as the firm was busy with country clients north, east, and west
of the city, their business in New York City was active. Between 1886
and 1908, Rossiter & Wright was commissioned to design 19 projects
in the city, including apartment buildings, town houses, apartment
renovations, commercial buildings and a combination church and
settlement house.

After the financial panic of 1893 eased in the middle of the decade, construction picked up in the city. In 1896, Rossiter & Wright designed a $17,000 frame house for George Strong in Manhattan. The same year it began the renovations for Elizabeth Schley's apartment at 812 Madison Ave., on the southwest corner of 68th St., adding two leaded glass windows and a beamed ceiling. Three years later, the architects joined two houses for the Schleys at 845-846 Fifth Ave., removing the second entrance and creating a passage to an existing conservatory. In 1898, they designed two projects at 105 East 34th St. for Charles Noyes, a young lawyer. The first was a four-story stone home, 20 by 56 feet, expected to cost $40,000, and the second was a four-story building with apartments, 20 by 50 feet, containing double-height studio spaces, expected to cost $12,000. They made renovations to buildings on the Upper West Side, including the construction of a bay window in 1899 in Helen Elderkin's apartment at 150 West 65th St. and in 1903 the installation of an elevator in the home at 6 West 70th St. belonging to Joseph Eastman, a prosperous butcher.[64] Then, as now, residential work in the city was filled with small-scale projects, building renovations as well as new construction. These projects were the routine work of the architects' office, updating the homes of a rising middle class, hungry for stylish leaded glass windows, conservatories, elevators, and bay windows, as well designing new buildings to line the city streets.

The partners did a considerable business in the commercial district downtown. In 1897, Rossiter & Wright designed roof alterations and fireproofing for a building at 19 Barclay St. owned by the National Railroad Publishing Company and designed a two-story brick building with offices and stores at Court St. for Frederick Barnum. The same year, they completed alterations to a building at 71-73 Franklin St. for the Warner Brothers' garment business and moved a building on Mott St. They designed a 10-story bachelor apartment building in 1899 at 32-34 West 49th St. They built a three-story fireproof building on Spruce St. and a two-story frame stable for W. B. Lockwood at 45 Broadway. In 1902 they designed the Hegeman Building, a $100,000 six-story brick-and-stone building with stores and manufacturing lofts at 198 Broadway and another one next door at 200-202 Broadway for a similar price for Oscar Zollikoffer.[65]

Rossiter was his own client for this commercial building on land that had been part of his grandfather Parmly's estate. Tenants in the 12 story building included shops in the textile trades, such as Wilcox and Gibb sewing machines, a clothing manufacturer, a maker of ties, a maker of men's hats and a milliner.

The Royalton, commissioned by Rossiter's cousin Frederick Billings, Jr., was the firm's first big project in New York City and their first opportunity to demonstrate their ability to design in the Classical Revival style on a grand scale. It is now a luxury hotel.

In 1903 Rossiter built his own commercial building, a 12-story steel-framed brick building, at 656-666 Broadway, on the southeast corner of Bond St. The property was part of Rossiter's inheritance from his grandfather's real estate empire, located in the city's historic retail and wholesale dry goods center. Brooks Brothers and W. and J. Sloan built stores nearby in the 1880s. Rossiter's new building, constructed during a real estate boom in the area following the consolidation of the five boroughs in 1898, had stores on the ground floor and lofts on the upper floors for small-scale manufacturing, primarily in the textile trades, with several shops that made ties and hats for men and women.

The firm's most prestigious city commissions were completed between 1886 and 1908—The Royalton, at the time of its construction in 1897 the largest bachelor hotel in the city, and two apartment buildings in 1907 on the city's Upper East Side at the intersection of Lexington Ave. and 67th St.

The Royalton was built by Frederick Billings, Jr., Rossiter's cousin, who managed his father's estate following the senior Billing's death in 1890. Located at 47-49 West 43rd St., the 12-story building was one of the first in New York to run completely through the block, with entrances on both 43rd and 44th St. Alternatives to apartment buildings, bachelor hotels were popular at the turn of the twentieth century among wealthy single men, who rented their *pieds-à-terre* by the year to use during their frequent visits to the city. Unlike apartments, these units did not have kitchen facilities; they were more like the sleeping accommodations at the private men's clubs in the neighborhood, such as the Harvard Club and the New York Yacht Club on 43rd St.[66] The Royalton had 90 apartments for tenants overlooking the street frontages and additional accommodations for servants of the guests and the hotel on the interior of the floors.

The Royalton had a classically inspired façade, with an oversized Georgian double-height doorway with a broken-arch pediment. The architectural press took an interest in the fireproof building, with a full-page photo of the entrance running in the Yearbook of the Architectural League. *American Architect and Building News* and *Real Estate Record and Guide* also took note of the building, the *Guide* reporting that it cost $500,000.[67]

The firm's other high-profile projects during this period were high-quality cooperative apartment buildings, or co-ops, on the Upper East Side. In the early twentieth century, New York apartment buildings were increasingly popular with affluent buyers, who had previously insisted on single-family housing. As the number of inhabitants in the city grew, the cost of single-family homes, even row houses, was beyond the means of most families. New apartment buildings, designed by the city's leading architects, were a welcome alternative. In 1909, *Architects' and Builders' Magazine* claimed that well appointed, cooperatively owned apartment buildings were an attractive and less expensive housing option for those who had previously owned private houses worth from $50,000 to $150,000. Apartments were especially popular, the magazine reported, since many of the owners would be spending a greater time out of the city in their country homes. "The apartment-house idea presents an almost perfect solution of the problem. It provides a city residence, to be occupied or abandoned almost at a moment's notice, with little of the care and responsibility incidental to maintaining a whole house and with much less expense for accommodations of corresponding size and quality."[68]

A group of co-ops had been successfully developed on the West Side, including the artist-oriented 1903 studio building at 15 West 67th St., where Rossiter lived and was managing director. Fourteen studio apartments, so named because they had a two-story "studio" space in addition to rooms of the usual height in an apartment, and 20 smaller apartments shared the building in a combination of owner-occupied units and rental units. The income from the rental units was expected to cover the cost of the building's maintenance. William Taylor was the developer of the West 67th St. project that had been instigated by the painter Henry Ward Ranger with a decidedly artistic focus. The architects of that project, Simonson, Pollard & Steinman, designed additional studio apartment buildings on West 67th St. over the next five years. The artist Walter Russell, who was a Rossiter client in Washington and had been a director with Rossiter of the Central Park Studio building at 15 West 67th, described the amenities of a new co-op at 65th and Central Park West in 1918 that he was apparently trying to get Rossiter to invest in. Among the amenities of the new project, probably typical of co-ops in this market, were tiled kitchens with electric refrigeration and ice machines that were connected by fast-moving electric-powered dumb waiters bringing food from the central kitchen that served the building. Beyond that, there was a gymnasium and a "luxurious" swimming pool.[69]

Rossiter's experience with the studio apartments on the Upper West Side probably led to the firm's involvement with two cooperative apartment buildings on the Upper East Side developed by William J. Taylor, who became a specialist in building and managing co-ops in the city.

In 1907, two cooperative apartment buildings designed by Rossiter & Wright were built at Lexington Ave. and East 67th St. on the southeast and northeast corners of the intersection. The building on the southeast corner, entered from 67th Street, was a classical design clad in limestone, with heavier blocks on the façade of the first three floors and a classically detailed projecting cornice. Along with the artist Kenyon Cox, Rossiter was one of the "founders," as the original investors were called, of the 11-story building, which cost $750,000.[70] According to the *New York Times*, Taylor's projects appealed to middle-class buyers, who were in the market for apartments costing between $20,000 and $50,000. By February 1907, the *Times* reported that investors in a neighboring Taylor building at Lexington and 66th were cashing in their shares for a quick 10% profit, and the *Times* cautioned that such action would lead to financial speculation and ruin this emerging market.

ROSSITER & WRIGHT, Cooperative apartment building, 130 E. 67th Street, New York City, 1907. *Architects' and Builders' Magazine*, 3/09.

The partners designed this cooperative apartment building for William Taylor, a developer specializing in this new kind of housing for the middle class market. Rossiter & Wright hired the designer Charles Platt to draw the building facades. Platt was also designing elevations for the Taylor-sponsored project immediately to the south.

Rossiter & Wright invited the artist and designer Charles Platt to compose the building's façade. Platt was also designing the façade of the cooperative apartment building next door, on the southern half of the block, facing 66th Street, another Taylor project being designed by Pollard & Steinan. The two buildings' ground plans were complementary, as well as their façades. Each had a large central courtyard, which formed an oasis of light and air in the center of the block. Inside the Rossiter & Wright building, there were five duplex (two-story) apartments on the main floors, all facing the street, with two smaller, single-floor apartments facing the interior courtyard. Single-floor apartments and servants' rooms occupied the ground floor at street level. The duplex apartments typically consisted of a living room with fireplace, a library with fireplace, a dining room and a kitchen, as well as a private entrance hall with a stairway to the home's second floor, where there were four to six bedrooms. The single-floor apartments typically consisted of a living room, a kitchenette, and two bedrooms. The second cooperative apartment building designed by Rossiter &

ABOVE ROSSITER & WRIGHT, Cooperative apartment building, 901 Lexington Street, New York City, 1907. Collection of the Museum of the City of New York/ Art Resource, NY.

Across 67th Street to the north, Rossiter & Wright designed a second cooperative apartment building, again for the developer William Taylor. As suggested by the more modest entrance and the use of brick rather than the more expensive limestone for much of the exterior, this project was intended as a more affordable apartment option.

RIGHT ROSSITER & WRIGHT, Amity Baptist Church, 310 W. 54th Street, New York, 1908. *Architects' and Builders' Magazine, 1/1909.*

The church doorway was tucked behind an entrance courtyard with a school and dispensary to the right and a Deaconess home and hospital planned to the left. A tower gate at the street entrance was to also house a library. The entire complex was intended to serve as a settlement house for the notorious Hell's Kitchen neighborhood. Behind the Byzantine ornament on the doorway, a series of terra cotta vaults and a central dome, visible to the left, formed the exotic interior.

Wright, also developed by William Taylor, was located across 67th St., on the northeast corner of the intersection, with its entrance at 901 Lexington Ave. Though similar to the first building in the classical design of its façade, the building at 901 was smaller, with less than half the square footage, and, at $250,000, less costly. It was homelier, clad in red brick between the third and ninth floors. Inside, the ground floor contained single-floor apartments consisting, typically, of a living room, dining room, kitchen, two bedrooms, and a servant's room. The upper floors consisted of two apartments per floor: the apartment on the south corner of the building was a duplex with a living room, dining room, and library, all with fireplaces, a kitchen, four bedrooms, and two servants' rooms. The smaller single-floor apartments on the upper floors included a living room, a combination dining room and library, both with fireplaces, a kitchen, three bedrooms, and two servants' rooms.

Rossiter & Wright worked for Amity Baptist Church in the city, submitting designs for various church renovations for nearly a decade before the first of their plans saw fruition. Occupying the south side of 54th St. between 8th and 9th Ave., the new church complex was planned as a center that would serve the "west side tenement district," a sort of reformers' settlement house with a school, hospital, and library, according to the *New York Times* at the time the church opened in December 1908. Next door, the previous church building was converted into a school and dispensary, and during the construction of the new church the foundations were laid for a five-story hospital and Deaconess's Home to be built alongside the new church. A tower gate with a memorial library was also planned. The newly built church had a bowling alley and gymnasium in the basement. Contemporary reviewers described the style of the building as Byzantine, with a large dome "like the one on St. Paul's chapel at Columbia University." Completed in buff brick and terracotta, the church was a tour de force of barrel-vaulted ceilings lined in ribbed green tile.[71]

A NEW PARTNERSHIP

After 30 years, the firm had achieved success with a wide range of projects in the city and the surrounding suburbs and countryside. The partners themselves were of an age to consider retirement, both turning 66 in 1910.

In the spring of 1910, they sent a notice to clients that the partnership would be dissolved as of May 1, 1910. Rossiter would move his office to 15-17 West 38th St., the former Parmly home, and Wright would continue to maintain an office at 110 East 23rd St., where the firm had been located since 1907. Although retirement may have been on their minds, both architects lived for another 30 years and both continued to practice, although the pace of their work slowed and the projects they worked on were focused on the areas each man was personally suited to.

In 1910, Wright designed an apartment building in New York City at 400 Convent Ave., a large brick-and-stone building, 89 by 99 feet. He designed additional buildings at Branch Brook Park in Newark in 1914.[72] In 1921, he designed a $175,000 six-story apartment building for the Mutual Apartment Company on the site of the firm's former office at 110 East 23rd St.[73] As he limited his architectural practice, Wright played more golf, earning a high ranking in the Seniors' division of the PGA between 1910 and 1912, a point of great satisfaction to Wright as he reflected on his life in later years.

TOP ROSSITER & MULLER, Hepburn Library, **Madrid, New York, 1917.** Collection of the St. Lawrence Historical Association.

MIDDLE ROSSITER & MULLER, Hepburn **Library, Edwards, New York, 1919.** Courtesy of Mary Jane Watson.

LOWER ROSSITER & MULLER, Hepburn **Library, Norfolk, New York, 1919.** Collection of the St. Lawrence Historical Association.

Rossiter was busy with his ongoing projects at The Hotchkiss School and with other clients in Connecticut. In addition, he established a stronger relationship with A. Barton Hepburn, whose country home in Ridgefield, Connecticut, Rossiter & Wright had designed in 1902. Between 1913 and his death in 1922, Hepburn commissioned eight buildings from Rossiter— seven rural libraries and a college dormitory in northern New England.

Rossiter took on a new partner in 1913 to assist with this work. John Muller (1883-1964) graduated from the architectural program at Columbia College in 1907 and then studied at the École des Beaux Arts in Paris. In 1909 and 1910, Muller was the resident architect of Robert College in Istanbul, which was then affiliated with Columbia, where he designed a library and supervised other construction projects at the campus. He married the accomplished American sculptor Olga Popoff (1883-1980), who won a bronze medal at the Pan Pacific Exposition in San Francisco in 1915. According to his daughter-in-law, Muller spoke like a man educated in England, although he was the son of German immigrants who ran a grocery in Brooklyn.[74] Muller played football at Columbia and paid for his college education by working at the Henry Street Settlement house on the Lower East Side. He and Olga lived in Flushing, Queens, during the first decades of his work with Rossiter. In the beginning of their partnership, Rossiter continued to take an active role in the projects commissioned by his long-time clients, but by the 1920s, as Rossiter approached his 80th birthday, Muller assumed the lead with the clients and the designs.[75]

A. Barton Hepburn hired Rossiter to design a series of philanthropic projects about the time the new partnership was formed; indeed, the prospect of these buildings may have prompted Rossiter to take on Muller as a partner. Hepburn, the phenomenally successful banker who had grown up poor on a farm in upstate New York, determined to build libraries in the small farming communities where he'd spent his youth, beginning with a library for his birthplace, Colton, completed in 1913. A library for Madrid was completed in 1917, and following World War I, additional libraries were built in Edwards, Hermon, Norfolk, and Waddington, all in 1919; a final library was completed in Lisbon in 1920.[76] Hepburn estimated that each library cost him about $50,000, including land, construction, the purchase of the books, and the gift

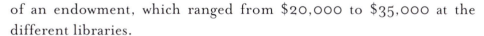

Hepburn Library—Colton, N. Y.

of an endowment, which ranged from $20,000 to $35,000 at the different libraries.

Although the design for each building was different, all but the last one was designed in a classical style and all had similar layouts. Each had a central "reception" room on the main floor, where the librarian could keep on eye on both public rooms—a reading room and a children's room—to either side. The book stacks were generally located behind the librarian's desk. Each building also had a lower level designed for community meetings, with a fully equipped kitchen. A few years later, in 1923, the *White Pine Series* of architectural publications ran a competition for libraries for towns like these with populations of less than 2,000. The contest rules codified Rossiter's plans in these libraries: there should be a reading room, a children's room, a reception desk allowing one person to supervise the public areas, an auditorium with a raised platform, space for 8,000 books, and good natural light. *White Pine* also suggested that a small historical museum be incorporated in the building if possible.

Hepburn had graduated from Middlebury College in Vermont in 1871, and in 1914 he donated funds to the college to build a dormitory, Hepburn Hall, to be designed by Rossiter & Muller. The classical

LEFT EHRICK ROSSITER, Hepburn Library, Colton, New York, 1912-13. Collection of the St. Lawrence County Historical Association.

TOP RIGHT ROSSITER & MULLER, Hepburn Library, Waddington, New York, 1919. Courtesy of Mary Jane Watson.

MIDDLE RIGHT ROSSITER & MULLER, Hepburn Library, Hermon, New York, 1919. Joel Finn photo.

LOWER RIGHT ROSSITER & MULLER, Hepburn Library, Lisbon, New York, 1920. Courtesy of Mary Jane Watson.

Hepburn also commissioned Rossiter & Muller to design a dormitory for his alma mater, Middlebury College. This building affirmed traditional American values through its Colonial Revival style.

brick building was sited on a hill overlooking a new college quadrangle that was under construction between 1912 and 1916. Built in yellow brick, apparently at Hepburn's request, the fireproof dormitory was later painted gray to be more consistent with the adjacent limestone buildings. Later, in 1940 and 1941, John Muller, acting for the firm Rossiter & Muller, was commissioned to design two more dormitories for the college, Gifford Hall and Munroe Hall, both in limestone. Mrs. James Gifford, the donor of Gifford Hall, also commissioned a home in Morristown, New Jersey, from Rossiter & Muller.

Rossiter & Muller designed substantial homes in Connecticut that were a departure from Rossiter's earlier designs. The first of these was Restmore, built between 1911 and 1913 as a summer residence in Southport, a neighborhood in the town of Fairfield, Connecticut, for Dr. Ira DeVer Warner. Warner and his brother were partners in the corset manufacturing company that had hired Rossiter & Wright to renovate a commercial building in New York in 1897. Warner had moved the company to Bridgeport, where there was plenty of room to expand the manufacturing operation and where he also built a substantial house. Warner was on the board of a bank in Bridgeport that hired Rossiter to design its building in 1910. Like other Connecticut manufacturers at the turn of the twentieth century, Warner was determined to build a summer house in the country. Warner's summer house, designed by Rossiter, was built in a rural area seven miles west of Bridgeport. According to the Warner family, the design of the house was based on the former residence of Cecil Rhodes in Capetown, South Africa, with distinctively shaped

At the top of Mill Hill stands "Restmore," part of the estate of Mrs. I. DeVer Warner, surrounded by one of the most spacious lawns in Fairfield.

Side view emphasizes details of Colonial Capetown architecture of the house, which is a replica of the home of Cecil Rhodes in Capetown, South Africa.

Dutch gables and wide tiled porches. Conceived at a time when Rossiter was experimenting with fireproof construction, the house was clad in hollow terracotta tiles covered with stucco and roofed in tile. The house was the center of a 200-acre dairy farm, with Rossiter-designed servant quarters and a carriage house. In 1913 Ira, and the dairy herd, died, and his widow did not pursue the dairy operation.

Rossiter also designed houses in bucolic neighborhoods being developed on the outskirts of Connecticut cities in the early 20th century for affluent urban clients. These houses were more formal than their country counterparts. They were sited on city lots in such a way that residents and their guests could enjoy a measure of outdoor leisure within a screen of privacy. Inside, these houses were fitted

EHRICK ROSSITER, Restmore, summer home for Dr. Ira DeVer Warner, the Southport neighborhood of Fairfield, Connecticut, 1910-1913. *Pictorial Fairfield,* c. 1940. Courtesy of Tod Bryant.

Rossiter had designed country homes and he had designed barns, but this was the only project where he designed a country home on 200 acres with its own working dairy farm and related barn and utility buildings, as well as a carriage house and a separate house for servants. The property, in coastal Connecticut, was seven miles from the Warner's winter home in Bridgeport, Connecticut.

ROSSITER & MULLER, Stedman-Johnson House, 1335 Asylum Avenue, Hartford, Connecticut, 1913. A.Y. Smith photo.

out with substantial rooms for entertaining and suites of bedrooms incorporating the latest hygienic technologies.

In Hartford, Connecticut, Rossiter was commissioned to design a Tudor Revival house for Elizabeth Stedman and her nieces Mabel and Eleanor Johnson. Completed in 1913, the buff-colored brick home occupied an entire block on Asylum Avenue, in an area then being developed for gracious estates on the edge of the thriving city. Elizabeth Stedman was the sister of the locally celebrated General Griffin Stedman, who died at the age of 26 in the battle at Petersburgh, Virginia, during the siege of Richmond, which led to the conclusion of the Civil War. Her nieces' father, Charles Johnson, was a Hartford lawyer who became Clerk of the Superior Court of Hartford County, a position of some prestige, from which he retired in 1907. In 1910, Elizabeth, then in her fifties, and her nieces, then in their mid-thirties, were living together downtown at 77 Elm St., along with two maids and an additional servant. The house they built on Asylum Ave. was a splendid new setting for three spinsters, with separate bedroom suites for each woman on the second floor. Elizabeth's suite had a morning room, where she was served breakfast, that had a bay window overlooking the entrance hall and stairwell. On the first floor, the entrance hall and grand stairway opened on to a small reception room with a piazza, a dining room, and a large music room with another open piazza, the fashionable name for an open air entertaining area. A two-story wing for the caretakers was built behind the porte-cochère in 1916. The property was a jewel in an exclusive

ROSSITER & MULLER, Residence for Dr. B. Austin Cheney, 755 Prospect Street, New Haven, Connecticut, 1918. *The American Architect,* May 25, 1923.

neighborhood: In 1930, when Mabel was living alone in the house with her staff, the property was valued at $147,000, three times the value of the adjacent houses.

In 1918, Rossiter & Muller designed a home in New Haven for Dr. B. Austin Cheney and his family. Rossiter probably met Cheney in Litchfield, where Cheney had purchased a summer home, Falcon's Flight Farm, in 1912. Cheney intended to run the Litchfield estate as a model dairy farm, and Rossiter is thought to have designed a dairy barn for the rural retreat. Cheney was an assistant professor of obstetrics at Yale Medical School when he began the Rossiter project in New Haven, his winter address. Nearly 50 years old at the time, he and his somewhat younger wife had two young sons, as well as a governess, a cook, and two maids living with them. The house, at 755 Prospect St., was executed in cut stone, random ashlar and stucco, and was sited on a corner lot with a plan that presented a formal façade to both streets. Guests arriving by car passed through an impressive gateway on Prospect Street, with urns set atop masonry posts. The main entrance to the house was located in a two-story crenellated tower at the 90-degree junction of the two main wings. Inside the entrance, a reception hall opened to the right into a music room with a bay window. At the back of the reception hall, a second vestibule and doorway opened to a low walled terrace, offering an entrance to pedestrians approaching from the side street. The living room, with a large bay window and a fireplace, overlooked the side street. The dining room was joined to the living room at the back of the house. To the left of the main entrance, the second wing contained a sequence of service rooms, including the kitchen and pantries as well as the maids' sitting room and porch. On the second floor, there was a bedroom suite for Dr. Cheney and his wife, a two-bedroom suite with a bathroom for their two sons, two guest rooms, each with a private bath, and four maids' bedrooms with a bathroom. The architects' drawings indicated the location of an elevator and a telephone. Tucked behind the house, with access from the side street, was another modern innovation: a garage for automobiles, one of only a few included in a Rossiter design.

During World War I and the years that followed, Rossiter & Muller also designed other homes in Connecticut cities and suburbs, including one for Stiles Goodsell in Bridgeport in 1917 and a brick home for Alton Terrell in Orange. In 1925, the firm also designed a home in West Hartford for Howard Gibb, Jr., perhaps a distant cousin of Rossiter and the son of one of his Long Island clients.[77]

The younger Gibb was a 25-year-old salesman for a stock broker and the heir to a dry-goods fortune in New York. His new home was in a neighborhood on the outskirts of Hartford, an enclave of stylish homes, with garages discreetly tucked behind the houses and accessed from a back alley. The colonial style house recalled the nearby historic Stanley Whitman house, which was included in influential books on historic Connecticut architecture published between 1879 and 1924.[78] Like the Stanley Whitman house, the Gibb home had diamond-paned casement windows and a projecting second floor that was embellished with drop pendants. At the Gibb house, Rossiter dressed up the drop pendants, placing them on brackets, and added other classical features, including dentil molding at the cornice and a Palladian window in the gable.[79]

Between 1916 and 1922 Rossiter & Muller designed at least four homes in Great Neck, on the north shore of Long Island within commuting distance of New York, during a period of rapid development in the several villages on the peninsula.[80] Muller lived in Flushing, Queens, about seven miles from Great Neck, and may have promoted the new business here. The partners also designed a three-story brick-and-stone commercial building, 75 by 200 feet, in Scarsdale, New York, in 1919.

Rossiter & Muller designed two churches during World War I, one in Washington and the other in Litchfield. The Washington project was a stone building for St. John's Episcopal Church, just off the town green, begun in 1917 and quickly completed in time for Easter services in 1918. With gothic windows and a buttressed nave and bell tower, the compact church was a quintessential English medieval design. The interior was embellished by two artists whose Washington homes had been designed by Rossiter—H. Siddons Mowbray painted images of the apostles and the stations of the cross along the nave, and Herbert Faulkner did the interior carvings.[81]

In Litchfield, Rossiter & Muller was commissioned by Henry R. Towne to design a new building for the Episcopal congregation of St. Michael's Church. The phenomenally successful Towne, who had been president of the Yale and Towne Manufacturing Company in Stamford from 1868 to 1916, moved to Litchfield in his retirement and took up various real estate development projects there as well as serving on the board of the local Village Improvement Society. His wife was the great-granddaughter of Benjamin Tallmadge, whose Litchfield house was the model for Rossiter's design of the 1907 Connecticut State Building at the Exposition in Jamestown, Virginia. After his wife died in 1917, Towne offered to provide St. Michael's with a church building as her memorial. The foundation was laid in 1919, but the substantial cross-formed church wasn't completed for another two years. Towne

Two Connecticut churches, one in Washington and the other in Litchfield, were done in the final years of Rossiter's active architectural career. These final two designs are among the best work of his career, confident, understated, and inspirational.

appears to have paid for the building directly, since the construction expenditures were not listed in the parish financial records. Rossiter & Muller designed a substantial stone church, again in an English medieval style. Estimated at $100,000, the building was reputed to have cost much more than this by the time it was finished. Mowbray, again, painted the interior murals. The woodwork included a gothic-inspired choir screen with drop pendants in the form of portrait busts by Muller's wife, Olga Popoff, and included portraits of Towne, Muller, and Rossiter.[82]

Several years later, the congregation set about building a parish house, which Towne had requested they do as a condition of his gift of the church building. Towne died in 1924, and when the building committee met with Rossiter and Muller soon after, they could not come to an agreement regarding the design for the parish house. The committee felt the architects' first design, for a two-story building, was too expensive; their second attempt was also rejected, and the parish turned to a Philadelphia firm with connections to a member of the building committee whose more modest design was ultimately built.[83]

The last major project of the partnership during the years Rossiter was active was a country resort, Skytop, built in the Poconos in northeastern Pennsylvania by a group of investors from New York, Philadelphia, and New Jersey. Modeled on a successful Quaker hotel at Buck Hill, Pennsylvania, the project was located in what was thought to be an especially healthful area of natural beauty. John Muller, a friend of one of the organizers, was the partner in charge, beginning the design work for the Lodge, the main hotel building, early in 1926. He recruited the nation's leading landscape design firm, the Olmsted Brothers, to survey the property intended for the resort, approximately 2,500 acres, and to design the grounds, which were to include a golf course and other outdoor sporting activities. The Lodge was designed in stone, as requested by the organizers, who thought that material would make the building look as though it had grown out of the surrounding mountains. The Lodge retained the colonial massing that the architects had used in dormitory projects at The Gunnery and at Middlebury College, symmetrically organized here under a high gambrel roof with a series of small dormers. The organizers authorized the start of construction before the funds were secured from investors, and when the funds were not forthcoming, the original design for the hotel was reduced in the midst of construction, eliminating the east wing and reducing the height of the west wing. Following the first season of operation in 1928, construction began again, with an extension to the dining room and the west wing, the construction of a power house, a garage for guests' cars, and dormitories for hotel employees and guests' chauffeurs. A swimming pool was added soon after. John Muller and later his son Peter Paul Muller remained involved with architectural projects at the resort for many years.

The Great Depression of the 1930s brought a halt to both private and civic construction. The final Rossiter & Muller project to receive national press was the firm's work for the Department of Education in Scarsdale, New York. Rossiter & Muller had worked in Scarsdale in 1919, designing a substantial $200,000 brick-and-stone commercial building, 75 by 200 feet, for a private client. The 1939 project[84] was a planning proposal for the town's junior and senior high schools to address progressive theories in education developed since the schools' construction. Among the planned additions were two gymnasiums, locker rooms for boys and girls, an additional auditorium and music rooms, separate cafeterias for the junior and senior schools, and various laboratories, shops, and classrooms. Muller, the likely author of the article, emphasized the importance of creating a master plan for big civic projects, such as the one presented, so that the actual construction could be accomplished through incremental steps as funds were made available. It was a wise approach in the challenging financial times of the 1930s and reflected the incremental process the firm had experienced at The Hotchkiss School and Skytop in the past.

Rossiter may have kept a hand in the partnership through the 1920s, since he continued to correspond with his contacts at The Hotchkiss School until their projects at the school were concluded in 1925, and he probably helped with the firm's design of homes for members of his family, including new houses for his daughter, Edith, now Mrs. William Bevan, in Ruxton, Maryland, in 1924; and for his cousin's daughter Mrs. Truman Troxel in Concord, New Hampshire, in 1928.[85] (Rossiter's undated designs for homes for his sons, Frank, in Boonton, New Jersey, and Kensett, in Norwalk, California, were probably done earlier in the architect's career.)

ROSSITER & MULLER, Skytop, Buck Hill Falls, Pennsylvania, 1925.

In 1924 at the age of 70, Rossiter was ready, at last, to retire, although he continued to work on small projects until 1931. He began writing a history of heroes and villains who passed through Litchfield County during the Revolutionary War. The chatty 87-page essay, *Washington's Journey Through Litchfield County, 1780,* illustrated with pictures of colonial houses where Washington was entertained, was published by the Litchfield County University Club in 1930.

In retirement, he traveled. It had been his practice, at least since the early years of the twentieth century, to travel to Bermuda in January for several weeks, but now his winter holidays were more wide-ranging.[86] In November 1925 he and his wife sailed to Europe, returning the following April. In 1927 and 1928 they traveled again to France for the winter. He and his wife returned from the 1928 voyage in the company of their Washington neighbor Annie Halsted, who had purchased the house in Washington that had been built for Frank Heath in 1903. In 1930 the Rossiters traveled to Italy, and the following winter they went to England. In the winter of 1932, they traveled in France and Germany.[87]

There is no record of later winter trips to Europe, and the Rossiters began spending the winters in Florida instead. In 1933, Rossiter donated paintings from his personal collection to the local museum in Winter Park, which suggests that the couple felt at home in the sophisticated winter colony there.[88] They rented rooms in the small Pechmann Inn, which accommodated only six to eight couples in the season. Among the other residents at the inn were Dr. and Mrs. Richard Burton, probably the son of Rossiter's client in New Jersey and Long Island. Rossiter admired Winter Park's evocative architecture and ambitious art galleries. He took an active role in his new seasonal community, joining the University Club and the Garden Club there and writing occasional columns for the local paper. Admired by their new associates in Winter Park, the Rossiters' seasonal social activities were mentioned in the local paper until 1938.

In 1937 Rossiter admitted in a letter to the son of his long-time Washington caretaker that he was losing his eyesight. He spent his final years in White Plains, New York, in the home of his son Kensett, where he died in 1941 at the age of 97. Three years later his widow, Mary, gave an additional 92 acres of land at Steep Rock to the conservation group in Washington that Rossiter had established in 1925, adding to his legacy as the founder of the Steep Rock Association. In 1948, Mary died and was buried next to her husband on a hill in Washington, next to his last building in town, St. John's Church, overlooking the Shepaug valley and the Steep Rock preserve.

EHRICK ROSSITER, Poem inscribed in the guest book at his daughter's home in Maryland, 1927. Rossiter family archives. Courtesy of David Kensett Rossiter.

CHAPTER FOUR: ROSSITER AND HIS CLIENTS

Then, as now, the business of architecture was a matter of social connections as well as technical accomplishment and style. Rossiter's client list emerged from the wellspring of his club activities, including The Gunnery graduates, the Litchfield County University Club, and the Century Club in New York. Satisfied clients engaged the architect for additional projects and renovations and recommended the firm to family members and friends. Rossiter's background assured potential clients that they were in good hands with a designer who was well educated, well versed in the arts, active in cultured circles in New York City, and who possessed a country house and garden of his own.

Most of Rossiter's clients were members of the rising middle class, who had earned social standing and prosperity from the new occupations that flourished as the country became more urban. They were bankers, traders, railroad officers, real estate developers, doctors, and lawyers; they were the artists and musicians who were part of that social circle; they were the board members of the churches and schools that this network supported. They were not the super rich, like the Vanderbilts or the Roosevelts, with inherited wealth and summer homes in Newport, the Berkshires, or Long Island, spending hundreds of thousands of dollars on their second or third house. Rossiter's clients were not even at the next level of such architectural ambition. The celebrated writer Edith Wharton, for example, spent more than $250,000 on her estate in the Berkshires at the turn of the twentieth century. She was one of many people building expansively then. By 1910, there were 15,000 families in the country with annual incomes of more than $50,000, enabling them to purchase and maintain a substantial country house, according to architect and critic Fiske Kimball. Kimball assumed that such a house would cost $100,000 to purchase and $7,500 annually to maintain.[1] Rossiter's most affluent clients spent a quarter of that on their country houses, and the builders of houses in suburban developments—his firm's bread and butter business—spent much less, with their houses costing between $6,000 and $20,000.[2]

Whether the building project was intended for a suburban development or a country retreat, Rossiter's clients were motivated by the same aspirations that led wealthier builders: they wanted to remove their families from the perceived dangers of the new urban environment and to create a safe family life close to nature. The appeal of a house in the country was widespread, encouraged by popular media, and it motivated home builders at all price levels. New magazines, such as *Country Life in America* and *House and Garden*, emphasized the benefits of the simpler and healthier life away from the city. The wealthy had their exclusive resorts, such as Newport and Bar Harbor, and their private country clubs with the newly popular golf courses. They formed new organizations, such as the D.A.R., that confirmed their colonial ancestry, as if reasserting their birthright to the rural American life. The less affluent could also pursue country-like experiences through the new public parks in the cities and parks in the suburbs developed by the trolley lines, which hoped to boost traffic on their lines on the weekends. The growth of scouting and the environmental conservation movement reflected a broad interest in country life within the upper and middle classes. Members of the middle class could buy a house in the country, or at least in the suburbs, according to a 1901 issue of *Country Life* magazine. "For $100, an acre of land can be bought here and there within easy access of our great cities. You can build a comfortable summer lodge for the remaining $400 if you have the knack; and you can make it attractive outside and inside if you have the art. If you have $2,000 and upwards to spend, you can make a permanent country home and have enough land to consume your energy for digging and experimenting." These were Rossiter's clients.

Generally, the Rossiter & Wright clients in the suburbs of New Jersey were young men, in their thirties and forties, with a houseful of children and servants, while the clients in northwest Connecticut were older men, several of them only a few years from retirement.

Those clients who chose summer homes in northwest Connecticut were drawn from Brooklyn, New York, and Hartford, Connecticut, attracted by a short commute on the trains and by the region's reputation for education and wholesome entertainment, including choral singing and country fairs. In northern New Jersey, clients interested in suburban real estate development, parks, golfing, and seaside recreation called on the firm.

Clients commissioned the firm to remodel homes in the city and to design suburban and weekend homes in the country. Clients often returned to the firm to commission additional buildings for their manufacturing operations or new community projects, such as schools, churches, and parks. Nearly two thirds of the 350 projects designed by the partners were for homes. They designed new houses and remodeled existing ones, and they built the ancillary estate buildings, such as gate houses and gardeners' cottages. In addition to its single-family residential work, the firm also designed 4 apartment buildings, 19 commercial buildings, 11 libraries, 7 park buildings, 2 town halls, 26 schools, 18 churches, and 10 clubs. Their clients had confidence in the architects' versatility, expecting them to be able to build anything from apartment buildings to churches to barns. Rossiter's clients considered their architect to be competent in all forms of building; they didn't look for a designer specializing in particular building forms, such as schools or commercial buildings.

Rossiter and his clients were social peers. In the early stages of his work for The Hotchkiss School, the Rossiters entertained the headmaster, Dr. Buehler, at their home in Washington, and the Rossiters and Buehlers dined together in New York before an evening at the theater. Edith Rossiter went to school with the daughters of his clients and was a bridesmaid in at least two of their weddings. Client meetings were arranged at the Century Club, on those frequent occasions where the client, like Rossiter, was a member of the club.

A friend and biographer of the artist Dwight Tryon, who was one of Rossiter's early clients, remembered that the artist and the architect discussed poetry. "In the enjoyment of literature there was no one with whom Tryon was more in sympathy than the architect E. K. Rossiter, of New York. To be present at one of their meetings was an event to be remembered. Each had a remarkable memory for quotations and for books they had read. The conversation was sparkling and witty."[3]

Rossiter shared his clients' aspirations for a project. For the little library at Homer in the Finger Lakes region of New York, he not only donated his design services but also encouraged the library trustees to believe in the importance of their mission. In 1896 he wrote to the library trustees that he was sending two options for the new building they were considering, but, he added, "...far more than this, do I wish you every possible encouragement and success—not the immediate material success only that will enable you to realize your first bright hopes, but the later success that will surely come when the bread now cast up on the waters returns on its homeward voyage with its valued increment in the shape of happier and better lives. Should these drawings then contribute ever so little towards lightening your labors it will be unnecessary to add that I shall regard my last visit in the Glen with especial good fortune."[4]

Although the building was inexpensive and promoted by influential clients,[5] its construction was delayed and was only approved by local taxpayers after the library was joined with a venture to build a new one-room school for the region. Rossiter prepared a new design for the combined structure. While the committee still struggled to raise the funds and to persuade the townspeople to support the project, Rossiter offered further encouragement. "[Even if the building remains only an architect's sketch] rest assured that I have had all the sport and satisfaction that I am entitled to with the scheme. I shall still wish though for your 'innings', as we used to say in our ball days when the other side took the bat, and I hope the score card will show a profitable return for your labor."[6]

This kind of congeniality facilitated the architect's work with his clients, because the projects were an extended partnership. In addition to providing architectural designs, Rossiter coordinated a variety of separate tasks during the construction project, as a general contractor would today. At Dr. Warner's summer house in Southport, Connecticut, these tasks included the layout and construction of the driveway, the selection and delivery of stone and tile, the excavation and water systems, the finish plaster and painting, each of which was excluded from the builder's scope of work and fell to the architect rather than a general contractor to arrange.

Surviving correspondence at The Hotchkiss School, spanning nearly 20 years, gives a window into the practical matters that defined the relationship between the architect and his clients. The letters between Rossiter and headmaster Buehler describe their mutual balancing of interests with regard to cost and appearance, the challenges of new technologies and new concerns about health and safety, the delicate negotiations about the architect's fees, the sometimes meddlesome design directives from the headmaster and the board, and the surprising range of services the architect provided to his clients.

Since Buehler was required to raise the funds for every new building on campus, generally costing between $10,000 and $20,000, he was determined to build as inexpensively as possible, but he was also anxious not to impair the competitive position of the school. He cautioned Rossiter that the final buildings could not "look inferior to other schools." Rossiter suggested a number of ways to reduce the building costs, such as using roughcast rather than brick or stone, using cement rather than stone for exterior trim like corner quoins, and using cement rather than tile for flooring in certain utilitarian rooms. He recommended gambrel-roofed buildings as an inexpensive way to achieve an additional floor. Rossiter described in some detail the way to build a foundation out of concrete rather than stone, to save money. Have a skilled carpenter build the cribbing, the molds for the concrete pour, he suggested, but do the rest of the work with men "to whom the ordinary wages are paid." He continued: "In order to cheapen the work, I always suggest filling the cribs as far as possible with small field stones."

The headmaster had his own thoughts about ways to make the buildings less expensive—make them smaller. Responding to Rossiter's plans for a small field house that the architect estimated would cost $3,500, Buehler directed him to combine the lounge, the dressing room, and the locker rooms, designed as three separate spaces, into one room of only 15 by 15 feet, thereby making the building, and its cost, smaller. He also suggested that Rossiter reduce the plumbing specified for the building; Buehler believed the 50 boys in the field house could do nicely with two showers, one sink, one toilet, and two urinals. He announced, for the first time, that the budget for the project was $2,500. The building was apparently built to the diminished specifications, but Rossiter was asked to draw up plans a few years later to enlarge the field house, adding a separate locker room and toilets for the visiting teams.

Often Rossiter responded gracefully to the limitations placed on his design work for the school. Regarding the possibility of creating a small, low-budget track house on campus, he replied, "Though diminutive in size, it has an important place in the minds of the boys and I feel it will be an ornament to the grounds." On occasion, he objected to the design constraints placed on his projects by cost-conscious trustees. "After I had followed the suggestions made at the time of our recent interview, which were along the lines of the most rigid economy, it seemed to me that the result was a most unhappy one, and that by stepping the roof of the proposed Covered Way [in order to follow the grade of the sloping ground] we were forced into producing a very disjointed and unattractive building, the result appearing to me like a freight train in a moment of collapse occasioned by a land slide, or perhaps the simile of Coney Island bath houses running up hill from the water would be more appropriate."

When it came to the expansion of his own home, the headmaster was less constrained in his budget, requesting that more expensive maple be substituted for the pine floors Rossiter had specified and suggesting that new mantels should be acquired for the bedrooms rather than reusing the old ones as the architect had proposed. The headmaster had raised the funds for a more expansive building, where he would be entertaining potential donors and the parents of prospective students, and it was important to him that the house be imposing.

The headmaster, his wife, the trustees, and donors showered Rossiter with directives that often look far beyond a client's prerogatives. A trustee insisted that a particular contractor not be used on the job because of a personal dispute he had with the contractor over a private job. The headmaster's wife instructed the architect about the arrangement of shelves in the service areas. She wanted to be sure that the sink in the kitchen of their new house, which would be the domain of staff, would not be porcelain. She wanted the exterior doors, the entrance hall, the stairway, and the dining room of the new headmaster's house to be painted white rather than the oak and black birch Rossiter had specified. It was. Buehler had determined opinions about a number of matters in buildings across the campus, including suppliers, materials, and the layout of rooms. Sometimes a directive given by Buehler was reversed by the trustees after Rossiter submitted his initial designs. Rossiter soldiered on.

There were delays when designs were submitted but the money was not available. The expansion of the infirmary in 1914 was delayed by two years while Buehler raised the funds for the project. The addition to the headmaster's house, a project costing more than double the usual campus projects, was planned by the architect and the headmaster over five years before the funds were raised and the project was completed.

The tasks Rossiter performed on the school projects were varied. In addition to providing designs and specifications, he solicited the contractors' bids and prepared their contracts, supervised their work, and paid their monthly bills. He selected and ordered refrigeration units, sinks, dumb waiters, boilers for the power plant, and filters for the swimming pool. He secured and shipped building supplies to the school, including sections of metal ceiling and barrels of nails. He selected the paint colors, tiles, and wallpapers for the interior decoration of the rooms. He purchased the furniture for the headmaster's office, although, as might be expected, Buehler had specific instructions about which model of desk he wanted and which store should supply it. Rossiter bought lighting fixtures, ornamental hardware, and important room embellishments. Among the decorations were brass plaques and braziers that were shipped from Italy, at a price Buehler agreed was "extremely cheap." Rossiter purchased carvings for the school from an English supplier, including inspirational mottos for the dining room, and a set of the coats of arms of Oxford colleges and carved oak awards for the debate team.

He directed minor repairs on school buildings as well as major renovations and new construction. Reluctantly, he added a fire escape to the upper floors of the main building, where the boys' sleeping rooms were located but admitted that he hated the way the fire escape looked so he recommended only one, to be shared across a landing. On occasion, he turned work down because he felt the project too mundane. Requested to design an expansion of a school cottage, he replied, "I would, of course, be very glad to serve you in this matter as well as in all others, but it seems to me that Mr. Raynsford [a school employee] is quite capable of handling this little 'chore' himself. If he has any doubt about it I could arrange to make a visit, but it hardly seems worth your while to employ me for a matter which scarcely admits of more than one solution, determined very largely by existing conditions and the proportions of which are already prescribed."

Rossiter visited the campus every two weeks while projects were underway, arriving by train, frequently in conjunction with visits to review projects for other clients in the area, including the Stoeckels in Norfolk, Mrs. Black in New Milford, or Miss Johnson in Hartford.

Rossiter's fees were based on a percentage of the contractor's fees for individual projects. The percentage varied depending on whether he was doing "alterations," which were probably minor jobs such as the addition of electricity or showers in an existing building or installing vents in the chapel ceiling to improve air circulation, or whether he was doing "new work," which was probably the design and construction of additions to existing buildings as well as the design and construction of new buildings.

In the first years of his work for The Hotchkiss School, 1905 and 1906, his fee was 2 1/2% for new work (probably projects with larger budgets) and 5% for alterations; he also charged "10% for painting," which might have been the development of a paint scheme rather than the supervision of painting contractors. In 1907 he charged 10% for extensive renovations and the extensions to the recitation hall, a classroom and the gym. His rates continued to rise. In 1909 he wrote that he had been charging "6% on all country work, somewhat below the rates of AIA, of which we are members," suggesting that he had been giving the school a discount but was about to raise his rates. His commission for the work on the headmaster's house in 1910 was 15%. By 1925, the firm's rates and fee structure had changed again, with a distinction made between the fees charged for design and supervision (10%) and the fees charged for the design work only, without on-site supervision of the construction (8%).

From finishes to furnishings, Rossiter was deeply involved in every aspect of the buildings he designed. He was amenable to fairly extensive input from his clients, such as the Buehlers, on matters that may have seemed to the architect to be more a matter for his professional determination, not the client's. The kind of give and take in his projects was probably made easier by the architect's personality and his social parity with his clients.

Nevertheless, even in northwest Connecticut, Rossiter faced competition from architects whose personal connections to potential clients grew stronger as Rossiter grew older. Richard Henry Dana (1879-1933), an architect and professor at Yale, was hired to design new campus buildings in the 1920s for The Gunnery and to design a country house, Topsmead (1923-1925) for heiress Edith Chase in Litchfield. Alfredo Taylor (1872-1947) began to work in Norfolk, Connecticut, when his wife's mother moved there in 1903. Moving to the town as a summer resident himself in 1904, the inventive architect eventually worked for the best clients in Norfolk, doing work for the Stoeckels by 1914. Cameron Clark, the Yale roommate of William Van Sinderen's son Adrien, designed the Van Sinderens' new Washington home Glenholme in 1924 and the Washington Town Hall in 1931. Meanwhile, Robert Wakeman Hill, a Waterbury architect who was also Connecticut's state architect, began designing public projects in Litchfield, including the new court house in 1890, following a disastrous fire in the village two years earlier, and the new firehouse, commissioned by Julius Deming Perkins and given to the town in 1896. Henry Towne, who commissioned Rossiter to design the Episcopal church as a memorial to his wife in 1918, hired the nationally recognized designer of country houses, Aymar Embury, to design his retirement home on South St. in Litchfield in 1915. As Rossiter entered the last years of his career, he began to lose projects even in his own backyard to younger architects with impressive credentials and stronger social connections to the new generation of builders.

CHAPTER FIVE: STYLE AND IMAGE

Rossiter's clients were affluent, but most were not wealthy. They were conservative in their architectural choices, building homes and civic buildings in styles that had been new 20 years earlier. By the time the Rossiter projects were built, these styles did not challenge the status quo or call attention to the builder as a tastemaker. Instead, these somewhat dated designs confirmed the client's good taste. Clients seemed comfortable with Rossiter's free-handed mix of concurrent styles, combining elements of several historical styles on both the exteriors and the interiors of his buildings rather than focusing on a rigid rendition of a particular style.

Today we have named these styles the Queen Anne Revival, the Colonial Revival, and the Tudor Revival. However, these styles were in a fluid state when Rossiter designed his projects. Rossiter, like many architects at the turn of the twentieth century, believed that his skill was in freely adapting historical styles to modern needs. He and his fellow architects would have been puzzled by our current struggle to assign tidy style names to their individual projects.

Today, "naming the style" enables us to check off a list of features on a building, in a sort of architectural bingo game. But Rossiter and his contemporaries designed buildings that embraced a spirit of improvisation with historical precedent and were not confined by the same sense of clear-cut stylistic boundaries.

The variety of style names used in the late nineteenth century was bewildering. In 1883, Rossiter reflected: "Modern styles cover a wider range, and embrace a larger school of purely eclectic designers than ever before. They have not yet crystallized into any very definite forms. They are respectively called Queen Anne, English Domestic, Colonial, or Free Classic as the different supposed characteristics of these various styles are thought to predominate, but they all elude any definite architectural analysis. Buildings that are recognizably definable in any distinct style are rare."[1] Indeed, Rossiter thought this fluid stylistic environment was a good thing: "There is no reason why we should not learn all that we can from the past, and recall from oblivion all that is good and adaptable to modern life. This is what is now taking place, and it cannot be denied that our houses are, in consequence, gradually assuming a more homelike and picturesque character much to be preferred to the manufactured style so monotonously prevalent at one period."[2]

Others agreed with Rossiter that the style names were quixotic and imprecise. Architect, teacher, and critic Aymar Embury noted that "the use of the old work [that is, historical styles], changed and modified with the greatest possible freedom, is the key-note of modern architecture....[and] it has advanced furthest in the country dwelling-house....Architects are employing a number of different historical styles modified and modernized to suit the conditions and needs of today. Exact reproduction of old work is apt to be dry and tiresome [unless the architect improves on the design for modern purposes].... The classification [of prototype] will be necessarily a very loose one; probably almost every modern home owes something to two or more of these styles."[3] A writer in *Architects' and Builders' Magazine* summed it up with some exasperation: "The different designs [illustrated] are variously denominated as 'English domestic' design, 'Spanish' design, and what not: but we will leave it to our reader to name the styles as he chooses."[4]

Architects and critics at the time were comfortable with a fluid definition of historical styles. In this discussion of Rossiter's eclectic designs, however, we will use the modern names of the styles that were fashionable during his four decades of practice.

The Queen Anne Revival style is now recognized as a wood or brick design that featured asymmetric massing, often with turrets, bays, and porches. Clustered brick chimneys rose above the roof. The exterior surfaces were highly decorated, with glazed and patterned brick and terracotta tiles. Wooden clapboards, shaped and scalloped shingles, and ornamental bargeboards and turnings festooned houses and porches. Gables, sometimes projecting from the exterior walls as well as the roof, were decorated with faux half-timbering and stucco. Commonly, the surface cladding changed with each floor, creating a lively play of patterns. Casement and double-hung windows were often made up of small leaded panes. While this elaboration of form and decoration was made possible by newly available and industrially processed millwork from commercial lumberyards, the style was thought to be inspired by medieval English architecture.

In 1955, the distinguished architectural historian Vincent Scully suggested that the Queen Anne Revival could be further understood by dividing these style clusters into the Stick style and the Shingle style. In his analysis, the Stick style, beginning in the mid-nineteenth century, emphasized the "structural fact of wood" with the new light balloon frame of construction expressed in the cladding, a thin skin of wooden clapboards articulated into panels with vertical "stick" borders. The Shingle style evolved from the organic, vernacular houses of the medieval tradition, with a flexible floor plan and extended verandas, but in this newly defined variant the exterior was entirely covered in shingles. Scully pointed out that these Shingle style houses were conceived as a horizontal unity, with windows grouped in horizontal bands; roofs extending in a long continual sweep rather than being broken into a cluster of gables and towers; and porches subsumed into the body of the exterior walls, rather than extending out past the walls and rooflines. Typically, these houses were organized around an open floor plan, such as the hearth-centered entrance hall of the houses in the Queen Anne style.

Generally, homes in these related Queen Anne styles in the northeastern United States were built after the Civil War. George Sheldon, a contemporary architectural publisher, noted that the Queen Anne Revival was no longer "fashionable" by 1885; nevertheless, it continued to be popular in the northeast and across the country until the end of the century, and Rossiter's clients built houses in this fashion until after the turn of the 20th century.

Other subgroups of various medieval styles have also been identified by twentieth-century historians, including the Romanesque Revival, the Richardsonian Romanesque, and the Arts and Crafts style.

The Romanesque Revival, another medieval style popular in the second half of the nineteenth century, was considered particularly appropriate for churches, schools, and libraries built in stone. Inspired by the heavy masonry buildings of the Middle Ages in Europe, these buildings were characterized by round-headed windows (as opposed to the pointed arched windows of the Gothic Revival, which were fashionable before the Civil War), arcades, buttresses, squat columns, and pyramidal spires on square towers. The architect H. H. Richardson expanded the Romanesque Revival with robustly rusticated masonry, horizontal bands of windows, exaggerated arches over recessed doorways, and circular towers embedded in exterior walls. In this configuration, the style was later known as the Richardsonian Romanesque.

In England late in the nineteenth century, architects like C. F. A. Voysey advanced another variation on medieval building designs, leading to the English Arts and Crafts style. Intending to recall a traditional hand-crafted cottage, these designs also featured open and informal floor plans; steep roofs, often reaching down to the top of the first floor; plain exterior walls; and cottage-inspired doorways, dormers, and windows. More popular in England than America, these "aesthetic movement" designs were nevertheless published in magazines in both countries and influenced country house design in America at the turn of the twentieth century.

The second broad stylistic category adopted by Rossiter and his clients was The Colonial Revival, which took hold of the public imagination following the Centennial celebrations of 1876. The Colonial Revival was part of a growing nostalgia for America's past in the face of great changes, including immigration, urbanization, and industrialization. In contrast to these disturbing modern developments, the past was imagined to have been a society of virtue, simplicity, and taste. The Colonial Revival influenced the redesign of towns at the turn of the century with newly reclaimed town greens and fostered colonial designs for furniture, interiors, and gardens as well as architecture. Architecturally, the Colonial Revival was characterized by a return to symmetry in the building mass and façade and classical decorative elements for doorways, windows, roof treatments, and interior woodwork. The colonial architecture of the early settlements on the east coast was rediscovered and published in various professional and popular magazines, encouraging public interest. Late in life, Rossiter's partner Frank A. Wright recalled that he had organized tours of the colonial houses of New England for members of the Architectural League in the mid 1880s, a process famously undertaken in 1877 by youthful architects who were later partners in the blockbuster firm McKim Mead & White. New England's colonial houses fueled the rediscovery and appreciation of America's architectural past, as Rossiter learned when he studied the historic Deming and Tallmadge houses in Litchfield in 1887 and 1907.

At the same time, American architects and their clients were better informed about the classical styles of Europe, which were the foundation for early colonial styles in the northeastern United States, including the American Georgian and the Federal styles. In the second half or the nineteenth century, architects studied abroad and their clients took the Grand Tour; both groups saw first hand the classical styles of Europe. They read the new illustrated architectural publications in the United States. As a result of travel and study, they were increasingly discerning about the history and accuracy of period details of classical architectural ornament. Within the Colonial Revival, various Classical Revivals could be distinguished and offered an opportunity for architect and client to demonstrate their sophistication and their nuanced understanding of the various classical design sources: American Colonial, Georgian Revival, Dutch Revival, and the ancient Greek and Roman classical motifs. Variations on the "Colonial Revival" style were popular for another 50 years.

Among the hallmarks of the Colonial Revival architecture generally were Palladian windows, a mullioned window flanked by narrower side windows, with an arched fan light over the center section; pedimented doorways with sidelights; fan lights; corner quoins that imitated projecting cut stone blocks; elaborately molded cornices, sometimes with dentil or other classical molding details; balustrades with posts, sometimes topped with urns; and gable, hipped, or gambrel roofs, often with dormers.

The Tudor Revival, adopted with gusto by Rossiter in the years after he formed his partnership with the European-trained Muller, was an extension of America's earlier attraction to English medieval domestic architecture. Indeed, some of the Queen Anne style buildings incorporated features, such as half-timbering, which were also described as Jacobean or Tudor Revival in the late nineteenth century. Early in the twentieth century, perhaps as a result of Americans' renewed fascination with English aristocratic society, Tudor Revival designs once again became fashionable. This time around, many of these buildings were masonry. As before, the buildings featured antique leaded casement windows, though in a taller version than those found in Queen Anne Revival buildings; Tudor arches (flatter than a gothic arch but retaining a central peak); steeply pitched roofs often with revealed roof beams at the gutter; and the half-timbering also popular in the earlier revival. The more substantial size of these designs in the early twentieth century were often powerful statements about architecture and stature, with castle-inspired crenellated walls and parapets projecting above the roof line at the gable ends. Homes, churches, and schools in this style were particularly fashionable in wealthy suburbs in the 1920s and 1930s, as well as in college buildings, libraries, and apartment buildings.

Other building types and styles were also fashionable during this period.[5] However, Rossiter and his clients favored styles that were conservative symbols of a reassuring past. They were not attracted to Four Square country houses, bungalows, Beaux Arts extravaganzas, or French châteaux. Rossiter knew his market.

Rossiter & Wright and The Queen Anne Revival

Rossiter and Wright were proponents of the Queen Anne Revival in the first two decades of their practice, from 1880 until 1900, although they also designed a few houses in a wide-ranging and eclectic medieval style in the early years of the twentieth century.

Having trained under an advocate of the Gothic Revival style at Cornell, Rossiter admired the Queen Anne style because he recognized its affiliation with gothic architecture. "The general form and arrangement of these [Queen Anne] buildings was after the Gothic manner: i.e. they were designed from the inside; the plan was the first consideration and was made to meet the practical requirements of the times, while the exterior was left in a great measure to take care of and adapt itself to the plan."[6]

With this in mind, Rossiter and Wright designed houses that organized space so that their floor plans would meet the requirements of modern lifestyles. They covered the houses in the fashionable shingles and porches of the 1880s and dressed them up with medieval decoration. The earliest of their designs in this style were for cottages, studios, schools, and churches, the designs published in 1880. Their final work in the Queen Anne Revival style was done for the Spofford house in Norfolk, Connecticut, in 1898 and the half-timbered home for Safford Goodwin Perry in Washington, Connecticut, in 1908.

The Queen Anne Revival was evident in Rossiter & Wright's earliest designs, published in the *American Architect and Building News* in 1880. These projects included a school in Cold Spring, New York; a studio for the painter R. Swain Gifford in Nonquitt, Massachusetts; and a church in Netherwood, New Jersey. The school was a simple two and a half-story building with a dormer and a gabled entrance pavilion, covered with shingles. A clustered chimney added further Queen Anne features to the picturesque building. The stone studio designed for Gifford had both gabled and hip roofs with crested tiles, a clustered chimney, and an entrance porch. It was a more elaborate, and probably more costly, version of the Queen Anne style in masonry.[7] The Netherwood church was a compendium of "medieval" Queen Anne details, with a cross wing, a square tower with a round-headed arcade, and a spire,

ROSSITER & WRIGHT, Low Priced Cottages at Fairmount, NJ, 1881. *American Architect and Building News, 8/6/1881.*

The architects designed small but fashionable cottages in the Queen Anne Revival style for the new suburbs growing up around Newark, New Jersey.

a recessed porch, lancet windows, and a horizontal band of casement windows covered by a shed roof.

Rossiter & Wright published their designs for houses in the Queen Anne Revival style throughout the 1880s. In 1881, their "Low-Price Cottage" in Fairmount, New Jersey, was a small, inexpensive house, yet it featured a number of Queen Anne details. It had a cluster of roof gables, including one over the entrance porch, a substantial chimney and leaded windows, with clapboards on the first floor and shingles on the second, as well as a patterned screen in the roof gables.

Another house designed for a client in Fairmount, the images published the same year, was larger and more elaborate. Two elevations of the home were published along with several wall treatments for interior spaces and detailed patterns to show carpenters how to execute the decorative wood finishes inside and out. Overall, the design could have been a salesman sample of Queen Anne features with an exuberant accumulation of clapboards, shaped shingles, turned posts, beaded railings, framed paneling, leaded windows, scrolled and shaped window

borders, sunbursts, half-timbered gables, clustered chimneys…and carved flower pots perched over an ornamental window header. Inside, the relentlessly patterned woodwork continued with banded railings in the main hall stairway, boxed panels along the stairwell and the overmantel (with locations provided in the panels for paintings and mirrors), a tiled hearth in the hallway, and glazed and shaped brick on the hallway mantle. The stair rail wrapped around the bottom post like a soft stick of licorice. While the overall massing of the house was fairly straightforward, the profusion of porches, bays, oriels, built-in benches, and gable projections gave the house a somewhat frenzied appearance.

At the same time, Rossiter and Wright published a series of designs that illustrate how the Queen Anne style could be adapted for houses of increasing cost, from $500 to $4,000. At the low end of the range, for $500, a plain house with two rooms and a second floor over one of the rooms had asymmetric gables in several directions. For $1,500, a house with three rooms on the first floor and two rooms on the second floor provided another desirable picturesque roofline. In addition, an

ROSSITER & WRIGHT, Study for a Country House, c. 1880. Author's collection.

A more ambitious design for a seaside house, probably published in *American Architect and Building News*.

ROSSITER & WRIGHT, Suburban Cottage for $4,000, 1883. *American Cottages.* New York: William T. Comstock, 1883. Reprinted in William T. Comstock, *Country Houses and Seaside Cottages of the Victorian Era,* Mineola, N. Y.: Dover Publications, Inc., 1989.

entrance on the side of the house had another gabled porch, while a bay window on the façade broke up the mass of the house in a pleasing nod to the Queen Anne. For $1,800, a client could have a house with a cluster of gables created from the intersection of the roofs of two wings, each two full stories, with a continuous skirt of porches surrounding the first floor. This house was embellished with the clustered chimneys, ornamental shingles, and half-timbering of the more elaborate Queen Anne style. For $3,500, a house could have half-timbering in the gable, multi-paned windows, second-floor balconies and bay windows, and ornamental brackets on the projecting gables and over the decorative canted corner windows. For $4,000, an owner might build a larger house (five rooms on the first floor and three main rooms on the second floor), with even more elaborate decorative details, including multiple chimneys, towers with turrets, and an entrance porch across the side of the house where the circular drive entered from the street.

Happily, the houses that Rossiter & Wright actually built for clients were more restrained than these speculative house designs. An 1883 house designed for David McClure in Red Bank, New Jersey, had a more simplified Queen Anne exterior, with bracketed supports under projecting gables in the roof line gables, two clustered chimneys, and a second-floor balcony over the porch roof above the main entrance.

Frank Wright's 1884 home in South Orange, New Jersey, reflected a measure of restraint within the Queen Anne style. A two and a half-story house, it featured generously formed half-timbered gables at the roof line, a clustered chimney, a bay window on the first floor, a modest gabled entrance porch, and a turreted oriel on the second floor, nicely shifted 90 degrees.

The Washington, Connecticut, carriage house that Rossiter converted to a temporary summer home for his family was much more elaborately embellished, with arched porches, bracketed projecting gables, and a prominent chimney ornamenting the exterior.

The most elaborate of these country houses in the Queen Anne style were created in Washington, Connecticut, in 1885 for Rossiter's clients Richard Barnes and his brother-in-law Lucius Barbour. As published in 1885, the Barnes house retains some of the fussiness of Rossiter's earlier published work, with the gables, turrets, and oriels compressed onto the roof line of the expansive porch. However, a photograph of the house, as built and viewed from the other side, shows it to be a more relaxed and graceful design. The large gables rest on the wide porches and the house seems to be anchored on the hillside perch by the sculptural chimneys. In the photograph, the fussy details of the windows and the shingles recede. *(See page 43)*

Rock Gate, the house designed in Washington for Barnes's brother-in-law Lucius Barbour, is perhaps the partners' best domestic work in the Queen Anne style. *(See page 44-45)* Rossiter used powerful geometry to organize the façade, a lesson he may have learned from his time in the workshop of H. H. Richardson. While retaining the porches, chimneys, and turrets of the Queen Anne, this Shingle style design was pulled together under a high pitched-roof line with a long sweep to the east and joined windows that created a series of horizontal bands at

ROSSITER & WRIGHT, The Rock Gate, carriage house for Lucius A. Barbour, Washington, Connecticut, 1885. Joseph West photos, Collection of the Gunn Memorial Library and Museum, Washington, Connecticut.

ROSSITER & WRIGHT, Carriage house for Charles Merritt, Danbury, Connecticut. Nd. Collection of the Danbury Museum and Historical Society, Connecticut.

the second story. A wide Richardsonian arch announced, yet sheltered, the entrance behind the road-facing porch that was recessed into the façade. On the opposite elevation, an explosion of open and closed circular porches, bays, and wide paired windows projects into the glorious western views across the Shepaug valley.

The Shingle style also influenced Rossiter's design for Hickory Hearth, Mrs. William Black's weekend house in nearby New Milford. Wrapped in shingles, the house had exaggerated sweeping roofs and deep porches, a suitably stylish design for the country house of a wealthy sophisticate in 1895.

Elements of the Colonial Revival began to slip into the late Shingle style houses designed by Rossiter & Wright in the 1890s. The Black house featured a Palladian window in the main gable. Palladian windows, dormers, and gambrel rooflines—elements of the Colonial Revival style—were also incorporated in the otherwise expansive shingle-clad house Rossiter designed for Col. W. E. Hughes in Dallas, Texas, in 1890,[8] and for William Hamilton Gibson in Washington, Connecticut, in 1892. *(See page 65)* The 1903 Washington home for Rossiter's brother-in-law (replacing an earlier home, Heathcote, that burned on the site) was a shingle-covered house with earlier style open porches, cone-topped towers, and bays (design elements taken, perhaps, from the earlier house?), but the rectangular footprint, gambrel roof, and dormers were features of the newer Colonial Revival style.

In the final decade of the nineteenth century, the expectations of suburban developers became more predictable, and Rossiter & Wright responded with convenient and stylish houses for their middle-class clients loosely based on elements of the Queen Anne Revival style. Many of these homes were substantial two-and-a-half-story houses with hipped roofs and towers at the entrance or towers projecting in pairs from either end of the façade. These houses were tasteful adaptations of the popular fashions, bringing together the clustered chimneys and leaded windows of the Queen Anne Revival with the towers and arcades of the Richardsonian Revival. Among the examples designed by Rossiter & Wright during these years were houses in Rumson, Morristown, and Montrose, New Jersey; the Washburn house in Worcester, Massachusetts; and several projects illustrated in the annual yearbook of the Architectural League. Rossiter's own home in Washington,

ROSSITER & WRIGHT, Rock Gate, summer home for Lucius A. Barbour, Washington, Connecticut, 1885. *American Architect and Building News,* 11/21/85, Author's collection

The quintessential expression of the Queen Anne Revival, seasoned with elements of the Shingle Style.

Connecticut, built 1888-1889, was influenced by this aesthetic, at least on the street façade. To the west, toward the view, Rossiter designed a series of porches under a sweeping roof, in a sort of Shingle style informality...or simply a response to the delight of the view. A house designed for Frank Wright in Short Hills, New Jersey, in 1900, also displayed a lingering affection for the Romanesque Revival, with heavy stonework at the entrance flanked by capped towers.[9] *(See page 59)*

At the turn of the century, Rossiter & Wright designed the last of its houses in the Queen Anne Revival style. In Washington, Arthur Woodruff's 1895 Orchard Terrace was a tight cluster of bays, gables, porches, and shingles. Larger homes in the late iteration of the style were designed for the Sterlings in St. Louis, Missouri, in 1892, the Spoffords in Norfolk, Connecticut, in 1898, and the Perrys in Washington, Connecticut, in 1908. *(See pages 65, 67)* All three houses had steeply pitched roofs with stacked gables over the façade. Leaded casement windows were grouped in the main front gable, and the disparate decorative elements were organized in bold geometric patterns.

The firm's institutional designs in the nineteenth century also emphasized the Queen Anne Revival and its related medieval cousins. The Worthington Memorial Chapel at Irvington-on-Hudson, New York, of 1882 was a cross-form chapel with Tudor parapets projecting above the roof lines at the gable ends and cone-topped towers tucked into the corners. *(See page 30)* The 1883 proposal for the Marsh library at the University of Vermont was a bold gathering of wings and porches with round-headed windows and arcades surrounding an off-center tall squared clock tower. *(See page 31)* More suggestive of Elizabethan England, the 1884 Village Hall built in South Orange, New Jersey, was a hipped-roof structure organized in a manor house "H" plan, with half-timbering in the gables and an oddly elongated tower on the corner. *(See page 57)* The Romanesque fashion was evident in Rossiter & Wright's successful design for the Newburgh Academy in 1886, which featured a symmetric block with a central front gable, flanked by massive round-headed arches and a pair of cone-topped towers. *(See page 29)* The row houses designed for West 81st St. in New York in 1886 also incorporated motifs inspired by the architectural romance with Romanesque and Tudor styles, with round-headed windows, bays, and parapets. *(See page 50)*

ROSSITER & WRIGHT, Eames & Young, G. E.
Sterling Residence, St. Louis, Missouri, 1892.
The Inland Architect and News Record, 6/1893.
Ryerson and Burnham Libraries Book Collection, The
Art Institute of Chicago. Digital File #IA2105_1279
© The Art Institute of Chicago.

The firm designed the last of its Queen Anne Revival public buildings
in the 1890s. The 1891 Setauket Library on Long Island had a little bit
of everything—a deep roof line that reached low to the first-story façade
(an Arts and Crafts reference?); a brick façade that featured corner
quoins (a Georgian Revival reference?); an entrance that was set under
a round-headed door (a Richardsonian reference?), and a prominent
two-story central gable decorated with half-timbering and leaded
windows (a Tudor Revival reference?). *(See page 83)* The architects'
final institutional projects designed in medieval fashions were the 1896
president's house at Vassar College in Poughkeepsie, New York, and
the Hackensack Library in New Jersey in 1900. Executed in red brick,
the Tudor style house at Vassar had parapets extending above the roof
line at the projecting side gables. *(See page 81)* Polygonal towers fronted
the walls under the front gables and were lined with horizontal bands
of small-paned windows. The stone-walled Johnson public library in
Hackensack was also furnished with parapets at the gable ends. *(See page
60)* The entrance, at the junction of the two cross wings, was set into a
crenellated square tower.

In their heyday of designing Queen Anne Revival, Rossiter and Wright
did a series of buildings with bold half-timbering, offering a bright
patterned contrast on the elevations of the upper floors, including the
renovations to the Van Ingen house in Washington, Connecticut; the

1891 Emma S. Clark Library in Setauket, New York; the 1894 Village Hall in South Orange, New Jersey; and the 1908 house for the Perrys in Washington. These were, perhaps, their most distinctive buildings in the style, although the architects were enthusiastically embracing the eclecticism of the era.

Rossiter & Wright and The Colonial Revival
The Colonial Revival was introduced into the work of Rossiter & Wright when the firm undertook the expansion of the historic Julius Deming house in Litchfield in 1887. The architects' most prominent commissions in New York City, for the Royalton Hotel in 1897 and for the cooperative apartment buildings in 1907, were also designed in a Classical Revival style. *(See pages 86, 89, 90)* By the turn of the century, many of the firm's country houses were conceived in a classical vocabulary, from small gambrel-roofed cottages, to grand columned estates, providing homes in the style for clients with a range of budgets. The firm also remodeled earlier homes for clients who wanted to update to the more fashionable Colonial Revival style and designed libraries and school buildings in the newly popular American variation on the classical style. The Colonial Revival remained popular well into the twentieth century, and Rossiter & Wright and later Rossiter & Muller continued to design projects in this style into the mid-1920s.

Rossiter had previously deplored the rectangular symmetry of the classical styles, but he now took an interest in the colonial period, which grew in popularity after the celebrations of the American Centennial. Later, in retirement, Wright recalled that he had organized tours of New England colonial houses for members of New York's Architectural League as their interest in colonial buildings grew. Rossiter was president of Washington's Village Improvement Society, formed, as similar organizations in New England, to enhance the colonial appearance of the village green during a wave of nostalgia for an imagined simpler time, centered on the New England country town. Rossiter had studied the colonial style when he renovated the eighteenth-century Deming house in Litchfield in 1886. He also revisited Connecticut's colonial architecture when he designed the Connecticut State Building for the 1907 Jamestown Exposition in Virginia, an adaptation of the eighteenth-century Tallmadge house, which stood across the street from the Deming house in Litchfield.

Rossiter's in-depth introduction to the colonial style came when he was commissioned by J. Deming Perkins to remodel the home of his grandfather Julius Deming on North St. in Litchfield. Litchfield was then consumed with colonial enthusiasm as New Yorkers gathering in the historic village for the summers set about remodeling the town's houses, village center, and green with architectural embellishments and landscaping inspired by an imagined colonial precedent. They were creating an ideal colonial village a century after the fact. Perkins was a Litchfield native who worked in New York before returning to the village after his marriage in 1868. In Litchfield, he worked to bring the Shepaug Railroad from New York to Litchfield and later served as the Litchfield representative to the state senate. He inherited his grandfather's house from his maiden aunt in 1887 and set about expanding it with Rossiter's assistance.

Rossiter came to measure the house in August 1887. Both client and architect recognized the challenge of renovating the historic house, then nearly a century old. *(See page 47)* "It is quite a problem as to how to enlarge it without spoiling it, but it will solve itself after a time," Perkins wrote to a family member. Rossiter's plans were delivered to Perkins at his home in New York the following February, and Perkins reported to family members, "We are much pleased with the changes, as Rossiter plans them, and shall hope you will all like the 'extended' house. We do not change the style of architecture—we could not do that—but add materially to the accommodations by extending the main house to the east."[10]

Rossiter enlarged the classical house to accommodate Perkins's requirements for the gracious lifestyle of an American country house in the late nineteenth century, while at the same time honoring the historic character of the eighteenth-century home built by the client's grandfather, a prominent Litchfield figure during and after the Revolutionary War. The "colonial" house was a classical Georgian design, with a central hall and two interior chimneys, rather than a colonial design with a center chimney. The house had a symmetric façade with a slightly projecting pedimented entrance pavilion, four engaged single-story columns surrounding the doorway, and a balustrade and Palladian window above. Corner quoins, a light Federal style balustrade at the edge of the shallow hipped roof, and dentil moldings on the

The Julius Deming House, Litchfield, Connecticut, before the Rossiter & Wright alterations of 1887.
Archives of the Litchfield Historical Society, Litchfield, Connecticut.

The 18th century Deming house gave Rossiter first-hand experience with "colonial" precedent in American architecture.

cornices at the roof line and over the windows added to the historic appeal of the house. To expand the house, Rossiter enlarged the service wing at the back of the house and converted the attic into living space lighted by new dormers. On the south side of the house, facing the driveway and gardens, he added a two-story gabled extension flanked by two large bays on the first floor. The face of the double-height extension duplicated the front entrance, mimicking its arrangement of columns and Palladian window.

Over the next 30 years, Rossiter and his partners designed homes in various colonial or classical revival styles throughout the northeast. Generally favoring a symmetric ground plan and façade, they embellished these houses with a consistent range of classical detailing, including columns, balustrades, corner quoins, urns, fanlights, and Palladian windows.

One group of houses was designed with gambrel roofs, considered to be a colonial feature suggesting the Dutch heritage of New York and New Jersey. This roof line also had the advantage of providing extra room under the roof at the attic or second floor, depending on the number of stories in the house, offering additional space for a modest cost. Rossiter first adopted the gambrel roof, perhaps a matter of economy as well as aesthetics, for the summer home and studio of the painter Dwight Tryon, a simple pair of shingle-covered structures built on the shore of Buzzards Bay at South Dartmouth, Massachusetts, in 1887. The colonial gambrel roof on the Tallmadge house in Litchfield, across the street from the Deming-Perkins house, may have inspired Rossiter's interest in the form; he later used the Tallmadge house as the model for his design for the Connecticut State Building at the 1907 Jamestown Exposition. *(See page 78)*

Gambrel roofs were incorporated into Rossiter's more substantial Gibson house in Washington, Connecticut, in 1892, *(see page 65)*, otherwise a house in the Queen Anne style, and also into the 1893 Holiday House in Washington, the summer boarding house where

ROSSITER & WRIGHT, Main Building, The Ridge School, Washington, Connecticut, 1904. Joseph West photo, Collection of the Gunn Memorial Library and Museum, Washington, Connecticut.

The buildings for the new boys' school in Washington were intended to evoke a virtuous American domesticity, best expressed in the Colonial Revival style, seen here in the gambrel roof, dormers and overall symmetry. The school was later converted into The Mayflower Inn.

ROSSITER & WRIGHT, Vanholme, the summer home for William Van Sinderen, Washington, Connecticut, 1905. Joseph West photo, Collection of the Gunn Memorial Library and Museum, Washington, Connecticut.

The summer home for Van Sinderen, a descendant of a prominent colonial family in Washington, was designed in a Colonial Revival style, with its gambrel roof and Palladian window.

The architects adapted their Colonial
Revival gambrel-roofed cottage, popular
in Washington and Norfolk, to a homey
student infirmary.

working girls from New York were invited for a fresh air holiday, built
as a charity project of the Van Ingens. In 1895, Rossiter & Wright
designed a small summer house with a long, flared gambrel roof for
the Van Sinderen family in Washington, Connecticut. *(See page 131)* A
gambrel roof covered the 1903 house for the Heaths in Washington.
Compact summer homes with broader gambrel roofs were created for
the Richmond Paine family in Norfolk, Connecticut, in 1906 and the
Wersebes in Washington in 1907. *(See page 76, 130)* A similar, undated
home for the Robbins Stoeckel family was built in Norfolk, probably
at the same time. These small homes were ornamented with columned
entrance porches, shed roofs, and dormers. Each was sited on a high
ridge and provided with plenty of windows to take advantage of the
country breezes and long views. The Hotchkiss School 1905 infirmary
was designed in a similar style.

Another variation of the Colonial Revival houses designed by the firm
at the turn of the twentieth century sat on squared footprints, with

classically inspired hip roofs or gable roofs lined with dormers. These houses were decorated with a liberal use of columns, Palladian windows, and expansive porches wrapping the first floor. Examples were designed for suburban settings, including the 1892 Shedd house and the 1894 Palmer house in Rumson, New Jersey; the 1898 Brown-Keeley house in White Plains, New York; and Prospect Hill, the summer house of the Gold family in Washington. (*See page 72*)

At the turn of the century, Rossiter & Wright began to accent their Colonial Revival houses with columned two-story entrance porches. These may have been an adaptation of the double-height columned entrance at the Royalton Hotel in New York, which their team designed in 1897. They returned to this urban-scaled classical façade in the two cooperative apartment buildings designed at Lexington Ave. and East 67th St. in 1907.

One of their earliest suburban double-height entrance porches was designed for the 1898 home of Charles Lane Poor on Shelter Island at the eastern end of Long Island. (*See page 79*) An avid sailor and member of the New York Yacht Club, Poor was then the editor for the New York Academy of Sciences and later a professor of astronomy at Columbia University. His Rossiter & Wright-designed house was a boxy shingle-covered colonial overlooking Long Island Sound. Single-story porches projected toward the Sound at a 45-degree angle from either side of a double-height entrance porch supported by columns, with a balustrade marking the second floor. Early photos show racing flags fluttering from the porches, giving the house itself the appearance of a ship rigged for sailing.

In Washington, Rossiter designed a double-height porch for the 1898 Senator Orville Platt house, with double-height columns at the front corners of the porch and a pair of single-height columns supporting a balustraded balcony at the porch's second floor. (*See page 71*) It was the first of a series of fully developed double-height entrance porches in northwest Connecticut.

The double-height entrance porch appears repeatedly in the firm's work in the first decade of the twentieth century, particularly on homes

ROSSITER & WRIGHT, The Senator Orville Platt House, Washington, Connecticut, 1898. A.Y. Smith photo.

The Platt house was one of the first Rossiter & Wright houses to incorporate the double height front porch.

intended for summer retreats or retirement. There were a number of variations on the theme, but the oversize classical motif was designed to impress. The 1900 Charles Deming house in Litchfield had a double-height entrance portico supported on paired columns, while the 1903 Cunningham house down the street displayed a double-height circular porch with a balustraded balcony at the second floor. *(See page 79)* The Hepburn 1903 weekend estate in Ridgefield, Connecticut, had clustered corner columns at the double-height porch facing the street and a second double-height porch facing the gardens behind the house.

ROSSITER & WRIGHT, The Charles Beach House, New Milford, Connecticut, renovations in 1910.
A.Y. Smith photo.

The architects were hired to embellish the Beach's colonial house on the New Milford green, adding the double height porch.

The Ashton Harvey home in Short Hills, New Jersey, built sometime before 1904, had a circular double-height porch, reminiscent of the porch at the Cunningham house but without the second-floor balcony. The 1904 William Peters house in Mill Neck, on Long Island, had a double-height recessed porch overlooking Long Island Sound. Rossiter's design for the Connecticut State Building at the 1907 Jamestown Exposition, based on the Tallmadge house in Litchfield, modified the original to include a porch-like, double-height projection, delineated with pilasters on either side and topped with a gable. The eighteenth- century Charles Beach house at the south end of the green in New Milford, Connecticut, was remodeled in 1910, adding a grand columned double-story portico with a full balcony between the columns at the second floor. The same year, Rossiter designed a double-height portico with columns for the brick colonial house he designed for his cousin Richard Billings in Vermont. The circular double-height porch at Whitehouse in Norfolk was probably built in 1906; the second-floor balcony there was tucked back toward the facade, the roof top of the porch serving as a balustraded balcony. (*See page 74, 78, 79, 80*)

ROSSITER & MULLER, The Oaks, home of E. H. Fallows in Norfolk, Connecticut, after 1913.
Photo: Frank H. DeMars. DeMarsImages.com.

Rossiter & Muller added a Mount Vernon-style double height porch to the front of this colonial home in Norfolk, and second floor sleeping porches to the back. Edward Huntington Fallows, a New York lawyer, was the first President of the Norfolk Golf Club.

The double-height entrance porch was extended in two Rossiter projects so that the two-story porch stretched across the full front of the house, a deliberate reference to Washington's home Mount Vernon. Standish (later known as Edgewood, *see page 73*), in Washington, Connecticut, designed in 1910 for a proud descendant of Miles Standish, was a classic Colonial Revival house, symmetrically arranged and fitted out with first-floor bay windows and sleeping porches on the second floor, overlooking the garden. In addition to the bay windows and sleeping porches, a columned two-story porch ran the full length of the house, with a Chinoiserie balustrade across the top. At the Fallows house in Norfolk, Rossiter took a modest colonial, and added corner quoins, dormers, and a Palladian window in the gable, and added a two-story porch across the full length of the front, topped with a balustrade matching the one on the Washington house. On the back of the Fallows house, a two-story porch accommodated second-floor balconies and sleeping porches.[11]

Beyond the gambrel roofs and double-height porches in Rossiter's Colonial Revival houses, other characteristics of the style abounded in the projects designed in the first decade of the twentieth century. Many of the larger houses had dentil moldings at the cornices, corner quoins or corner pilasters, fanlights, and Palladian windows. In early photographs, shutters frequently appear at the windows. While earlier examples still incorporated the diamond-pane windows of the older Queen Anne style in either casement or sash form, clear glass sash windows became more prevalent as the decade progressed. Sometimes two or three sash windows, often with geometric leaded glass, were grouped together to form a wider expanse of glass, or were set into three-sided bays, opening the wall to admit more light into the house. Porches and balconies abounded, particularly in the suburban and summer houses, to accommodate family members and guests as they gathered outside for the evening breezes.

Schools, libraries, and community buildings for suburban and country projects incorporated many of the same design features, encouraging a sense of domestic familiarity in a village setting. The school projects in New Milford, Washington, and Lakeville, Connecticut, borrowed extensively from Rossiter's domestic designs in the Colonial Revival style.

At the Ingleside School in New Milford, new buildings were added to the campus that updated the 1899 Weantinaug Hall designed in the old-fashioned Queen Anne style. The 1903 Foundation House was a shingle-covered colonial block with symmetric projecting wings at either end. The 1906 Ingleside "bungalow," a club for visiting alumnae, was a gambrel-roofed, shingle-clad residence with porches surrounding the first floor on three sides.

In Washington, both The Gunnery and The Ridge School built colonial-style buildings at their campuses in 1904. The Gunnery's Bartlett Hall dormitory was a symmetric gambrel-roofed house with large third-floor dormers, a classical entrance porch, and shingle cladding. (See page 68) The Ridge School buildings designed in 1904, including its main building and two residential cottages, Colton and Chapin, were designed with gambrel roofs, shingles, dormers, and

EHRICK ROSSITER, Muwagha Lodge, Washington, Connecticut, 1916. Collection of the Gunn Memorial Library and Museum, Washington, Connecticut.

This plain summer house in the Colonial Revival style was built for Arthur Shipman, a Trustee of Steep Rock Association and founding partner in the Hartford law firm Shipman and Goodwin.

ALTERATION & ADDITION
TO COTTAGE AT WEST SIDE
HOTCHKISS · SCHOOL ·
LAKEVILLE · CONN ·

- FRONT · ELEVATION -
SCALE ¼ INCH ONE FOOT

- ROSSITER & WRIGHT -
ARCHITECTS
110 EAST 23ʳᵈ ST · NY CITY

PROPOSED ENLARGEMENT OF HEADMASTER'S HOUSE—FRONT OR SOUTH ELEVATION

HEADMASTER'S HOUSE, The Hotchkiss School, Lakeville, Connecticut, 1910. Archives, The Hotchkiss School.

In the Colonial Revival, the entrance hallway was reduced in size, allowing the principal entertaining rooms to be expanded. Here, the entrance hall, largely occupied by the stairway, proceeds to the Master's Study, where visitors would descend a short stairway into the impressive Tudor Revival reception room. To the left of the entrance hall, the dining room was separated from the basement kitchen, which delivered food to the main floor dining room by way of a dumb waiter in the pantry.

porches to intentionally suggest the best of cottage living in the country. *(See page 131)* The 1910 expansion of the headmaster's house at The Hotchkiss School in Lakeville was designed as a gracious Colonial Revival home, though at a larger scale to accommodate the public role it played in the school's activities and ambitions.

Clubhouses in these sophisticated country towns also adopted the Colonial Revival style, with the 1906 Music Shed in Norfolk and the 1907 Washington Clubhouse in Washington similarly conceived with columned porches at a gabled entrance and a large cupola in the roof at the intersection of the cross wings, although the music shed was covered in shingles and the clubhouse was originally covered in roughcast and embellished with pedimented windows. *(See pages 68, 75)*

Rossiter's designs for libraries, in spite of the common functionality of their interior spaces, illustrated the architect's ingenuity within a limited range of decorative motifs. Beginning with the Gunn Library in Washington in 1907, *(see page 69)*, and continuing with the Hepburn libraries in upstate New York—in Colton, Edwards, Lisbon, Waddington, Madrid and Norfolk,—Rossiter varied the design elements to give each of the buildings its own distinctive image while generally sharing the same classical elements. *(See pages 92-93)* The first two libraries were faced with Richardsonian fieldstone and finished with classical projecting pediments and elegant cupolas. The later libraries, located in adjoining towns in upstate New York, were designed in brick with sophisticated classical detailing at the windows and entrances. The upstate New York libraries were all sited with high basements, allowing light into the public spaces below and permitting impressive entrance stairways in spite of their small scale. Although three of these libraries have parapets at the end gables, all but one of the New York libraries are clearly classical designs, with columned pediments at the front doorways.

The Colonial Revival style was also selected for the 1916 Hepburn Hall at Middlebury College in Vermont. *(See page 94)* Like the earlier, wooden Foundation House for the Ingleside School, Hepburn Hall was organized around a symmetric central block with projecting wings at each end. The brick dormitory in Middlebury featured a variety of colonial details, including a hip roof, dormers, cupola, and a classically appointed central entrance doorway. The restrained elevations were set on a rusticated foundation and delineated with bold masonry belt courses placed at the second and fourth floors, giving visual interest to the façade.[12]

With the emphasis on the Colonial Revival, Rossiter also changed his thinking about the appropriate colors for domestic architecture, turning to a lighter palate than what he'd promoted for the Queen Anne style. In 1907 he suggested to the headmaster of The Hotchkiss School that the campus buildings should be painted a "mellow" gray, matching the color of roughcast, and that the woodwork should be painted ivory. He recommended that the blinds (shutters) should be painted the same color as the trim, rather than the dark green that they were then painted. He reflected that green was a cold color and that the buildings would look better with ivory shutters. Mindful of promoting the school, he pointed out that "the postal card color is more cheerful" in gray and ivory. He recommended that the shingles and clapboards be painted the same color and that roofs not be stained a color but be allowed to fade out to a simple weathered gray. "In my mind...[it is] in better taste than any artificial colored roof."[13]

The firm continued to work in the perennially popular Colonial Revival style into the 1920s, when Skytop, the 1928 resort in northeast Pennsylvania, was designed. *(See page 101)* The stone hotel with a dormered gambrel roof recalled the conservative values of the colonial era and appealed to the clients' goals for an exclusive, "high class" retreat in nature.

Rossiter & Muller and The Tudor Revival
Early in their practice, Rossiter & Wright designed several Queen Anne revival projects in masonry that could be considered as part of the Tudor Revival style, including the All Saint's Church in New Milford, Connecticut (1882), the Worthington Chapel in Irvington on Hudson, New York (1882), the Presbyterian churches in Oceanic and South Orange, New Jersey (1882), the president's house at Vassar College in Poughkeepsie, New York (1896), and the Johnson Public Library in Hackensack, New Jersey (1900). Like their other work in the Queen Anne revival style, these buildings incorporated Tudor Revival elements as part of an eclectic mix of design details in the Queen Anne manner.

After the turn of the twentieth century, however, the Tudor Revival regained popularity in the United States, particularly among Anglophiles. College buildings, churches, and suburban housing for the upper middle class embraced an association with aristocratic English traditions by adopting this architectural style. After 1912, Rossiter's new partner, John Muller, who had trained at Columbia College and the École des Beaux Arts in Paris, brought a new vigor and authority to the firm's Tudor Revival work. The Tudor Revival designs after Muller joined the firm crackle with confidence, combining a strong sense of massing, and bold Tudor detail. They were also larger and more expensive than the earlier buildings.

The first project in this newly invigorated style was the 1913 Stedman-Johnson house in Hartford, Connecticut. *(See page 96)* Occupying a full block in the fashionable west end, the house looked like a Masterpiece

ROSSITER & WRIGHT, Doorway at Cheney House, New Haven, Connecticut, 1919. Photo by A.Y. Smith, 2011.

Theater set. It was imposing, with a steeply raked slate roof silhouetting a pair of matching Tudor gables with parapets facing the street at either side of the central entrance. Bold finials sat at the crest of each parapet. Another Tudor-shaped parapet projected above the front door. Banks of windows were set in deep limestone surrounds surmounted with a Tudor style molding. An oversized stone doorway, Georgian rather than Tudor in style, implied that the house had evolved through many generations.

The 1918 Cheney house in New Haven, Connecticut, was designed as another bold geometric mass, dramatically set behind stone pillars on the prominent city street. *(See page 97)* Three wings, gabled with parapets, converged on the entrance tower, where a visitor approached through an arched, paneled door hung with heavy ornamental hinges under carved stone quatrefoils above the doorway. Paired casement windows were set into heavily molded stone surrounds. The exterior

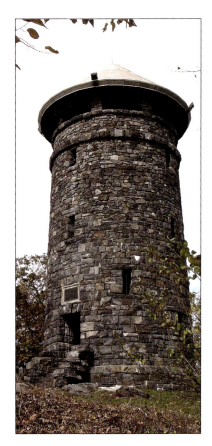

ROSSITER & MULLER, Haystack Mountain tower, Norfolk, Connecticut, 1929. Photo by Alan Levere, Department of Energy and Environmental Protection, State of Connecticut.

walls were alternately covered in stucco and random ashlar, as if the house had withstood a medieval siege or the passage of centuries. Even the three-car garage had a clustered chimney, parapets on the end walls, and Tudor arches over the garage doors.

The Episcopal churches designed by Rossiter & Muller during World War I in Washington and Litchfield, Connecticut, fully expressed the Tudor Revival style. Compared with All Saints Episcopal church designed by Rossiter & Wright in New Milford, Connecticut, in 1882, the new designs were much stronger in both massing and composition, even though all three churches were similarly composed of a nave with parapets on the gable ends, buttresses, a square tower, and cross wings. At the smallest church, St. John's in Washington of 1917-18, the tower joined the nave in a more integrated manner than the New Milford church, while the taller spire, bolder buttressing, and large tracery window at the entrance made the Washington building soar. *(See page 99)*

St. Michael's Church in Litchfield, Connecticut, 1919-1921, was the firm's most successful design in the Tudor Revival style. The largest of the firm's three churches in northwest Connecticut, the composition included the expected Tudor Revival features—masonry, gothic windows, parapets, a square tower, and buttresses. While the churches in New Milford and Washington were sited on open lawns, the Litchfield church was located at a prominent site in the village center. By pulling the elements of the building together on the narrow lot, the architects created a powerful, almost massive, structure. Lightening the composition with a large tracery window in the front gable facing the street and in the paired large round-headed windows in the tower, the church was heavy and light, powerful and aspirational. *(See page 99)*

The firm's final project in the Tudor Revival style was the observation tower at Haystack Mountain, in Norfolk, Connecticut, commissioned in 1929 by Mrs. Stoeckel in honor of her father, replacing an earlier tower that Robbins Battell had given the town, which had disintegrated. The circular, rusticated masonry tower was covered with a broad roof above an observation gallery at the top. Looking like an ancient survivor from the Middle Ages, the tower emphasized its mass and simplicity with small slits of windows marking the interior ascent, perfect for shooting arrows at an attacking army.

Interior Finishes

Over the course of a century of continued occupation, the interiors of Rossiter's projects still extant have been renovated again and again to suit modern fashions and lifestyles. Some of the houses were burned and rebuilt; others were extensively remodeled and redecorated. Walls, floors, and woodwork were removed, sometimes within a decade of their original construction. Consequently, most surviving buildings are unreliable indicators of the original interior finishes and floor plans.

Fortunately, there are period publications that show the interior finishes and floor plans of the earliest projects, and a handful of architectural drawings and historic photographs reveal the interior finishes of later projects soon after they were completed.

Just as Rossiter promoted an eclectic aesthetic at the beginning of his career in *Modern House Painting*, the Queen Anne Revival, Colonial Revival, and Tudor Revival styles mix indiscriminately on the firm's interior finishes over 40 years. New fashions were reflected in the interiors more quickly than on the exteriors, and the firm mixed styles inside and out. Queen Anne Revival houses featured Colonial Revival interiors, and Colonial Revival houses incorporated Tudor Revival interiors. The elaborate houses of the architect's final years included one with a Colonial Revival exterior and Tudor Revival interior, another with an emphatically Tudor Revival exterior and elaborate Colonial Revival finishes on the interior. The late, elaborate homes have Tudor Revival details in the main rooms and Colonial Revival finishes in the bedrooms.

Drawings for three New Jersey houses, published between 1881 and 1883, illustrate Rossiter & Wright's preference for domestic interiors in the Queen Anne Revival style. The small, diamond-paned casement windows and hearth-centered spaces provided cozy rooms. Woodwork covered the walls with built-in drawers and bookcases, open shelves for the display of *objets d'art,* and multi-paned glass cupboard doors to showcase, as the architects specified, "bric-a-brac." Boxed panels filled the walls below the chair rail in halls and stairwells and covered the chimney breasts above the mantels, with provision made for mirrored insets and the placement of paintings. Eastlake-inspired posts, circular

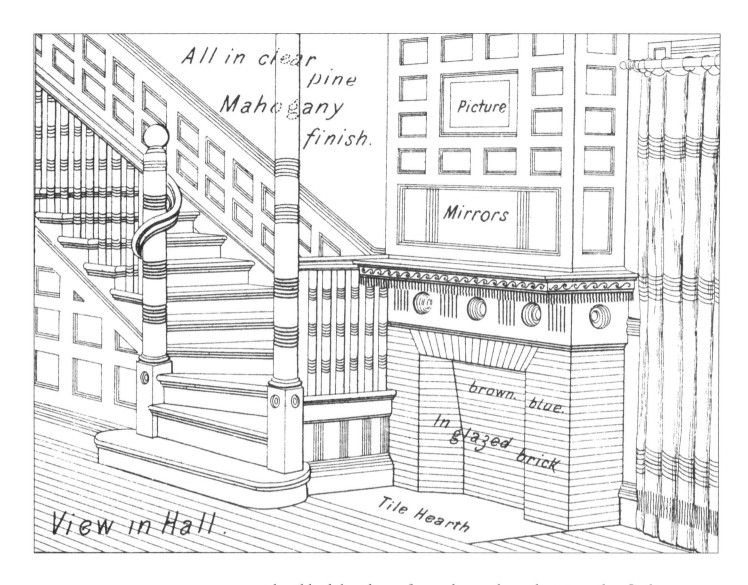

All in clear pine Mahogany finish.

Picture

Mirrors

brown. blue. In glazed brick

Tile Hearth

View in Hall.

ROSSITER & WRIGHT, Interior drawings for a house in Fairmount, New Jersey, 1881. William T. Comstock, *Modern Architectural Designs and Details*, New York, 1881. Reprinted as William T. Comstock, *Victorian Domestic Architectural Plans and Details*, Mineola, NY: Dover Publications, 1987.

with ribbed banding, formed newels and stair rails. Ceilings were finished with an astonishing array of boxed "beams" in busy rectangular patterns. Glazed brick, colored and decorated with mottos, covered the front of the fireplaces. In two of three surviving drawings, the fireplace opening was a large round-headed arch. Large arched openings, set on pilasters or springing from short bookcases, divided major first-floor rooms. In Wright's own 1884 home in South Orange, a heavy curtain hung from a brass rod in the opening of the archway between the library and the dining room; other drawings for houses indicated that such a curtain, both decorative and functional, was common. Notes on the drawings suggested that the interiors should be painted in deep, rich colors—red-and-green painted plaster over the mantel in one house, brown-and-blue glazed brick on the fireplace in another.

ROSSITER & WRIGHT, Interior drawings for a house for Frank A. Wright, South Orange, New Jersey, 1884. *Building*, May, 1884.

The interiors in Rossiter & Wright's designs for houses in the Queen Anne Revival style were filled with pattern and machine-crafted details. Fireplaces, often dramatically shaped and faced with colorful glazed brick, were a central feature in entrance halls and principal rooms. Ceilings were dressed to suggest panels and walls were covered with raised panels below a high chair rail. Heavy drapery hung from brass rails in the archways that separated the principal rooms.

ROSSITER & WRIGHT, Interior of the Atwood House at the Water Witch Club, Monmouth County, New Jersey, 1897. Collection of Mary Jo (Burke) Kenny, Monmouth Hills, Highlands, New Jersey.

Both functional and decorative, the fireplace remained prominent even at the informal summer cottages at Water Witch.

ROSSITER & WRIGHT, Rock Gate, dining room in the Barbour-Seccomb house, Washington, Connecticut. Photo taken after 1895. Collection of the Gunn Memorial Library and Museum, Washington, Connecticut.

ROSSITER & WRIGHT, Rock Gate, entrance hall in the Barbour-Seccomb house, Washington, Connecticut. Photo taken after 1895. Collection of the Gunn Memorial Library and Museum, Washington, Connecticut.

Elements of the Queen Anne Revival persisted in Rossiter's interiors, including diamond paned windows, patterned ceilings and dog leg stairways with multiple landings, producing a romantic and cozy atmosphere.

Photographs taken at the Barbour house in Washington soon after it was sold to the Seccombs, a Brooklyn family, in 1892, show that the entrance hall was finished in such a style.[14] Highly polished wood panels covered the walls in the stairwell and the boxed ceiling. However, the post and turnings on the high balustraded screen at the stairwell and the pilasters to either side of the stair closet were classical, anticipating the Colonial Revival. Other rooms also blended features of the Queen Anne Revival, such as diamond-pane glass cupboard doors, with the Colonial Revival, seen in the high wainscot paneling, boxed-beam ceilings, and molded ceiling cornices.

ROSSITER & WRIGHT, Laneholme, for Charles Lane Poor, Shelter Island, New York, 1898. Photos from the Lane family collection, courtesy of Ward and Lane Poor.

Laneholme, on Shelter Island, had a Colonial Revival interior, with a white painted classical columns ornamenting the primary rooms. What would have been a cozy inglenook in a Queen Anne Revival design was here updated with large windows over the seats to either side of the fireplace, framed by Ionic columns.

Rossiter's interiors in the Colonial Revival style were recorded in photographs taken shortly after the turn of the century in several rooms then recently completed. Laneholme, the 1898 summer home for Charles Lane Poor at Shelter Island, off Long Island, was one of the architects' first interiors in the new style. Large windows filled the rooms with light. The walls were simply covered with middle-toned wallpaper and paint and accented with white-painted trim. Arched openings still served as dividers between main rooms, but the white-painted arches were supported by fluted pilasters with ionic capitals. Ceilings were embellished with unpainted but highly polished boxed

beams in the colonial style. An open balustrade at the top of the interior wall brought more natural light into the center hallway. Elsewhere in the house, a raised alcove with a rusticated stone fireplace was an updated medieval inglenook, light-filled with banks of diamond casements in bay windows over window seats on either side of the fireplace.

Kirby Corner, the 1898 home for Senator Orville Platt, was photographed for his widow in the early twentieth century, capturing the Colonial Revival interiors of its first owner. Wallpapers in middle-tone patterns cover the walls on the first floor, accented with white-painted classical pilasters, archways, cupboards, and ceiling cornices. On the second floor, light-colored walls were lined with restrained colonial moldings at the doorways and baseboards; thin picture moldings were fitted just below the coved ceilings. Elegant Federal style mantels, painted white, recalled the refined sensibility of the nation's early decades.

ROSSITER & WRIGHT, Kirby Corner, the home of Senator Orville Platt, Washington, Connecticut, 1897. Photos taken by R. A. Warrender, after 1915; in the collection of the Gunn Memorial Library and Museum, Washington, Connecticut.

Virtually next door to the Barbour/Seccomb house, but designed a decade later, the Platt house was completed in the patriotic Colonial Revival style for the senator and his wife. A wide hallway and open-well stairway were at the center of the symmetrically arranged house. Large windows let more light into the rooms, which were covered in light wallpapers and trimmed in light-painted classically-inspired columns and mantels. While leaded glass remained, it was reconfigured to suggest the light elliptical designs of the Federal era, rather than the diamond panes of the medieval era.

The 1904 Ridge School in Washington, Connecticut, was also photographed shortly after its construction—probably for promotional purposes—showing another aspect of the architects' perspective on the Colonial Revival interior. Although these campus buildings were designed as school facilities, they were deliberately intended to convey a cottage-like domesticity. The interiors of Chapin, one of the residential cottages, had plain walls, painted in light colors with a reflective sheen. A rusticated stone fireplace was surrounded by short built-in bookcases, leaving room above for pictures to be hung from a simple picture molding. The dining room at the main building was also finished with plain light-toned walls, and a wooden plank ceiling was painted in a light, reflective color. Pairs of polished but unpainted side posts met boxed ceiling beams, joined with a simple bracket, an architectural pun intended to evoke the interior of the ship the *Mayflower*, which brought the Puritans to New England. Built-in bookcases at either side of the doorway and a high display shelf along the main wall were fitted with front rails, as if to secure the contents on the rolling seas.

Surviving drawings indicate that Rossiter and Wright designed the interiors for their projects rather than leaving the work to the finish carpenters or buying ready-made woodwork and mantels. Therefore, surviving houses—the Stedman-Johnson house and the headmaster's house at The Hotchkiss School in Lakeville—with their interiors relatively intact, along with the main floor of the Gunn Memorial Library in Washington, offer additional evidence of the kind of interior finishes favored by the architects during the Colonial Revival. Both houses have main rooms finished in an elaborate Tudor Revival style, but the bedrooms and other secondary rooms were finished in the Colonial Revival style. At The Hotchkiss School, these colonial areas include the entrance hallway, the dining room, and the bedrooms, and at Stedman-Johnson, they include the dining room and the bedrooms. The bedroom woodwork, painted white in both houses, includes a Greek key molding in the frieze of the ceiling cornice, and, at The Hotchkiss School, it appears at the chair rail and at some of the doorway cornices. Both houses have elegant classical mantels, with urns, columns, and other lightly lyrical classical motifs. The front hallway at The Hotchkiss School was decorated with raised panels under a high chair rail, and the stairway was composed of a series of spiraled balusters and a spiral twist newel similar to those found at Rossiter projects in Washington, New

ROSSITER & WRIGHT, The headmaster's house,
The Hotchkiss School, Lakeville, Connecticut. A.
Y. Smith photos.

Milford, and Norfolk.[15] The dining room at the Stedman-Johnson house was finished with a classically inspired yet inventive chimney breast that had a glass-fronted cupboard above the fireplace along with the more customary side pilasters and multiple rows of dentil molding at the cornice. To either side of the fireplace, classical pilastered doors opened onto a cupboard on the left and onto the pantries and kitchen on the right. A chair rail with a dentil molding above a paneled wainscot finished the remaining walls. The woodwork was not painted. The Gunn Library interiors, also unpainted, were embellished with fluted Ionic columns, boxed arches supported on fluted pilasters, and dentil molding at the deep cornices. Curiously, a sort of Tudor diamond carving was applied to the columns between the windows.

The most elaborate interiors in the Stedman-Johnson house and the headmaster's house at The Hotchkiss School were in the Tudor Revival style. In the Stedman-Johnson house, the Tudor Revival style dominated the main entrance and stairwell, along with the adjacent music room, the largest room in the house. Rossiter's Tudor Revival details are shown on the original architectural drawings of 1913. The 1910 master's study in the headmaster's house at The Hotchkiss School, designed to intimidate students and impress potential donors, was also a Tudor Revival statement, documented in a 1913 photograph. Judging by the awed memories of students, faculty, and donors in the generations since, it served its purpose.

The Stedman-Johnson house entrance hall and The Hotchkiss School master's study are lined with similar boxed panels. Applied split spindles and pierced foliate patterns on the mantels and the newel posts appear in both of these nearly contemporary projects. These Tudor Revival rooms were dramatic. In Hartford, an impressive two-landing stairway filled the entrance hall; to the right of the entrance, the large music room and an adjacent inglenook were both finished in Tudor Revival paneling. In the Hotchkiss project, the master's study was set several steps below the first floor, with the entrance opposite an imposing fireplace covered in Tudor Revival paneling. A high diamond casement window in the dining room looked across the master's study to window seats set in the north wall overlooking the piazza and the lake. These were large rooms intended to impress, and they still do.

In Rossiter's late work, the Tudor Revival was the style of choice for the public entertaining rooms, as demonstrated in the Master's Study at The Hotchkiss headmaster's house and in the entrance hall and the "Music Room," the largest room in the house at Stedman-Johnson house.

Rossiter & Wright and, later, Rossiter & Muller weren't creating textbook designs in carefully defined styles. Instead, the firms were mixing and balancing traditional and contemporary fashion to suit the lifestyles and budgets of their clients.

EHRICK ROSSITER, The Tudor Revival entrance
hall in the Stedman-Johnson house, Hartford,
Connecticut. A. Y. Smith photos.

CHAPTER SIX: BUILDINGS FOR MODERN LIFE

Recently, a world-renowned architect who lives in a Rossiter-designed house in Washington, Connecticut, described the virtues of his country houses. The siting is magnificent, he pointed out, the rooms are filled with light, and the passage from one room to another is graceful and expansive. Some of this grace is the result of Rossiter's abilities, and some is a result of the way houses were configured at the turn of the twentieth century. Interior spaces were organized to enhance family life by balancing separate zones—for private family activities, public hospitality, and live-in servants' quarters. In addition, new technologies for lighting, heating, cooking, and personal hygiene were transforming middle-class housing. Like the best of his peers, Rossiter was juggling evolving social expectations with the new technologies for healthy living.

Siting a house was the first design challenge. Urban lots and densely clustered developments within commuting distance of the city left the architect little discretion about the placement of the house on the lot. These housing developments depended on the installation of newly engineered public sewers, drainage systems, and water supplies to accommodate the housing density and resulted in the arbitrary placement of buildings on small lots. In more suburban and rural settings, however, the architect needed to consider the house placement carefully.

Rossiter sited his houses in a manner consistent with the best thinking of the day.[1] It wasn't just about the views. Mindful of the effect of weather on the comfort in a house before the days of sealed insulation, reliable heating, and air conditioning, he placed his houses on high, dry land, sloping where possible to the southeast or southwest. Sheltering trees or high ground to the north or west helped protect a house from cold winds and damp. Drainage, through a perimeter trench filled with gravel or architectural tile around the base of the foundation, helped secure the foundation and reduce moisture in the house. Bracing the frame against the wind at each floor and adding air spaces between the frame and the masonry to reduce moisture in the house were techniques of the new technology of home construction for improved comfort.

OPPOSITE AND ABOVE Ehrick Rossiter's garden at The Rocks, his summer home in Washington, Connecticut. Joseph West photo. Collection of The Gunn Memorial Library and Museum, Washington, Connecticut.

The sunken garden was the site of dramatic tableau, staged by the Rossiters for the entertainment of Washington guests. The various stone structures housed firewood and gardening tools, while adding a romantic accent to the garden vistas.

The public approach to the house was carefully considered. Visitors arriving by horse-drawn carriage needed an appropriately scaled entrance, perhaps with a porte-cochère to provide weather protection as visitors got in and out of the carriages. The public entrance needed to be prominently located and embellished, while the service entrance to the kitchen needed to be discreetly located, out of sight but convenient. Unlike the garages of today, located for convenient access to the house, the carriage house and stable needed to be sited at a suitable distance, preferably downwind, from the main house.

Landscaping and gardens helped mediate the transition from public to private spaces between the house and the street. At the front of the house, landscaping separated the house from the public thoroughfare and provided shade, privacy, and a screen from the dust kicked up by traffic on the street. Gardens planted along the house foundations could provide shade and cooling for the porches and interiors in the summer months. Gardens at the back of the house could include screening between the areas where the family and their guests gathered, particularly in warm months, and the working areas near the kitchen and laundry. The best gardens offered the homeowner a "cheerful place to spend his afternoons in seclusion."[2]

In the northeast, architects recommended that gardens be planted with hollyhocks, for color and height along the house foundations. Mindful of the advantage of colorful blooms in several seasons, they recommended that iris be planted for spring blooms and asters for the fall. Shrubs, including azaleas and rhododendrons, were popular— azaleas for their great varieties of color and rhododendrons for their evergreen foliage. Rose of Sharon was also planted for its size and color.

For those who could indulge in more elaborate domestic landscaping, vistas were encouraged. Vistas alone were not enough, however; they should be broken up with "objects of interest and terminated by some more or less important feature," such as a sundial, sculpture, or reflecting pool. Gardens had their own architectural requirements: boundaries should be strengthened with pergolas, walls, and changes in level, as created by terraces or a sunken garden. Pergolas were particularly popular "when overgrown with vines, shaded by trees, pierced through with spots of sunlight and casting shadows of irregular

and delightful form." However, a pergola had to be carefully placed; it "cannot simply happen anywhere, like a postage-stamp set in the middle of an envelope, but must bear some definite relation to the whole layout of the grounds." And there must be some place to sit. Vantage points in the house or on its porches were planned so that the homeowner and guests could look over the garden to admire its form and color.[3]

Many of the Rossiter houses in northwest Connecticut included such gardens. Rossiter's own home at Washington included a number of fashionable garden features, including a sunken garden and a pergola, Japanese-inspired stone gates, and large ornamental vases, reflecting Rossiter's interest in Japanese and Chinese art.[4] Among the flowers in Rossiter's garden were hydrangeas, scarlet geraniums, and scarlet gladioli.[5] Many of Rossiter's clients in northwest Connecticut were also avid gardeners; the elaborate gardens at the homes of Louis Vaillant, William Van Sinderen, and Seymour Cunningham are recorded in photographs at the Archives of American Gardens at the Smithsonian.

Ehrick Rossiter's gardens at The Rocks, in Washington, Connecticut. Joseph West photos, Collection of the Gunn Memorial Library and Museum, Washington, Connecticut.

The headmaster's house at The Hotchkiss School also looked over a formal garden at the back of the master's study, and there were extensive gardens at the Carl Stoeckel house in Norfolk and Barton Hepburn's house in Ridgefield, documented by early twentieth century photographs. There probably were more gardens, whose records are now lost, but clearly the value of a garden was well understood by Rossiter and his country clients.

Dr. S.G. Perry's gardens at The Gables, in Washington, Connecticut. Joseph West photos, Collection of the Gunn Memorial Library and Museum, Washington, Connecticut.

Inside the house, Rossiter's room arrangements reflected how proper social life was to be conducted. These floor plans changed with evolving standards about etiquette and the interaction among visitors, family members, and servants.

Contemporary floor plans have survived for a handful of projects from the 1880s and for several houses built in the early twentieth century, documenting the size, function, and arrangement of the rooms as originally conceived by the architect and his clients. Over 40 years, the designs range from early competition designs for small houses to the mid-sized homes and country estates of the late nineteenth century and the large city mansions of the early twentieth century.

The floor plans of the earlier homes reflect the prevailing interest in "convenient arrangement," much discussed in architectural competitions and magazines in the 1880s.[6] These principles of house planning were also published in 1887 by Charles Frances Osborne, who taught at Cornell in 1888 and would have been familiar to Rossiter and Wright. Among these principles were the clustering and separation of public and private spaces (that is, visitor versus family spaces), and the clustering and separation of family spaces from servant spaces. Spaces for family activities were expected to offer style, comfort, and privacy. Spaces for visitors and for servants needed to be designed to protect these family spaces from intrusion while presenting the family in the best light.

One in four households in New York City had live-in servants after the Civil War, including most of Rossiter's clients. Servants were confined to the areas where the household work was done—the basement, the kitchen, and the back stairs—and to their sleeping areas, initially in the attic or basement.

Although some middle-class families developed friendly relationships with their live-in servants, tensions over the social disparity were inevitable. Contemporary magazines chronicled the anxieties of the mistress trying to find and retain qualified help while her husband worried about theft. Meanwhile, the servants struggled with long hours, physically demanding work, curtailed social lives, and isolation from their own families. They were housed in the least desirable parts of the house, sharing small spaces and limited comforts.

Stylish houses after the Civil War were labor intensive for housekeepers. Window screens were a luxury in the 1870s, so dirt and insects floated in the open windows, regularly soiling the fashionable upholstered furniture and rugs. Until water was piped into the houses after the Civil War in urban neighborhoods and later in the suburbs and rural retreats, all household water was pumped by hand from wells and cisterns and carried by hand into the house. The demands for water increased after the war when the popular water cure made regular bathing more common.

In addition to separating rooms into zones for family members, visitors, or servants, separate circulation patterns also were desirable, keeping family members, visitors, and servants from passing one another in the hallways. At the same time, straightforward access to the rooms was expected. In the best designs, each principal room would be entered from a main hallway rather than requiring one to go through a room to enter another. In the 1880s, the main entrance hall was expanded to be large enough to impress visitors and to serve as a second parlor if needed. Room adjacencies, placing the kitchen near the dining room or the library near the dining room to serve as a smoking room after dinner, were carefully considered. The kitchen needed to be separated from adjacent rooms, including the dining room, by the double doors of a pantry, in order to contain the noise and smells of the kitchen. The kitchen, of course, would be placed within the zone designated for servants and their work. To the extent possible, preferred designs placed the principal family and visitor rooms on the first floor on the southern exposure, while the kitchen and related service rooms were on the northern side of the house.

Rossiter & Wright's smallest published house design, an 1883 cottage costing $500 to $800, had only two rooms: a living room and a bedroom and two closets on the first floor; and one room on the half floor above for additional sleeping or storage space. This floorplan was simply utilitarian.

Rossiter & Wright's designs for larger houses, ranging in price from $1,000 to $4,000, were able to accommodate the principles of "convenient arrangement" more easily, but a house with a design that met these standards was not really available for less than $1,800. For $1,000 to $1,500, the homeowner could build an 860 square foot

ROSSITER & WRIGHT, $500 house, 1883.
American Cottages. New York: William
T. Comstock, 1883. Reprinted in William T.
Comstock, *Country Houses and Seaside Cottages
of the Victorian Era,* Mineola, N.Y.: Dover
Publications, Inc., 1989.

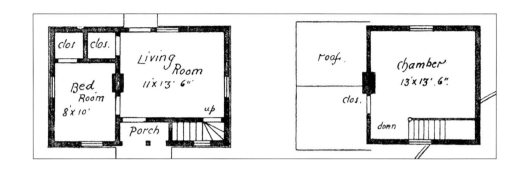

house with three rooms on the first floor—a living room opening onto the stairway, a kitchen with a storeroom, and a bedroom, unfortunately entered from the living room rather than a hallway. Upstairs, the stairway landing opened onto two bedrooms, each with a storage closet. For $1,800 to $2,000, Rossiter & Wright proposed a house of 895 square feet that had a larger entrance hallway, with a doorway to the living room on one side and one to the kitchen on the other, and an impressive front stairway. Upstairs, three bedrooms and a small auxiliary room each opened off the corridor. For $2,500, a 1,060 square foot cottage could be built, with a proper reception hall, dining room (divided from the hall by a curtained archway), kitchen (properly separated from the dining room by a pantry) and den, all on the first floor. Upstairs three bedrooms, each with a closet, and a bathroom were entered through separate doors in the hall. A back stairway descended from the kitchen to the cellar. For $3,500, Rossiter & Wright designed a 1,430 square foot cottage with a full complement of first-floor rooms—entrance hall, reception room, dining room, and kitchen; three bedrooms and a bath were provided on the second floor. Two rooms in the attic, presumably for servants, were reached by a back stairway that rose from the kitchen. At an estimated cost of $4,000, the largest and most expensive cottage, 2,000 square feet, had the most complete assemblage of rooms—with an entrance hall, library, parlor, dining room, and kitchen on the first floor and three bedrooms and a bathroom on the second floor. A service stairway, located behind the main stairway, rose from the pantry to the full-height attic, which presumably housed the servants. Such a house would sit on a lot large enough for a carriage to pull up to a porte-cochère at the side of the house, so that the main doorway and the entrance hall were at the center of the side of the house, leaving the two most formal rooms, the library and parlor, facing the street. This eight-room house form was typical of the Rossiter & Wright houses

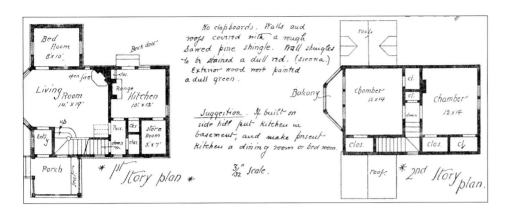

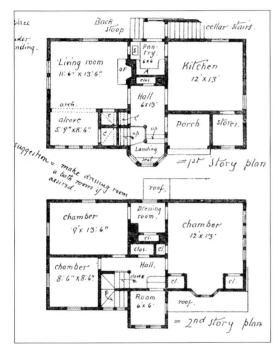

ABOVE ROSSITER & WRIGHT, $1,000 house, 1883. *American Cottages.* New York: William T. Comstock, 1883. Reprinted in William T. Comstock, *Country Houses and Seaside Cottages of the Victorian Era,* Mineola, N.Y.: Dover Publications, Inc., 1989.

CENTER ROSSITER & WRIGHT, $1,800 house, 1883. *American Cottages.* New York: William T. Comstock, 1883. Reprinted in William T. Comstock, *Country Houses and Seaside Cottages of the Victorian Era,* Mineola, N.Y.: Dover Publications, Inc., 1989.

BELOW ROSSITER & WRIGHT, $2,500 house, 1883. *American Cottages.* New York: William T. Comstock, 1883. Reprinted in William T. Comstock, *Country Houses and Seaside Cottages of the Victorian Era,* Mineola, N.Y.: Dover Publications, Inc., 1989.

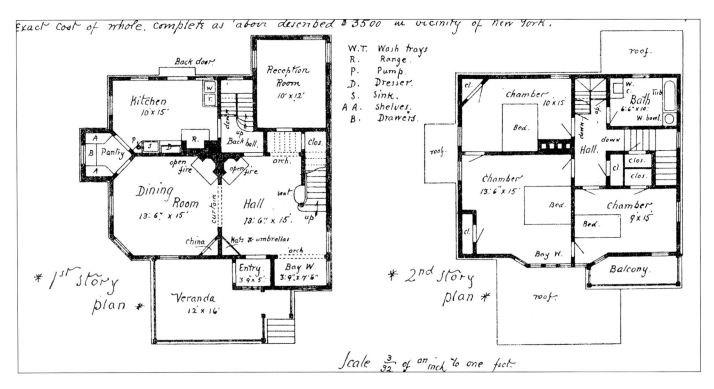

Exact cost of whole, complete as above described $3500 in vicinity of New York.

* 1ˢᵗ story plan *

* 2ⁿᵈ story plan *

W.T.   Wash trays.
R.   Range.
P.   Pump.
D.   Dresser.
S.   Sink.
A A.   Shelves.
B.   Drawers.

Scale 3/32 of an inch to one foot.

ABOVE ROSSITER & WRIGHT, $3,500 house, 1883. *American Cottages.* New York: William T. Comstock, 1883. Reprinted in William T. Comstock, *Country Houses and Seaside Cottages of the Victorian Era,* Mineola, N.Y.: Dover Publications, Inc., 1989.

RIGHT ROSSITER & WRIGHT, $4,000 house, 1883. *American Cottages.* New York: William T. Comstock, 1883. Reprinted in William T. Comstock, *Country Houses and Seaside Cottages of the Victorian Era,* Mineola, N.Y.: Dover Publications, Inc., 1989.

The house plans published by Rossiter & Wright in 1883 illustrated that smaller houses could be stylish, but only houses larger than about 1,000 square feet—with a budget of $2,500 or more—could accommodate rudimentary systems for heat and plumbing and layouts for fashionable room arrangements commensurate with those published in contemporary periodicals.

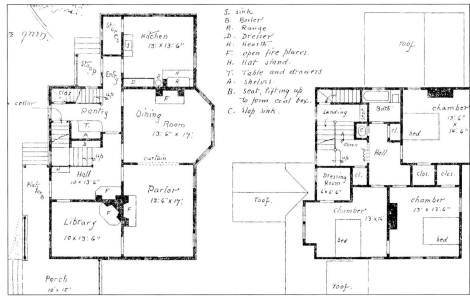

S. sink.
B. Boiler.
R. Range.
D. Dresser.
H. Hearth.
F. open fire places.
H. Hat stand.
T. Table and drawers.
A. Shelves.
B. Seat, lifting up to form coal box.
C. Slop sink.

Low priced Cottages at Fairmount N.J.

Rossiter and Wright Architects

2nd Story

1st Story

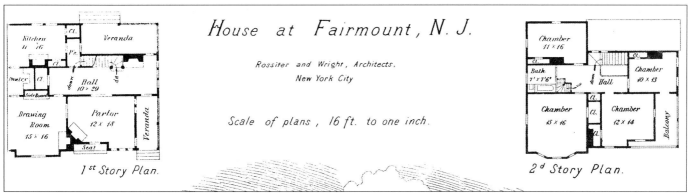

House at Fairmount, N.J.

Rossiter and Wright, Architects.
New York City

Scale of plans, 16 ft. to one inch.

1st Story Plan.

2d Story Plan.

built in the suburbs of northern New Jersey and western Long Island, priced at around $6,000, with the cost of the land included.

Rossiter & Wright's designs for clients were similar to the drawings submitted for architectural competitions. A 1,200 square foot cottage in Fairmount, New Jersey, published in 1881, had two main rooms on the first floor, a living room and a kitchen, along with a 6 by 8 foot bedroom and a pantry to the side of the kitchen, and two bedrooms on the second floor. It was compact, but it violated the principals of "convenient arrangement" since several rooms were accessible only by passing through other rooms. A larger house at Fairmount, also from 1881, with about 1,500 square feet, had a central entrance hall running the width of the house with a parlor and drawing room across the front of the house and a kitchen at the back of the house. With a pantry between the kitchen and the drawing room and a sideboard built into

ABOVE ROSSITER & WRIGHT, Cottage at Fairmont, New Jersey, 1881. *American Architect and Building News, 8/6/1881.*

BELOW ROSSITER & WRIGHT, House at Fairmount, New Jersey, 1881. William T. Comstock. *Modern Architectural Designs and Details,* New York, 1881. Reprinted as William T. Comstock, *Victorian Domestic Architectural Plans and Details,* Mineola, NY: Dover Publications, 1987.

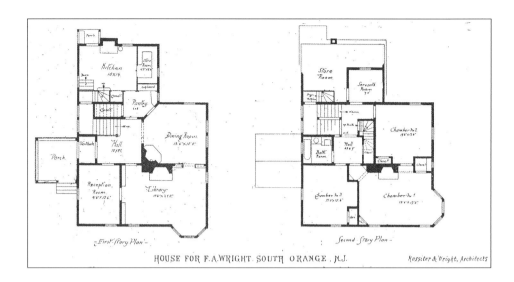

an alcove in the drawing room, the drawing room was probably used as a dining room. On the second floor, there were four bedrooms and a bathroom and a small stairway to the third-floor attic.

Frank Wright's own house in South Orange, designed in 1884, had only about 1,350 square feet on the first two floors, but it included all the desirable modern features of proper adjacencies and circulation. The main entrance to the house was located on the side of the house, and the entrance hall was positioned midway along that side. The first floor contained a large entrance hall with a double-run stairway and a reception room, library, and dining room each opening from the hall. A pantry separated the dining room and kitchen. A separate back stairway joined the cellar, the kitchen, and a servant's room on the second floor. There were three family bedrooms on the second floor, plus a bathroom, and another stairway led from the family hallway to the third floor. Closets and storage rooms were plentiful.

Fairview, a 2,000 square foot house in Red Bank, New Jersey, whose drawings were published in 1883, was a weekend house, unlike the houses Rossiter & Wright designed for clients in the suburbs of Newark. Overlooking the Navasink River, the house was designed with a floor plan departing from the typical work of the firm in the 1880s, anticipating the symmetric floor plans of the Colonial Revival. Still, the principals of convenient arrangement were apparent. The living room and dining room flanked the central hall, with the kitchen in a side wing next to the dining room; a pantry provided the passage between the two rooms.

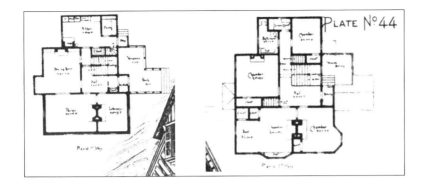

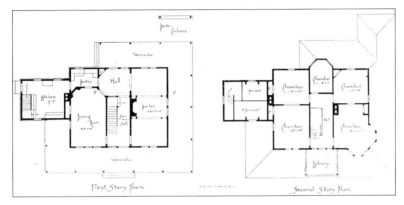

First Story plan.   Second Story plan.

ROSSITER & WRIGHT, First and second floor plans for the Telfair house, Flatbush, Brooklyn, New York, 1885. *The Builder and Wood-Worker,* 6/1884.

In the 1880s, houses built by Rossiter & Wright's clients in the suburbs of New York and New Jersey were usually organized asymmetrically, with the main entrance at the center of one side of the house. These houses were between 1,350 and 2,000 square feet and offered many of the features that were important to modern living, with plumbing in the kitchen and the single bathroom, a discrete separation between the dining-entertaining areas and the kitchen-working areas, and separate spaces for servants and family members.

ROSSITER & WRIGHT, Fairview, house at Red Bank, New Jersey, 1883. *Building,* October, 1883.

Fairview, a weekend house for a New York lawyer in Monmouth County had a floorplan in the more advanced and symmetric Colonial Revival style, but was organized around the same principals of utility and propriety.

Upstairs, five family bedrooms opened onto the central hall, two on either side and one in a bay window at the front of the hallway; two servants' rooms were housed separately above the kitchen with a service stairway at the end of the kitchen wing.

The partners designed larger homes for the summer estates built by New Yorkers in northwest Connecticut. These summer estates were more open to the natural vistas than were the suburban homes in New Jersey and Long Island, and they were also more informal than the much larger "cottages" of the very wealthy built in Newport or Lenox at the same time.

Rossiter's 1883 plan for his own summer home in Washington, The Rocks, was larger than those for the previous houses in New Jersey, with 2,600 square feet on the first two floors. The first floor included a large entrance hall with an expansive stairway, opening onto an octagonal parlor, a dining room, and a den, each oriented to the southwest, as well as a kitchen and pantry on the north side of the house beyond the dining room. On the second floor, there were to be four bedrooms, a bathroom, and another small room. A service stairway was tucked behind the family stairway, running from the cellar to the kitchen and up to the second floor. A third stairway provided access from the family hallway to the third floor. No plans were published for the third floor, but the elevation sketch shows two large rooms with window-filled walls and a balcony overlooking the valley to the west.

The home Rossiter designed in 1885 for Richard Barnes in Washington was nearly as large as The Rocks, with about 1,300 square feet on each floor. The carriage drive approached the house from the northeast corner, delivering guests to an entrance hall with a fireplace and a main stairway fitted into a cone-topped circular tower. Curtained archways separated the entrance hall from the dining room and the parlor, which faced southwest over the valley. The kitchen, with a service stairway to the cellar and the second floor, had a separate entrance at the back porch on the southeast corner of the house. A pantry was in place between the dining room and the kitchen. Drawings for additional floors were not published, but period photos show a high-ceilinged third floor with large round-headed windows that probably housed expansive family rooms for sleeping or socializing and that took advantage of the best hilltop views and breezes.

Rock Gate, designed in 1885 for the Barbour family in Washington, was also larger than the commuter homes in New Jersey's suburbs, with roughly 1,250 square feet per floor as originally built. An arched entrance greeted approaching carriages at the northwest corner of the house, and it opened onto a reception hall with a fireplace in an inglenook and an impressive two-landing stairway. The three principal rooms, each with a fireplace—the parlor, dining room, and den—opened from the entrance hall and faced the valley views to the south and southwest. A ten-foot wide piazza circled these rooms on the outside overlooking the view, providing an inviting open-air living room. A large kitchen, pantry, and laundry were positioned to the east end of the entrance hallway, along with a service stairway tucked between the kitchen and the main family stairway. A service entrance and porch were tucked into the east end of the kitchen. Drawings for the second and third floor were not published, but the drawing of the original elevation and period photographs indicate that the second-floor bedrooms, provided with bands of windows, a circular bay, a cone-topped oriel, and an open

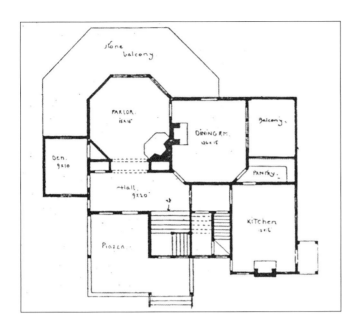

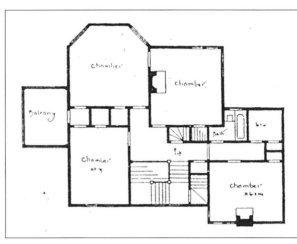

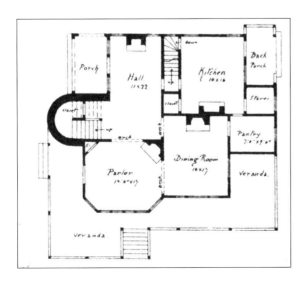

TOP ROSSITER & WRIGHT, First and second floorplans for Rossiter's house, The Rocks, Washington, Connecticut, as published, 1883. *American Architect and Building News*, 6/9/1883.

CENTER ROSSITER & WRIGHT, First floorplan for Rock Gate, the home of Lucius A. Barbour, Washington, Connecticut, 1885. *American Architect and Building News*. 11/21/85.

BELOW ROSSITER & WRIGHT, First floorplan for Westlawn, the home for Richard Barnes, Washington, Connecticut, 1885. *American Architect and Building News*. 6/27/85.

The summer estates in northwest Connecticut in the 1880s were larger, between 3,500 and 4,000 square feet on three floors, and more costly (up to three times more) than the suburban houses in New Jersey and New York. The rooms were also larger, with a more expansive flow to the interiors, although the same rules about room and use adjacencies were observed. Porches stretching across the width of these houses opened onto the celebrated views of nature.

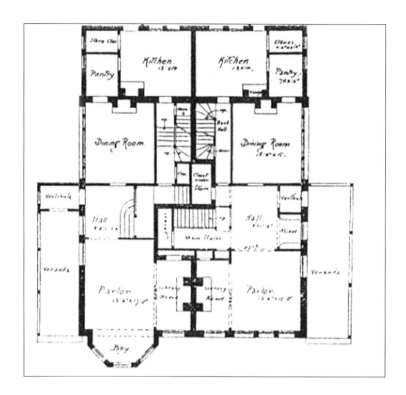

balcony, were probably intended for family members. The third floor, with small windows and steep gables, was probably intended for servants.

Urban houses designed by Rossiter & Wright in the 1880s showed a surprising consistency with the floor plans designed for the firm's suburban and country houses. The Van Kirk semi-detached houses designed in 1885 for a client in Pittsburgh were two houses, side by side, intended to look like one house from the street. Each house was approximately 3,000 square feet, with about 1,000 square feet on each of three floors. Each house was entered from a veranda on opposite sides of the combined house, leading to a hall positioned near the center of each of the houses. The floor plans of the two houses roughly mirror each other, having parlors at the front facing the street, with fireplaces in library alcoves set behind curtained archways in the parlors. Behind the entrance halls, there were dining rooms with fireplaces and pantries that led to kitchens in the back of the houses. Both houses had main stairways for the family and service stairways for the household staff. One of the houses had an alcove in the entrance hallway; the other had a bay window in the front of the parlor. These variations helped the two houses to appear as one from the street, rather than two identical row houses. Floor plans for the second and third floors were not published,

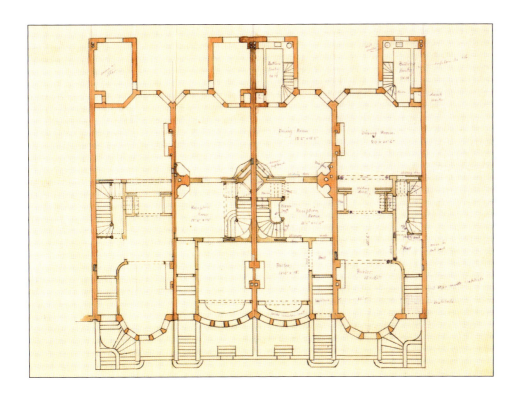

ROSSITER & WRIGHT, First floorplan for the Frankenheim row houses, 137-141 W. 81st Street, New York, New York, 1886. Levi Collection, Drawings and Archives, Avery Architectural and Fine Arts Library, Columbia University, New York.

Urban row houses in the Rossiter & Wright designs of the 1880s were able to accommodate the principals of "convenient arrangement" by dedicating the first floor to an entrance hall at the midpoint of the house, away from the street, with the Parlor in front and the Dining Room in the back. Service areas, including the pantry and kitchen and the service stairway, were tucked away behind the dining room.

but spacious gables and towers on the third floor suggested that family members were expected to occupy some of these rooms, with the servants probably relegated to the basement.

The four row houses designed in 1886 for West 81st St. in New York City were similarly laid out, with the entrance hall at the center of the narrow house plans, accessed from a side hallway entered from a doorway to the street. Each house contained approximately 1,200 square feet per floor, or about 6,000 square feet on the five floors. The four row houses were similar but not identical in their layouts, presumably because the architects accommodated the individual clients, named on the drawings, who were going to occupy these houses. The houses at each end of the row, 21 feet wide on the east end and 19 feet wide on the west end, had a "reception room" at the midpoint of the building with stairways on the end walls and access to the front parlor from the reception room through wide arched openings. Skylights in the stairwell brought light into the interiors. Sliding doors divided the reception area from the dining room at the back of the houses. The two middle houses, each 19 feet wide, had central "reception rooms" with rounded stairways on the shared wall and corner fireplaces on the opposite wall. Sliding doors separated these reception areas from the parlors at the front and the dining rooms at the back. Behind the dining room in each of the four houses was a butler's pantry, provided with a sink and a station for reheating food, and also containing a dumb waiter and the service stairs to the basement kitchen. The basements housed another dining room, probably intended for the use of the servants, as well as pantries, washtubs, and heaters. On the first two upper floors, each house had two rooms per floor; there were three rooms on the top floor, tucked into the roof. Bathrooms with a tub, sink, and water closet were located on the second and third floors over the butler's pantry, but to enter the bathroom one had to pass through a chamber, not a hallway. The architects and their clients opted for larger rooms and fewer hallways, in spite of the principles of convenient arrangement and concerns about privacy. The service stairway joined only the first floor and the basement, suggesting that servants' sleeping rooms may have been located in the basement. As with the elimination of the hallways, the elimination of the back stairway may have been intended to secure as much living space for the family as possible on each floor.[7]

By 1900, architectural competitions for domestic design featured more closets, fitted with shelves and hooks, and built-in storage cupboards. Plate glass for larger windows was more readily available in the United States,[8] and winners of the architectural competitions featured more windows and windows that were strategically placed on two walls in each room to provide cross ventilation. Separate stairwells for family and servants were more often placed in the same "spatial cavity," though still not open to the other. Kitchens were more fully equipped with plumbing and appliances, bathrooms multiplied, and rooms with plumbing were likely to be grouped vertically for greater efficiency.[9]

Rossiter & Wright's plans for two suburban houses in Mountain Station, New Jersey, published in 1910, show that these concepts were well understood by the partners and probably expected by their clients. These houses were larger than their suburban predecessors, approximately 2,500 square feet total on two floors, and were conceived as rectangular boxes with one room in each corner of the house, each accessed by the central hall. One corner room in each house was still named the Reception Hall, a term favored in the Queen Anne Revival drawings, and the kitchens were still provided with separate entrances, stairways, and pantries to keep them divided from the main household activities

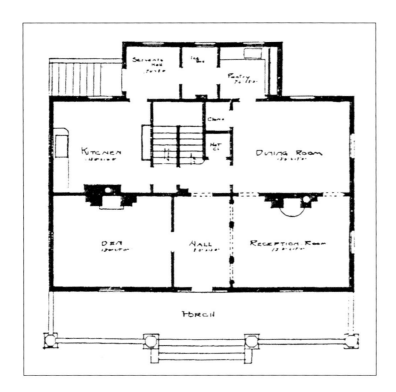

ROSSITER & WRIGHT, Floorplans for fireproof houses, Mountain Station, New Jersey, 1910. *Architects' and Builders' Magazine, 2/10/10.*

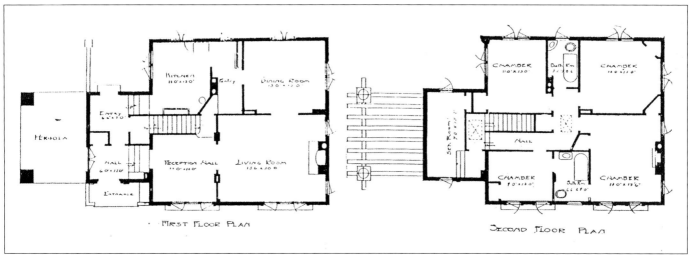

and near to, but not next to, the dining room. Cross ventilation was easily accomplished, since each room occupied a corner of the house and windows on two sides of each room added light as well as fresh air. Service rooms were assigned to a separate wing at the back of the house. Plumbing for bathrooms and kitchens was clustered to a greater extent than had been done 20 years earlier. In one design, skylights illuminated an interior hall and stairwell that otherwise would have been without natural light.

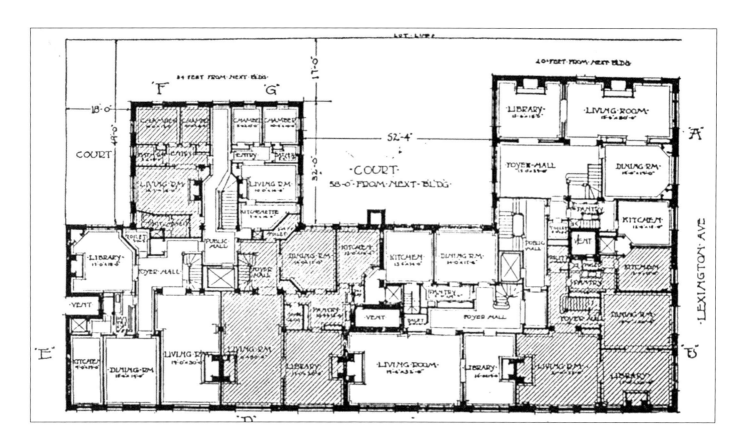

ROSSITER & WRIGHT, Cooperative floorplans, southeast corner of Lexington and 67th St., New York City, New York, 1907. *Architects' and Builders' Magazine, 3/09.*

The interiors in the Colonial Revival style were organized as rectangular blocks, with the principal rooms prominently positioned in each corner of the residence, while maintaining the separation of family spaces and service spaces.

Urban interiors after the turn of the twentieth century also incorporated the more rational house plan, with the rooms organized in a rectangular cluster and kitchens and bathrooms grouped together to share plumbing. Nevertheless, the separate zones for family, visitor, and servant activities still controlled the floor plan. The co-op apartments Rossiter & Wright designed in 1907 on East 67th St. were large. The biggest, at 3,200 square feet, included a foyer/hall (a new name for the reception hall), living room, dining room, library, kitchen, pantry, and a small room with a toilet and sink for visitors on the first floor and six rooms (four family bedrooms and two smaller staff bedrooms) with three bathrooms on the floor above. Service stairs were included, along with the prominent stairway for the family.

The footprint of the houses changed after the turn of the century. The houses of the last decades of the nineteenth century rose from irregular footprints, as the floor plans took shape based on an accretion of rooms inspired by a medieval pattern of organic development, with a central hall opening onto several rooms projecting into different wings and further varied with projecting bays. After the turn of the twentieth century, domestic floor plans were increasingly regular, with rectangular rooms lined up along straight hallways. Rossiter & Wright reflected these changes in their floor plans for the 1907 co-ops and the 1910 fireproof houses.

For the affluent, both their homes and the rooms within got larger in the early twentieth century. Eliminating the large reception hall made it possible to make the living room larger. Tastemakers proposed that a $15,000 house for a family of six, the market for many of the Rossiter & Wright houses after the turn of the century, should have a dining room of 15 by 17 feet and a living room half again as large, or 15 by 25.[10] These two rooms together were larger than the small cottages designed by Rossiter & Wright in 1881. In addition to the rooms' larger size, proper proportions for the rooms were also suggested: the living room should be longer than its width, providing several places for small groups to gather, to play cards and converse, and the room should feature a fireplace, bookcases, and a piano. The dining room, on the other hand, should be square, and should include a sideboard and a serving table.

The reception hall was discouraged in the new thinking because it was too drafty and too busy as a passageway to truly serve as a parlor; the new, smaller entrance hall, however, should still impress visitors. This hall should suggest the location of public spaces within the house but should not expose all of the rooms to visitors. Doors should be placed opposite each other, giving balance to the hallways, and open doorways should give way to interesting features such as additional doorways, windows, or stairs; in no instance should they open to blank walls.

Upstairs, the "improved methods of construction today" rendered attic floors more comfortable in the heat of the summer, so they were more often reserved for family members, especially if there were attractive views and "bright airy rooms" to enjoy. Servants were then relegated to "extensions above the kitchen," often in a wing of the house, or to rooms over the garage.

Rooms were bright and airy because of the larger windows available for domestic use. Rossiter took advantage of the larger windows and added "angle" windows (glass-sided bay windows) "to catch all the sun," as he wrote to the headmaster at The Hotchkiss School. In a number of houses, including the Poor house on Long Island, the headmaster's house at The Hotchkiss School, and the Stedman-Johnson house in Hartford, he put high windows, often leaded panels, into interior walls so that daylight from the exterior rooms would enter interior spaces from as many directions as possible. He added glass doors between the entrance hall and the reception room in the headmaster's house at The Hotchkiss School to increase the light in both, and in the 1912 additions to the infirmary he designed large windows to bring "sunny exposures in all rooms." Sliding doors in the Stedman-Johnson dining room were glass-paneled so as to admit light into the main hall.

In step with the new thinking about house design after the turn of the century, the homes and rooms in Rossiter's domestic designs grew larger. The rooms were organized on more direct sight lines, consistent with the concern that every doorway should open onto an "interesting feature." Entrance halls got smaller in proportion to the rest of the house. The entrance hall at the expanded headmaster's house at The Hotchkiss School was approximately 14 by 20 feet, mostly filled with the main stairway; but the master's study was approximately 25 by 45 feet and was lowered from the first-floor level to make the room more impressive. Rossiter wrote the headmaster that he lowered the floor "in order to gain more height and better proportions than if we ran the floor on a level with the 1st story of the cottage. This dropping the floor as indicated will lend a good deal of attractiveness to the room itself." The entrance hall at Stedman-Johnson in Hartford was large, but the adjacent dining room and music room were enormous. At the Cheney house in New Haven, the entrance hall (18 by 20, including the stairway) was the smallest public space in the house. The living room (23 by 36 feet) and dining room (19 by 26 feet) were properly proportioned and properly sized in relation to each other, following the contemporary design standards. The music room (18 by 30 feet) completed the public rooms on the first floor. Still, the separation of spaces between visitors,

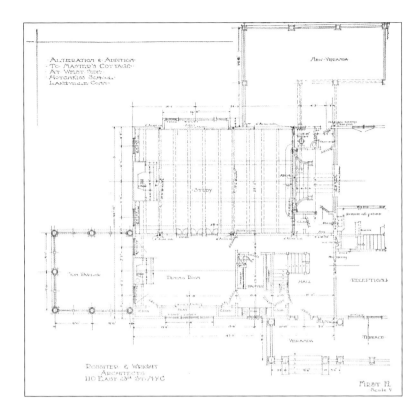

ABOVE ROSSITER & WRIGHT, floorplan for the Headmaster's House, The Hotchkiss School, Lakeville, Connecticut. **1910.** Archives of The Hotchkiss School.

BELOW ROSSITER & MULLER, floorplan for the Cheney House, New Haven, Connecticut. **1918.** *The American Architect, 5/25/21.*

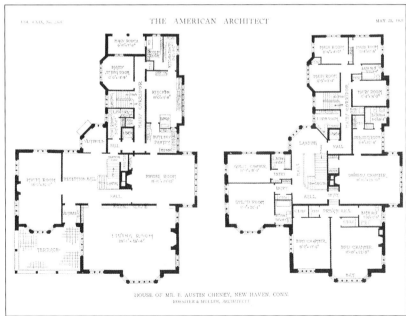

family, and servants was important. In a separate wing, the maids' corridor led to the kitchen, the butler's pantry, kitchen pantry, and cold room as well as the maids' sitting room, maids' porch, and the back stairway.

ROSSITER & WRIGHT, Hollow tile and stucco finished houses, Mountain Station, New Jersey, c. 1910.
Architects' and Builders' Magazine, 2/10/10.

The Fireproof House

In addition to spatial considerations, the architects were experimenting with modern materials to improve construction methods and home safety.

By the mid-1890s the partners began specifying a coat of "roughcast," a masonry slurry applied over a wood lath or wire mesh, for both aesthetic advantage and to protect the house from fire and moisture. (The wire mesh support was later found to melt in fires, and was banned in construction by 1915.) Within two decades, they were using a coat of stucco over a system of hollow tiles, a system advanced by the new steel-frame construction in commercial buildings, thought to provide further fire protection and a host of other advantages.

Like the plaster previously used between the framework in half-timbering, roughcast was a mixture of lime and cement mixed with sand and small gravel, a textured look that was thought to be particularly appropriate for country houses. In addition to its decorative advantages, the treatment was thought to offer some improvement over wood cladding for fire protection and was cheaper than masonry. In 1895, Rossiter covered his Washington home, The Rocks, with roughcast when he extended the house by 9 feet on the east wing and 15 feet on the west wing. The Barbour house, Rock Gate, was expanded before the turn of the century and also covered with roughcast, as was the new Washington home for Senator Platt, Kirby Corner. Other Rossiter & Wright projects in New Milford and Norfolk, Connecticut, and on Long Island were also covered in roughcast at the same time.

In 1910 Rossiter & Wright's designs for innovative houses, using hollow tile covered with cement stucco, were featured in a story on fireproof homes published in *Architects' and Builders' Magazine*. These houses, which had been constructed by the developer of Mountain Station, a commuter train stop in South Orange, New Jersey, were roofed in asbestos shingles, furthering their supposed advance in fireproof construction. Another hollow-tile stucco house was designed by the firm, probably at the same time, in Oakland, New Jersey.[11] Rossiter also specified the hollow-tile stucco system for the Warner house in Southport, Connecticut, in 1911.

At the time, manufacturers of Portland cement energetically promoted its fire- and water-retardant advantages, and contemporary periodicals showcased stylish new architect-designed houses with stucco or roughcast applications. Manufacturers emphasized that a coating of stucco or roughcast protected a house from both water and fire. They described the decorative possibilities of a stucco coating: it could have a smooth finish, a spatterdash finish, or a pebbledash finish. It was less expensive and more durable than plaster, which would crack; it was a scientific advancement that would prevent dampness in the home; and it provided improved soundproofing and insulation. Applied to interior walls in kitchens and bathrooms, it withstood repeated scrubbing and improved hygiene. Rossiter was intrigued by the possibilities of the new materials and used stucco and concrete for a variety of decorative and utilitarian purposes, including concrete floors at The Hotchkiss School and in outdoor parks and stucco walls in kitchens and bathrooms after 1895.

LEFT ROSSITER & WRIGHT, Hollow tile and stucco finished houses, Mountain Station, New Jersey, c. 1910. *Architects' and Builders' Magazine*, 2/10/10.

RIGHT ROSSITER & WRIGHT, Hollow Tile House, Oakland, New Jersey, c. 1910. Frederick Squires, *The Hollow Tile House*, New York: William Comstock, 1913.

Following their work with large-scale projects in New York City in the first years of the 20th century, Rossiter & Wright applied some of the fireproof building techniques used in commercial projects to small-scale domestic buildings. These techniques included the use of rough cast, also called stucco, and construction systems using hollow tiles that were thought to offer a light-weight structural support as well as insulation and fire resistance.

Technology for Healthy Living

Rossiter's house designs also incorporated new technologies for healthy domestic living. The adoption of modern utilities and plumbing and heating systems in the Rossiter & Wright houses was surprisingly slow. Even houses with highly decorative wall treatments were not provided with indoor plumbing in the 1880s. Rudimentary modern conveniences were introduced only in houses larger than about 1,000 square feet that were expected to cost more than $2,500. Bay windows were more readily available than bathrooms in these Rossiter & Wright designs.

In 1881, the least expensive Rossiter & Wright house, with only two rooms on the first floor, a living room and a bedroom, had no provision for either a kitchen or a bathroom, and no indoor plumbing. A larger cottage, of about 860 square feet, was to be heated with a corner fireplace in the living room, and a cooking range was available within this budget for the kitchen. But there was still no indoor plumbing.

With a slightly larger house, at 895 square feet, and double the cost, the designers called for a more elaborate five- or six-room house with a bay window and an arched alcove in the living room. Still, at this size and budget, there was no indoor plumbing, although the exterior finish "in the colonial style" was quite elaborate. The architects noted that a small dressing room adjacent to the largest bedroom, at 12 by 13 feet, could be converted to a bathroom if desired—at an additional cost.

Not until a house was larger, over 1,060 square feet, and expected to cost $2,500 or more, did Rossiter & Wright include indoor plumbing in the design. This house had a sink in the kitchen and a bathroom on the second floor, along with two fireplaces for heating.

At the next price level, $3,500, Rossiter & Wright offered a 1,430 square foot house with a cistern under the kitchen to collect water for household use and drainage to collect household waste into two cesspools. The kitchen had a sink, double wash trays for laundry, and a range for cooking. Upstairs, the bathroom included a bathtub, water closet, and wash bowl. The house was equipped with a portable hot-air furnace in addition to fireplaces in the front hall and the dining room.

The design for their largest and most expensive house in 1881, with terracotta tiles cresting the slate roof and gables covered in stucco, incorporated more modern conveniences, although the plumbing specified a second-floor slop sink, implying that residents would use wash bowls and chamber pots in their bedrooms rather than a sink and a toilet in the bathroom. At just over 2,000 square feet, the $4,000 suburban cottage included a sink, a coal-fired boiler, and a cooking range in the kitchen, while the second-floor bathroom housed a bathtub and water closet. Four fireplaces were provided to heat the primary rooms on the first floor, including the entrance hall, the library, parlor, and dining room.

Plans for actual clients confirm that Rossiter & Wright's less expensive houses did not have indoor plumbing or heating. A "low priced cottage at Fairmount, New Jersey" with approximately 1,200 square feet on two floors was designed without plumbing. A larger 1,500 square foot house in Fairmount had a bathroom on the second floor, with a tub and a water closet to be shared by four bedrooms. Frank Wright's own 1884 house in South Orange had a bathroom with a tub, a water closet, and a sink, to be shared by three family bedrooms, in spite of the relatively small size of the 1,350 square foot house.

Fairview, designed in 1883 for the McClure family on the Navasink River in Red Bank, New Jersey, was large, at nearly 2,000 square feet, and elegant. However, there was no indication of indoor plumbing or heating in the handsomely finished house, which was designed for weekend use by a prominent New York lawyer. Plumbing seems to have been an issue for the New Yorker, who was a vociferous opponent of a plan to pipe sewage from the town of Red Bank into the river 15 years later.

Floor plans were also published for three large summer houses in Washington, each with around 2,600 square feet on the two primary floors, designed in the mid-1880s. Only the preliminary drawing for Rossiter's house, The Rocks, shows a second floor, where a bathroom was planned, containing a bathtub and water closet. It is likely that Westlawn for the Barnes family and Rock Gate for the Barbour family had similar facilities on their second floors.

The design competitions sponsored by architectural periodicals in the 1880s suggest that the Rossiter & Wright designs were typical of the era, with smaller less expensive houses lacking indoor plumbing or heating. Larger houses, with seven or eight rooms, were beginning to incorporate second-floor bathrooms by the middle of the decade.

These larger homes also began to feature multiple fireplaces for warming individual rooms. These multiple fireplaces suggested more comfort and privacy for the family members who occupied separate rooms, and more work for the servants to tend to these fireplaces.

The turn of the twentieth century introduced a bewildering array of new and competing technologies for heating, lighting, and sanitation. The architect had to sift through the competing systems, persuade his clients of the merit and safety of his selection, and figure out how to gracefully incorporate the new technologies into the design. Coal-fired basement furnaces with giant octopus-like ductwork delivered hot air to room registers or heated water or steam to feed a web of piping for radiators; attic cisterns supported water pressure for the household's heating or plumbing needs; and competing methods for dealing with sewer gas and furnishing hygienic bathrooms required the architect's best skills in combining the practical and the aesthetic.

Heating a house had long been accomplished by fireplaces or stoves, aided by thoughtful siting. Heat generated by furnaces consumed less fuel than fireplaces or stoves and was more economical after the initial cost of purchase and installation. Furnaces for home heating, fueled by coal, oil, gas, or wood, were available by the mid-1880s, with extensive debates about which was the better fuel, which was the most efficient fuel, and how to deal with the necessary ventilation to ward off the danger of carbon monoxide poisoning. Room radiators bringing heat through steam or hot water were available after the turn of the century, also with several fuel options. But these systems required a reliable supply of water and steady water pressure, which was usually available only where the house was supplied by public water systems. And there were concerns about the safety of steam pressure, which if poorly installed might cause a radiator or boiler to explode. In addition, there was new competition from furnaces delivering hot air through ducts to large wall and floor registers by the second decade of the twentieth century. There was much to question with these new systems, and still plenty of questions about the older heating systems. Should the chimneys have a round, oval, or square pipe? How many stoves should a house have, since there were options for parlors, kitchens, and laundries? The "Torrid Parlor Heater," available for under $10, was one of thousands that could be purchased by mail order. Even with the many new home heating options, open fireplaces were still advised by architects like Rossiter, to provide ventilation that would counter the deleterious effects of the noxious fuels introduced to the house by the new heating systems themselves.

Kitchens became larger and supported more specialized activities. By the turn of the century, kitchen ranges offered a number of options, including baking ovens, broiling ovens, side broiling attachments, water-heating attachments, portable ovens, boilers, toasters, heaters for clothes irons, and more. Inventors and vendors promoted their refrigeration units, meant to keep food cool when filled with blocks of ice delivered periodically during the week, but troubles with these units included the risk of bacteria if the box was not well ventilated and regularly scrubbed, not to mention the risk of scalding the servant when the freezer was cleaned with steaming hot water.

Then there was the debate over home lighting devices. Traditionally in rural homes, tabletop lamps were lighted by burning various oils, while piped-in gas powered the lighting fixtures in city homes after the Civil War. By the 1880s, many city homes were lighted by gas, which provided more candle power than oil lamps at lower cost. Electricity was promoted as a better alternative for lighting in advertising that reminded homeowners of the shortcomings of gas or oil lamps. Unlike oil or gas lamps, electric lights did not give off the heat or the fumes that destroyed pictures, wallpapers, and other home decorations. Electricity did not require dangerous matches and was not affected by wind-driven drafts that blew through the house. On the other hand, many homeowners were justifiably worried about the dangers of electricity in their homes, and the current was often not yet available in suburban and rural areas.

Interior plumbing was a rapidly advancing technology at the turn of the twentieth century. By 1905, houses with a reliable indoor water supply were encouraged to have bathrooms and water closets (flushing toilets) even though there was some concern about the dangers of poisonous gas coming from sewer lines in the street as well as from poorly installed waste pipes in the house. With the discovery of the germ theory in the 1890s, there was a growing recognition that hygiene was important in fighting disease, and these concerns were heightened when the deadly "Spanish" flu epidemic broke out in the United States in 1918. The focus on hygiene prompted an increase in the number of bathrooms in American homes and the proliferation of new bathroom fixtures, new cleanable wall and floor surfaces, and new mechanisms for making the plumbing systems work more efficiently. Among the bathroom fixtures advertised in the Crane catalogue in 1905 were a variety of sinks, including a small laundry sink to be used for "personal items" (that is, underwear) near the upstairs bedrooms, sitz baths and foot baths, and dental sinks for the family bathroom so that the fastidious could avoid cleaning their teeth in the same sink where they washed their face and hands.

Writers and reformers encouraged home designers to adopt these advances. In 1907, Aymar Embury, a popular writer on domestic design, advocated lavatories (hand sinks) and water closets on the first floor, where visitors could go, also suggesting that these facilities be located at some "retired part of the house" to advance privacy. In addition, he advised, a toilet should be provided for servants in an area near the servants' daily household activities to keep them close to their household duties through the day.

By the early years of the twentieth century, Rossiter and his clients were up to date with these advances, since both the architect and his clients were city people and expected these amenities at their homes in the country as well as at their city homes. The long-planned expansion of the headmaster's house at The Hotchkiss School in 1910 included radiators and a telephone. There were seven bathrooms for the bedrooms on the second and third floors as well as a toilet for visitors on the first floor and one in the basement for the use of servants. Renovations to the campus infirmary in 1912 included fireproof stairs and gas stoves on each floor, and in 1914 the architects even replaced closets with metal wardrobes, which could be more easily moved for thorough fumigating to control contagion among the patients. The Hotchkiss School had its own electric generating plant and used electricity for much of its power needs, including the electric chandeliers installed in the dining room in 1906 (and for winching canoes into their racks in the boat house in 1915!). Colton, the residential cottage at the Ridge School in rural Washington, had electricity when it opened in 1905. The 1913 Warner house in Southport had a coal-fired furnace and a servants' toilet in the basement. The 1913 Stedman-Johnson house in Hartford had separate bathrooms for each bedroom suite, with blazingly white tiles and small (and, therefore, sanitary) grout lines as well as bright white appliances with virtually no cabinetry, to facilitate thorough cleaning. The 1918 Cheney house in New Haven was a paragon of hygiene, as befitted a university doctor, with what today we would consider a half bath on the first floor and separate bathrooms upstairs for the homeowners, their sons, each of their guests, and their maids. Cheney also installed other modern contraptions, including a telephone, an elevator, and a safe.

CHAPTER SEVEN: ROSSITER'S HOUSES TODAY

The designs of Rossiter & Wright, and those of Rossiter & Muller, are prized by the residents in the towns where the firms did their best work. As they did when new, their buildings continue to receive press even though the architects themselves have largely been forgotten by architectural historians.

Early on, Rossiter's work in Washington, Connecticut, was featured in a 1943 story in the regional periodical *The Lure of the Litchfield Hills.*[1] Author Wilbur Deming, the minister at the local Congregational Church, got the details of Rossiter's training, area of specialization, and even his name wrong, in spite of the short time that had elapsed since Rossiter's death. More recently, Alison Gilchrist wrote a well-researched essay about Rossiter's work in Washington that was published by the Gunn Memorial Library and Museum in 1997; Stephen Ketterer prepared a picture book about the Washington country houses, published again by the library in 2006; and Scott Tilden wrote an article about the local Rossiter houses for *The Magazine Antiques* in 2007.

Between 1982 and 1989, Dover Publications selected a number of Rossiter & Wright's domestic designs for republication in their illustrated books on the houses of the Victorian era and the Gilded Age.

In New Jersey, the role of Frank Wright is emphasized, appropriately, in architectural studies of local towns, including those published by Arcadia Press, and in National Register nominations.

Beyond publication, the best test of timelessness is the adaptation of historic structures to modern uses. Many of the partners' larger commercial properties have survived. In New York City, the Royalton Hotel was transformed by one of the early and much-celebrated makeovers of the Morgans Hotel Group, resulting in a very cool boutique hotel near Grand Central Station. The row houses on the Upper West Side, now divided into separate apartments on each floor, and the co-ops on the Upper East Side survive as prestigious residences. The commercial building at the corner of Bond Street and Broadway has been updated and continues to serve a busy neighborhood near Greenwich Village.

Other institutional buildings—including many libraries, churches, and schools—have been well taken care of and continue to provide a suitably sophisticated setting for the activities of their community-minded occupants. The headmaster's house at The Hotchkiss School has been beautifully maintained and renovated as the admissions office; the president's house at Vassar College is still used as the president's house; the Hepburn Hall dormitory at Middlebury College still exists, as does the Village Hall in South Orange; many libraries still in use in Connecticut, New York, and New Jersey and the churches still open in northwest Connecticut and New Jersey are all a tribute to the architects' ability to create environments that met the aspirations and needs of their clients for more than a century.

Residential properties have been lost, but many have survived. Many estate houses have been saved by non-profit organizations, such as the Episcopal Diocese of Connecticut, which owns the Stedman-Johnson house in Hartford; or the Yale Music School, which manages the Battell-Stoeckel estate in Norfolk; or the international non-profit organization affiliated with Yale University that now occupies the Cheney house in New Haven. Happily, the Stoeckel Trust and Yale University have taken steps to protect the historic, structural, and functional aspects of Whitehouse and the Music Shed in rural Norfolk, Connecticut, the summer home of the Yale University School of Art and Music, which has presented concerts there since 1941. However, the large urban residences face challenges, as their non-profit owners struggle to raise funds for the maintenance of these stylish historic buildings. The historic floor plans are problematic—the large public spaces are fine, but the small secondary rooms and inadequate utilities and facilities present many problems for the weekday staff, who outnumber the original inhabitants. In New Milford, Connecticut, one of the large houses has been converted into a funeral home; the parish house of the Rossiter-designed church is used for a children's day care center; the church itself serves as a Masonic Temple, available as a rental facility for weddings and celebrations.

In the historic weekend retreats in northwestern Connecticut and the Atlantic Highlands of New Jersey, the projects of Ehrick Rossiter and his partner Frank Wright also survive and offer a measure of grace to contemporary life there. The "cottages" in Water Witch, now

Monmouth Hills, in the Atlantic Highlands of New Jersey continue to enchant, with the breezes filtering through the vines on the multistoried porches of the houses perched on the high bluffs. The estates in Washington, Connecticut, have attracted new owners, whose aspirations parallel those of their predecessors. Like the original builders, the new Washington owners are mindful of these special places.

In Washington, a Rossiter history is an asset. A local realtor noted that houses attributed to Rossiter have a cachet. When a Rossiter house comes on the market, she reported, multiple bids are delivered from potential buyers; the house sells at a premium. The new owners, undeterred by the expense, often convert the multiple service rooms surrounding the historic kitchen into an open space replete with high-end appliances and the currently fashionable island for kitchen prep. Developers in up-scale markets in nearby Hartford and Fairfield counties advertise that their newly-built projects are "Rossiter" inspired, hoping to align their work with the romance and reputation of the Rossiter houses of the past.

Over the course of a half century, Ehrick Rossiter and his partners designed a full complement of buildings for an evolving America, including inexpensive suburban houses, exclusive city apartments and expansive country estates, as well as the churches, libraries, schools and recreational buildings that define the communities we know today. Within this diverse range, the architects' success was most evident in the homes for modern living they created for the rising middle class.

Stylish but unpretentious, these homes provided gracious environments for prosperous families in a world of rapid change. Artistic but practical, like Rossiter himself, these projects were intended to promote healthy families and communities. The success of these efforts is confirmed by the survival, and the celebration, of the Rossiter homes and civic buildings that continue to serve families and communities today.

ENDNOTES

Preface

1   The program at Cornell was the first four-year course in architecture in an American college, started in 1871, according to Elaine D. Engst, *125 Years of Achievement, The History of Cornell's College of Architecture, Art and Planning* (Ithaca, NY: Cornell University Library, 1996). M.I.T. offered architecture classes taught by the esteemed William Robert Ware beginning in 1868, according to the M.I.T. Libraries and Archives website, but it did not create a complete architectural curriculum until later.

Chapter One

1   The quote is from Emerson's 1836 book *Nature*.

2   For example, Thomas Pritchard Rossiter, *Washington and Lafayette at Mount Vernon, 1784 (The Home of Washington after the War)*, 1859 (Metropolitan Museum of Art, New York City); a series on the life of Christ (unfinished, and now unlocated) and *The Ideals* (current location unknown.) For a discussion of Rossiter's paintings and a list of known work, see the Thomas Prichard Rossiter and Rossiter Family papers, 1840-1957. Archives of American Art, Smithsonian Institution.

3   Susan Stein, "Some of the New York City Houses of Richard Morris Hunt," *The Magazine Antiques*, April 1986, pp. 846-53. The house design is believed to have been drawn in Paris when the Rossiters and Hunt were there in 1855. For more details on the lawsuit, see Robert A. M. Stern, Thomas Mellins, and David Fishman, *New York 1880, Architecture and Urbanism in the Gilded Age,* (New York: The Monacelli Press, Inc., 1999), pp. 609-10. The house was demolished before 1895.

4   A reporter for a New York newspaper described the home in detail. Two doors opened from the vestibule: one into a passage to the gallery with stairs leading to the studios on the upper floors; the other into the hall of the house for family use only. The house, 38 feet by 62 feet, with a 20-foot extension, was entered through a vestibule with two doors, one opening onto the hallway for the family's home and the other onto the gallery and the stairway to the studio. A large skylight in the roof illuminated the center of the building and an atrium on the first floor. The atrium opened onto the entrance hall, the gallery, the parlor and the dining room. The butler's pantry and service stairs, leading from the sub-cellar to the upper floors, were across the atrium from the main entrance and stairway. The parlor (saloon) was 20 feet square, the atrium 18 feet square, the dining room 16 by 18 feet, with a veranda, the gallery 20 by 36 feet. On the second floor, above the atrium, there was a gallery with a balustrade "uniting the two stories in one architectural motive. From this gallery eight doors open[ed] in the corners with panel space for pictures [in] between." Four of the doors opened to five bedrooms, a linen closet, and a dressing room. A bathroom and dumb waiter were also located on this floor.

The third floor had three bedrooms, a dressing room, and a bathroom at the front of the house, with a library (with a balcony) and portrait studio located at the back of the house. The fourth floor was devoted to a large studio with windows to the north and south as well as skylights. A circular stairway in one corner led to an observatory "for the purpose of studying sky effects." In the basement, there were rooms for servants, plus the kitchen, laundry, and storerooms. (Undated clipping from the *Home Journal,* in the Rossiter files at the Smithsonian's Archives of American Art, Box 11.)

5   Identification of the family members is included in the Rossiter papers at the Smithsonian. Sterling Rossiter, Ehrick's half-brother, died in 1883 while a student at Columbia.

6   Stern, Mellins, and Fishman, *New York 1880,* p. 610.

7   Thomas Rossiter's views on slavery are presented in *America Triumphant: Feeding the Emigrant and Freeing the Slave,* illustrating his celebration of the emancipation of the slaves as a great national accomplishment. See Gail Husch, *Something Coming, Apocalyptic Expectation and American Painting* (Lebanon, NH: University Press of New England, 2000). The painting may have been exhibited in Chicago in 1863, when the controversial Emancipation Proclamation was issued.

8   These are the dates of his attendance, according to most published sources. The school's records are missing. The school archivist recently suggested that Rossiter left in 1870 rather than 1871, which would have given him time to travel to England and study with a tutor in Ithaca before entering Cornell in the fall of 1871, as the Cornell records report. Rossiter's daughter, Edith, thought the sea voyage took place in the summer of 1871.

9   A warmly descriptive memoir of the school during Frederick Gunn's era was published following Gunn's death—William Hamilton Gibson, *The Master of the Gunnery* (New York: The Gunn Memorial Association, 1887). Rossiter wrote a chapter for the book describing Gunn's civic activities in Washington.

10   Rossiter family records, now in the Smithsonian's Archives of American Art, report that Anna was buried in the Parmly family cemetery in Rumson, New Jersey, but there is no record of her burial or gravesite there. The Grove Street Cemetery records in New Haven, Connecticut, state that Anna, Thomas, Mary, and Sterling were buried in Grove Street Cemetery in a vault at 31 Maple; the cemetery streets are named for trees.

11   Henry Ogden, 1889. Engst, *125 Years of Achievement.*

12   The college president and 22 professors were also members of the fraternity, and Samuel Clemens (Mark Twain), who had a summer home nearby, was an occasional guest. Jan Jennings, *Cheap and Tasteful Dwellings Design Competitions and the Convenient Interior,* 1879-1909 (Knoxville: University of Tennessee Press, 2005).

13   Jeffrey Karl Ochsner, *HH Richardson Complete Architectural Works* (Cambridge, MA: MIT Press, 1982).

14   Thomas Rossiter, the architect's father, and Richardson were fellow members

of the Century Association. Frederick Billings, Ehrick's uncle, commissioned Richardson in 1883 to design a library for the University of Vermont.

15   *AABN* 7/7/1877.

Chapter Two

1   Jennings, *Cheap and Tasteful Dwellings*.

2   Frank Wright claimed to be a founder of the Architectural League, but it was organized in 1881, before he was involved; he may have been one of those listed as an officer when it was incorporated in 1888. He was on the exhibition committee in 1886, 1891, and 1892; on the executive committee in 1887, 1888, and 1892; the secretary in 1888; on the catalogue committee in 1889, 1891, and 1892. Ehrick Rossiter was on the medals committee in 1889, 1891, and 1892; the awards committee in 1892; the executive committee in 1892, 1896, and 1897.

3   These were also published by William Comstock. *Architectural Perspective for Beginners* (1882, 1883, 1896, and 1904). This series of articles was published in six parts in the periodical *Building* in 1883. Among the topics were: Architectural Studies I (1885), Architectural Studies II: Store Fronts and Interior Details (1885) and Low-Cost Houses, Store Fronts and Interior Details, Stables, Sea-Side and Southern Houses, Out-Buildings (1886).

4   Adolf K. Placzek, in the introduction of the 1976 reissue of Henry-Russell Hitchcock's 1946 *American Architectural Books*, found 11 titles published in 1868 and in 1869, 15 in 1873, 15 in 1875, 16 in 1881, and 20 in 1882. Henry Russell Hitchcock, *American Architectural Books* (New York: Da Capo Press, 1976).

5   Ehrick K. Rossiter and Frank A. Wright, *Modern House Painting*, 2nd edn. rev. (New York: William T. Comstock, 1883), p. 6.

6   *Ibid.*, p. 7.

7   *Ibid.*, p. 12.

8   *Ibid.*, opposite Plate IX.

9   *Ibid.*, opposite Plate VIII.

10   *Ibid.*, opposite Plate X.

11   *Ibid.*, opposite Plate XVI.

12   *Ibid.*, opposite Plate XVII.

13   *Ibid.*, opposite Plate XVIII.

14   *AABN* 12/4/1880, No. 253.

15   For William Van Wyck. *RERG* 5/12/1883.

16   *RERG* 4/24/1888, No. 226.

17   *RERG* 5/12/1883 and *AABN* 4/18/1885.

18   The family connection to Tyrone has not yet been established, but the town

was then a center of lumber production, so Rossiter's father-in-law may have had associates in Tyrone. Illustrated in the annual exhibition *Yearbook of the Architectural League of New York* in 1887.

19 22 Westmoreland Pl. *Inland Architect,* 21:5 (6/1893).

20 The YMCA was illustrated in *The Builder and Wood-Worker* 8/1882; The Newburgh Academy was illustrated, with elevations and floor plans in *AABN* 4/10/1886.

21 *Newburgh Daily News,* March 18, 1893. The author is grateful to Hugh Goodman for providing this citation.

22 *AABN* 4/22/1882. The chapel is now the Saint Joseph of Arimathea Chapel of the Episcopal church in Greenburgh. The widow gave it to the church in 1893 to be used for the burial of bishops. Later additions were apparently designed by Hobart Upjohn, son of Richard Upjohn, the prominent architect and proponent of the Gothic Revival. The 2001 National Register nomination for this property erroneously attributed the original building to Richard Upjohn's son Richard.

23 *AABN* 10/27/1883.

24 Billings Farm and Museum, Woodstock, Vermont.

25 Kermit Carlyle Parsons, *The Cornell Campus: A History of Its Planning and Development* (Ithaca, NY: Cornell University Press, 1968), pp. 142-3.

26 Designs for the summer house in Washington were published in 1884 and 1885 (*RERG* 9/20/1884 and 11/15/1884 and *AABN* 6/27/1885). However, Barnes did not begin purchasing property in this location until 1884 and continued to buy land here over the next three years, so it is not certain when the Barnes house was built. Rossiter built a carriage house with an apartment for his own family across the street in 1884 and began construction on the Rocks, the Rossiters' main summer house in 1887

27 Wright married Elizabeth Hanford of Newark, New Jersey, in 1883; they had four children—Carile (b. 1886), Frances (b. 1888), Elizabeth (b. 1891), and their only son, Ehrick (b. 1896).

28 Dolores Hayden, *Building Suburbia: Green Fields and Urban Growth, 1820-2000* (New York: Pantheon Books, 2003).

29 *AABN* 12/4/1880.

30 *SA* 1/1883.

31 *AABN* 8/6/1881.

32 Jennings, *Cheap and Tasteful Dwellings.*

33 At 111 Irvington Ave. *AABN* 8/5/1882.

34 *AABN* 8/5/1882.

35 *Building* 5/1884.

36 The house was built for "Mr. Shane." *RERG* 9/20/1884. Other houses built in

South Orange in the 1880s were for B.B. Schneider at 255 Scotland Rd. (*YAL* 1888) and for Emma Grant (*YAL* 1889). A house may also have been designed in 1887 for C.E. Billquist, in 1887, an advocate of baseball and tennis in town.

37   *The Builder and Wood-Worker* 6/1881.

38   The Atlantic Highlands church is listed in Jennings, *Cheap and Tasteful Buildings*, p. 246, and it was originally noted in *Manufacturer and Builder* 12/1882; the church was moved to Leonardo, New Jersey, 10 years later, where it survives today. Thanks to Frank Greenagel for this information. The Long Branch chapel is illustrated in *Building* 4/1883.

39   *Building* 10/1883.

40   *RERG* 9/24/1888.

41   One was for J.V. Beckman, *SA* 1/1883, and the other for Alexander Gilbert, *YAL* 1887, No. 206, and *SA* 12/1890.

42   *YAL* 1888 No. 178, *AABN* 1891.

43   *AABN* 1891; in Summit, for R.D. Rickford: *ABM ill*, July–Dec,1889.

44   The source for the clipping about the stable is unidentified. A copy of the clipping was in a file kept by Chris Wood, a subsequent owner of the house. The "House to be Built" was published in *AABN* 6/9/1883.

45   In 1971, an elderly woman wrote a letter, now in the Gunn Memorial Library and Museum collection, that she had visited Edith Rossiter at Washington in 1906 or 1907 and that Ehrick Rossiter took the girls on a carriage ride into the valley and told her that he bought the land to save it from a lumber company, which delayed the building of the main house. Her memory may have been influenced by the frequent telling of the story by many in the twentieth century, or the story may be true.

46   The nine original trustees included many Rossiter clients (Adrian Van Sinderen, George Vaillant, Hamilton Gibson, Arthur Shipman, H. Siddons Mowbray, and Anne Van Ingen), as well as his son E. Winthrop Rossiter. Rossiter's widow donated another 92 acres to the Steep Rock reserve in 1944, after Rossiter had died. The Steep Rock Association currently owns 2,426 acres of land and holds conservation easements on another 2,348 acres.

47   The eastern façade was published in *YAL* 1887, No. 207. Photographs of the house taken by Joseph West at the turn of the twentieth century provide additional details. The West photographs are in the collection of the Gunn Memorial Library and Museum, Washington, CT.

48   Barbour was also the sponsor of the compilation of the state's vital records, beginning in 1900; the Barbour Collection of Vital Records is housed in the archives at the state library in Hartford.

49   *AABN* 11/21/1885 and *YAL* 1887, No. 121.

50   Mary Brinsmade, of Washington, was Van Ingen's wife Mary McLean's teacher

at the Packer Institute in Brooklyn; in addition, Amy Kenyon, a teacher at The Gunnery, was also a student of Mary Brinsmade. Alison Gilchrist has suggested that the lifelong friendship of these three women brought Van Ingen to Washington. *Return to Arcadia: Ehrick Rossiter's Washington The Architect, His Clients, and Their Houses* (Washington, CT: Gunn Memorial Library and Museum, 1997).

51 Illustrated in *AABN* 3/6/1880; reproduced in Vincent Scully, *The Shingle Style and the Stick Style: Architectural Theory and Design from Downing to the Origins of Wright,* rev. edn. (New Haven, CT: Yale University Press, 1971). Illustration #37.

52 The Van Ingen house was remodeled again in 1929 after the house was sold to Alfred Bourne. The blueprints for the 1929 renovation, by Roderick Barnes of New York, Richard Barnes's son and Alfred Bourne's brother-in-law, show these features as part of the existing property, although they don't appear in the 1879 Potter and Robertson design. The National Register nomination for the Washington Green historic district (1996) lists the carriage house and gate house as being constructed in 1920, although there is no documentation provided for that date and it seems more likely that these building were built during Van Ingen's era of building in the last decade of the nineteenth century. The Holiday House, illustrated in *YAL* 1893, was dismantled during World War I.

53 *YAL* 1889.

54 Perry (1844-1913) held several patents for dental advances for preparing crowns for teeth and for tooth separation along with other devices for dentists, and he published articles on the proper methods of performing root canal surgery and new techniques for dental cement.

55 His sons, a lawyer, a clergyman, a congressman, and one who ran the factory, continued to live in the house into the 1920s; the house itself survived until the 1980s.

56 Butler's barn was at 1134 Pacific St; Rossiter & Wright added a two-story brick extension on the east, 17 by 9 feet, and a two-story addition, 18 by 32, on the rear, as well as interior alterations, all for $8,000. *RERG* 5/13/1884 and 4/26/1884. The $3,500 brick stable, 44.8 feet by 32.8 feet, was on Dean St., east of Franklin, and had a slate-and-tin roof. *RERG* 3/15/1884. Also illustrated in *AABN* 1/16/1886. Barnes's 1887 stable was on the east side of Claremont Ave, south of Fulton St. It was a two-story brick stable with coachmen's quarters, 20 by 40 feet, having a tin roof and brick and iron courses, costing $3,000, apparently similar to the Butler stable. *RERG* 12/13/1897.

57 At 145-147 Mulberry St. for Thomas Hays. *RERG* 4/22/1889.

58 *Building* 7/28/1888.

59 The drawings for this project are in the Levi Collection in the archives at Avery Library, Columbia College, New York. Interestingly, one of the houses was designed for the father of a future architect who became a partner of Alfredo Taylor, who did many projects in Norfolk, CT, including later work for former Rossiter clients there. Ann Havemeyer kindly shared this information with me.

60 In the *New York Times*, August 13, 2006.

61 Ibid. Christopher Gray quoting Robert A. M. Stern in *New York 1880*.

Chapter Three

1   Barry Bergdoll, in his report nominating 130-134 East 67th St. to the New York Landmarks Preservation Commission (January 1980), found that Platt designed the façade of the 67th St. project, although contemporary publications list Platt only as the designer of the 66th St. project. *Architectural Record* 7/10/1907 and *Architects' and Builders'* Magazine 3/1909. One critic thought the façade of the building at 67th St. was less successful than the one at 66th St., probably the result of accommodating a different floor plan. Platt designed homes for Rossiter's cousin Laura Billings Lee, in New York City, in 1904, and in Vermont, in 1906; he had previously designed terrace gardens for her family's home in Woodstock, Vermont, as early as 1894.

2   Curiously, Wright does not appear in the federal census as a resident of New Jersey, although a 1910 City Directory lists him as a resident of Hobart St. in Short Hills. His only appearance in the federal census is in 1910, when he is listed, with his wife and four children, as a resident of an apartment building at 26 West 113 St. in Manhattan.

3   The *New Milford Gazette*, 1896 article on Rossiter. In the Rossiter file at the Gunn Memorial Library in Washington, CT.

4   These houses were for David Dodd (1890), at 344 Montrose Ave, *YAL* 1890, No. 166; D.H.A. Mandeville (1890, the billiard room addition), *YAL* 1890; H.A. Page, (1891), *YAL* 1892, No. 275; R.S. Sinclair (1891), *YAL* 1892, No. 275; H.G. Tomas (1891) *YAL* 1892, No. 275; W.T. Baird (1891) *YAL* 1892, No. 275; H.W. Ferris (1894) *RERG* 7/7/1894 and *SA* 1/1897; J.G. Mindt (1895); Maxwell Smith (1896) *SA* 10/1896; Livingston Middleditch (1898) *SA* 3/1898; Montrose Realty & Improvement (1905), *RERG* 1905. Rossiter & Muller designed a home in South Orange for Charles Thorling, according to Rossiter's daughter, Edith, sometime after 1913. Thorling was also a client on Long Island.

5   *YAL* 1895, *AABN* 1894.

6   *AABN* 7/14/1894.

7   Montrose for E.W. Given (1891) SA 3/1891; Frank Brewer (1893); and Norman Ward (1905) *RERG* 7/1/1905.

8   *Architects' and Builders' Magazine* 10/1910.

9   For Edward Page, published by William Comstock in 1913.

10 Titled Prospect Place, the building was 92 by 45 feet and was built for C.W.L. Roche, who commissioned a home from Rossiter & Wright at the Brantwood Park development. *RERG* 12/1/1900.

11 For Robert Dunn Douglas, *YAL* 1896, No. 337; *RERG* 11/16/1895.

12   Jennings, *Cheap and Tasteful Dwellings.* The houses were designed for Charles Finch (1896) a two-story frame house costing $20,000 *YAL* 1898, No. 837; *RERG* 11/7/1896; F.R. Littell (1905) *RERG* 1905; and on Hobart St. in Short Hills, Goodview for Frank A. Wright at 407 Hobart (1900) *YAL* 1900, No. 858; Ashton Harvey (1904) 395 Hobart; unknown owner at 325 Hobart. Another house at Brantwood was published in *House and Garden* 6/1906, p. 301.

13   It's not clear why Wright would build two new houses, one in Short Hills and the other in Middlebrook Heights at Bound Brook, within two years; perhaps the Bound Brook house was built to sell. Wright published the Short Hills house in *YAL* 1900 as "the residence of Mr. Frank A. Wright." Records at the Millburn-Short Hills Historical Society gathered by Lynne Ranieri show Fred [sic] A. Wright, architect, living at Hobart St. in Short Hills in the 1910 City Directory. Historical Society notes also indicate that he may have sold the Short Hills house in 1914.

14   *YAL* 1893, No. 264.

15   For H.M. Bingham. *SA* 10/1900.

16   *The American Architect* 12/23/1914.

17   For Mrs. R.H. Rickard (1889) *YAL* 1889, No. 115; for the Rev. F. Landon Humphries (1890) *YAL* 1890, No. 144; and for A. S. Van Winkle (1892) *YAL* 1892, No. 218. After 1913, Rossiter & Muller designed a home for James Gifford.

18   For Mrs. Frances P. Curtis (1890) *SA* 11/1891; C.F. Abbott (1892) *YAL* 1892, No. 337; an unidentified owner (1894) *SA* 2/1894; D.M. Moore on Central Ave. (1895) *RERG* 10/26/1895; John Bushnell (1897) *RERG* 10/27/1897; George A. Strong (1903) *SA* 7/1903; and a Mr. Chapman (1895) *YAL*.

19   George Lamont was also active in the Bound Brook community, buying a house there for the residents to use as a library. The other houses in Middlebrook Heights were designed for C.R. Cushman and Charles H. Cook, of Trenton, who built two frame dwellings for $10,000 each. *RERG* 9/11/1897 and *RERG* 10/18/1897.

20   The bank was 38 by 53 feet and was valued at $10,000. *RERG* 8/13/1898. See also *RERG* 9/11/1897 and *YAL* 1897, No. 227, and 1898, No. 801 and 833.

21   The Englewood homes included one for Col. H.W. Banks (1887) *YAL* 1887, No. 94, and the $6,000 house for Alvin Holman (1900) *RERG* 3/3/1900.

22   For Duncan D. Chaplin (1895) *YAL* 1896, No. 71; *The American Architect* 6/7/1916; for H.H. Palmer (1897) *RERG* 10/16/97; and the church addition (1899) *RERG* 2/18/1899.

23   *Brickbuilder* 9/1899.

24   The library, 70 by 50 feet, was valued at $35,000. *RERG* 4/21/1900. Rossiter's daughter included the Johnson homes on the list of her father's projects she prepared after his death. The house for Johnson's son was designed by Rossiter & Muller.

25 Poor (1898) *RERG* 7/16/1898 and 8/13/1898, a two and a half-story frame house valued at $6,000-$10,000; golf club (1900) *YAL* 1900, No. 857; Charles Reese (1900) *RERG* 12/22/1900, a two and a half-story frame house 42 by 50 feet.

26 *RERG* 9/21/1895. The client was E. Knowles.

27 The client for the two projects was Thomas McCarter. The residential building on Spruce St. was a three-story brick building, 45 by 65 feet, perhaps an apartment building (1900), and his stable, a two-story brick building, 34 by 42 feet. *RERG* 12/15/1900.

28 Caroline Bournoville was the owner of the four two-family houses at Webster and Reservoir Ave. Each was a two and a half-story frame house valued at $4,000. *RERG* 8/24/1901.

29 The shelters were 35 by 35 feet and 30 by 60 feet and were built for $15,000 in 1905. *RERG* 12/9/1905. For an octagonal shelter by a wading pool, built for $4,000, see *House and Garden* 10/1906. For the boat and field house, see *RERG* 3/10/1906. For the bandstand, see *The American Architect* 12/23/1914.

30 In Rumson, the firm designed houses for William and Georgiana Shedd (82 Buena Vista Rd., Rumson, 1892), Marie Stuart Palmer (54 Rumson Rd., Rumson, 1894) and Thomas Carmichael (1898). Randall Gabrielan, *Rumson, Images of America* (Dover, NH: Arcadia Publications, 1996). Coincidently, Rossiter's mother's family, the Parmlys, owned property in Rumson. Rossiter's grandfather Eleazer Parmly, the dentist and New York real estate investor, purchased Bingham Hall, an eighteenth-century estate, and added to it so that his extensive country property reached from the Navasink River to the Shrewsbury. In 1996, the house was still standing at 139 Bingham Avenue, Rumson. At his death, Eleazer left the property to his son Ehrick, whose son Dalton later divided the property for the Parmly Park development. I am grateful to Randall Gabrielan for sorting out this story.

31 *RERG* 11/12/1898.

32 One of the Water Witch houses, for example, cost $5,000 when some of the Washington houses cost four times that amount.

33 I am grateful to Mary Jo Kenny for sharing her extensive knowledge of the history of the Water Witch Club and her photo files. The Seabury Jones home was a two and a half-story frame house 50 by 60 feet, for $5,000. *RERG* 11/12/1898. Bowling alley and billiard room: *YAL* 1896, No. 60; F.A. Wright house *YAL* 1896, No. 359. See also the National Register Nomination for the Water Witch Club Historic District prepared by Tomkins Historical Research in 2002.

34 Allenhurst, *RERG* 11/23/1897; Other houses in Monmouth County were built for Daniel Cooney (1885); Emmet Olcott (1886); Mary Hecker [or Heckler], Navasink Beach (1889); Dr. James Green, Long Branch (1892); Marie Stuart Palmer, Long Branch (1893-4); M.H. Burch, Deal Beach (1895); Marie Stewart (sic) Palmer, Sea Bright (1899); Elizabeth Earl Hanford, Belmar (1901). Monmouth County Archives, courtesy of Mary Jo Kenny.

35 In 1922, The Gunnery, which had been privately owned by Frederick Gunn and then by his son-in-law John Brinsmade, was purchased by a group of investors and converted to an all boys' school. One of these investors, Henry Van Sinderen then bought The Ridge School and converted it into an inn. Today it has been reconstructed and is open as the Mayflower Inn, a luxury hotel, spa and restaurant. The Van Sinderens and Bournes provided funding to construct five new buildings for The Gunnery that formed a quadrangle on the campus; they were designed by New York architect Richard Henry Dana, who was teaching architecture at Yale when Adrian Van Sinderen, another of the investors, was a student there.

36 Mrs. Black also took the girls to her cottage, Lazy Lodge, on Lake Waramaug, which may have been designed by Rossiter in 1879. She committed suicide on the Isle of Wight in 1910; the Ingleside school buildings were sold to Canterbury School in 1915, which expanded the campus onto land north of the site of Mrs. Black's home and school. All of the Rossiter buildings on the Canterbury campus were later lost to fire.

37 The date of the Van Sinderen house, Vanholme, is often given as 1898, but the land records show that Van Sinderen first bought property here in Washington in 1905. He died in 1906. Van Sinderen's wife was Mary Brinsmade, of the extended Washington family. In 1924, the Van Sinderens' son Adrian, who attended The Ridge School, built a larger summer home, Glenholme, next door to his parents' house, with designs by the Fairfield architect Cameron Clark (1887-1957), who had been Adrian's roommate at Yale.

38 Documentation confirming that Rossiter did the turn-of-the-century renovations at Whitehouse is elusive, in spite of an extensive search of family records. Other architects also worked for the Battels and Stoeckels. J. Cleaveland Cady (1837-1919), the architect of the 1883 Metropolitan Opera House in New York City, provided designs for the expansion of the Robbins Battell house in 1880. The New York architect Henry Kilburn designed a barn for the Stoeckels in 1898. Alfredo Taylor (1872-1947) who was working in Norfolk by 1903, also worked for the Stoeckel estate after 1940. Ann Havemeyer has located newspaper accounts of extensive renovations at the house in 1900-1901, an extension of the library undertaken in 1902, electrical work and work on the organ in 1903, and the raising of the roof by half a story in 1906. Edith Rossiter believed her father did the renovations of Whitehouse for the Stoeckels in the early years of the 20th century, while he was working on the Music Shed. Rossiter was active in Norfolk then, designing a dozen projects in town between 1898 and 1908. Mrs. Stoeckel commissioned Rossiter to design a new tower roof and an oaken door for Norfolk's Battell Chapel, and church members also commissioned a new porch, pulpit, lighting and other interior renovations in 1927 and 1928. Mrs. Stoeckel also commissioned an observation tower at Haystack Mountain in 1929. Alterations to a home were commissioned by Robert Wehner in 1931.

39   The Stoeckel property, including Whitehouse and the Music Shed, was bequeathed to a trust at Mrs. Stoeckel's death, and it is today the location of the Yale School of Music's annual Norfolk Chamber Music Festival. See Ann Havemeyer and Robert Dance, *The Magnificent Battells: An Architectural Legacy* (Norfolk, CT: Norfolk Historical Society, 2006).

40   The tower is now part of a state park. The original architect's drawings for the tower are in the files of the Connecticut Department of Energy and Environmental Protection, which administers the park.

41   I am grateful to Joan Baldwin, Curator of Special Collections at The Hotchkiss School, for her careful attention to the architectural history of the school and her assistance during my research on campus. The financial summary of the architectural program was provided by Ms. Baldwin, along with her excellent guidance on the documents and photographs for these projects existing in the school archives.

42   Rossiter designed a stable for Mr. Scoville, a trustee and member of the building committee, at his elaborate estate in nearby Taconic in the early years of his work for the school.

43   John Hoysradt. Archives of The Hotchkiss School.

44   In subsequent years, Cass Gilbert and then Henry S. Waterbury of the New York firm Delano & Aldrich were the architects for new school buildings. All that remains of Rossiter's work on campus is the headmaster's house (now known as Harris House and currently used as the school's admissions office), the boat house and the barn.

45   In addition to the projects described in this paragraph, Rossiter's daughter also thought Ehrick had designed the South St. home of Mr. and Mrs. Henry Towne, but that house was designed by Aymar Embury (1880-1966), according to a 1924 letter from John Lancaster to John Buel in Litchfield, which discusses the Towne house. I am grateful to Rachel Carley for sharing this information with me.

46   A note in the architectural files at the Litchfield Historical Society attributes the home to Rossiter, and it is stylistically similar to other work known to have been designed by the firm.

47   Cunningham was also the president of the Electric Railroad Company of Rome, Georgia, a railroad promoter, like several of Rossiter's clients. Cunningham was also a great advocate of the motor car, driving a Pierce Arrow from Litchfield, Connecticut, to Charleston, South Carolina, in November 1910, an era when long-distance roads were virtually nonexistent.

48   Stephanie Cunningham's memoir, in the collections of the Litchfield Historical Society, was written sometime after 1940. She mistakenly believed the house was built in 1893. A respected contemporary historian Alain White reported that the house was built in 1904, which conforms more closely to the development of Rossiter's style and his activity in Litchfield.

49   A recent publication suggested that Rossiter also designed the 1890 Litchfield firehouse, an attribution perhaps based on the fact that the donor of the firehouse, J. Deming Perkins, hired Rossiter to renovate his grandfather's house in Litchfield in 1887. However, the firehouse was designed by Waterbury architect Robert Wakeman Hill, who also designed the 1889 courthouse in Litchfield, across the street from the firehouse. Thanks to Rachel Carley, author of *Litchfield, The Making of a New England Town* (Litchfield, CT: Litchfield Historical Society, 2011).

50   Hepburn succeeded J. P. Morgan as the head of the Chase bank advisory board. During his decade of architectural projects with Rossiter, he also donated funds for the construction of a hospital in Ogdensburg, New York, and for the founding of the Graduate School of Business at Columbia College in 1916. He was killed when struck by a bus on Fifth Ave. in 1922, cutting short a retirement that had been spent as an active benefactor of educational and community causes. In his will he gave away another $3 million in charitable bequests, including $2 million to colleges and libraries.

51   The Danbury houses were renovations and a carriage house for Charles Merritt at 350 Main St. (possibly 1883) and $3,000 worth of renovations, including a new kitchen and veranda, for Arnold Taylor (1900). *RERG* 12/1/1900. The Bridgeport house was for Judge M. B. Beardsley (1904) *RERG* 8/20/1904.

52   The building was at 1122-1126 Main St. *RERG* 5/21/1910.

53   In Ardsley-on-Hudson, for Mrs. H.W.M. Richardson (1906); in Bedford, for J. Lounsbery (1895) *YAL* 1896, No. 46; and a one-story brick-and-frame extension for a laundry and servants' quarters at the home of Dr. George M. Lefferts (1900) *RERG* 12/22/1900. The drawings for the Lefferts extension are in the B.J. Farrand records at UC Berkeley. In Brewster, for S. B. Howes, the firm moved his stone-and-brick house back 33 feet to improve the landscaping (1883), costing $8,000 *RERG* 7/26/1884, and in 1893 made further alterations to the house *YAL* 1892, No. 86, and *RERG* 8/13/1898; in Mt. Vernon, NY, a house, Chester Hill, for the violinist Gustav Danureuther (1894) *SA* 12/1894; in White Plains, NY, the home of G.W. Cummings (1898), two-story frame, 72 by 40 feet with extensions, $15,000 *RERG* 1/19/1898, and the Brown house (see next endnote); in Yonkers, NY, a home for Dr. S.G. Perry (1892) *SA* 6/1892. The firm also drew the renovations for an extension of a house at 2200 Edsall Place, Spuyten Duyvil in the Bronx, for W.H. Yale of Dobb's Ferry (1890) *RERG* 12/27/1890.

54   The Brown house was at 12 Greenridge Dr., built for the manager of the Keeley Institute and the president of the village of White Plains *RERG* 1/29/1889. Thanks to Miriam Varian, local history librarian in White Plains.

55   Lamont may have been introduced to Rossiter through the architect's Billings cousins in Vermont, whose father had earlier been president of the Northern Pacific Railroad, where Lamont was vice president after 1898. Rossiter and Billings were working on the Royalton Hotel in the years immediately preceding

the Lamont commission. Rossiter's daughter, Edith, was a bridesmaid along with Frances Lamont and Catherine Burton at a Millbrook wedding in 1908.

56   *RERG* 4/21/1900 and 7/14/1900.

57   A house for A.L. Casey at Linden Ave. (1890) 22 by 52, $5,000 *RERG* 8/16/1890; two two-story frame houses at 194 Poplar Ave., east of Highland Ave. for Walter Tomkins (1899) *RERG* 1/14/1899, each 30 by 63 feet, costing $8,000; a two-story frame house at Beach and 44th St. (1899) 41 by 31 feet, *RERG* 1/14/1899; a summer house for R.H. Field (1901) *SA* 10/1901; a two-story frame house for W.B. Vansigo (1902) 33 by 46 feet, *RERG* 3/15/1902; a summer home for the Seagate Improvement Co. (1902) *SA* 6/1902; a 24- by 12-foot extension to a house at the corner of Maple and Seagate Ave. for the Seagate Import Co. (1904) *RERG* 12/17/1904.

58   In Port Washington: a stone-and-frame house for Miss F.M. Danielson (1903), $6,000 *RERG* 12/9/1903; in Mill Neck: Three Harbors Hill for William H. Peters (1904) *RERG* 10/1/1904, a two-story frame-and-stone house 110 by 50 feet, $45,000; in Oyster Bay: the Hawirt House stable for William H. Peters (1900), $15,000 *RERG* 3/21/1900; a two-story coach house for William H. Peters (1900), 25 by 45, and two-story stable for William Peters *RERG* 5/16/1900 (it seems likely that these several descriptions and notices may refer to the same project; why would Peters built three stables and/or carriages houses in one year?); $80,000 house for Timothy Williams (1900) *RERG* 5/9/1900. (Williams also built a Tudor style home named Shorelands across the bay in Lloyd Harbor in 1903, designed by another architect); in Lloyd's Neck: a home for Charles Thorling, also a Rossiter & Wright client in New Jersey; in Quogue: a two and a half-story roughcast house, 78 by 38, for F.B. Austin (1902) *RERG* 10/18/1902; in East Hampton: a two and a half-story frame house for W.B. Lockwood (1901) *RERG* 6/15/1901; and in Islip: a cottage in the Brentwood neighborhood *House and Garden* 6/1906 and a home for H.D. Timmerman (1904) *RERG* 11/26/1904.

59   The Charles Lane Poor house (*RERG* 1/29/1898), built for a Johns Hopkins professor, burned as a result of a chimney fire in 1911, with a loss of $30,000. The Poor family built other notable houses in the area, some of which have survived. Thanks to Lane Poor and Ward Poor for information on the several family houses. The Gibb house, demolished by fire within a year of construction, at a loss of $56,000, *The New York Times,* 8/16/1910. Thanks to Robert MacKay, director of the Society for the Preservation of Long Island Antiquities, for assistance with tracking the Long Island houses.

60   One of the larger houses was for G.W. Cummings (1898) *RERG* 4/23/1898; the other two houses were for R.L. Burton (1901) *RERG* 7/23/1901.

61   August 8, 1908.

62   *RERG* 11/23/1901; *YAL* 1903, No. 584; *SA* 1/1904 and 2/1904.

63   *YAL* 1891, No. 165.

64   The Strong house: *RERG* 10/24/1896; Schley: *RERG* 9/19/1896 and 2/4/1899; Noyes: *RERG* 1/8/1898 and 6/25/1898; Elderkin: *RERG* 6/24/1899; Eastman: *RERG* 5/2/1903. Eastman was listed in the 1910 census as a butcher, but a wealthy one with a governess for his children and multiple servants. Elderkin was probably related to John Elderkin, who was a benefactor to the Rossiter-designed library in Setauket, New York.

65   National Railway: *RERG* 4/17/1897; Barnum: *RERG* 5/29/1897; Warner: *RERG* 9/25/1897; firm moving building at Mott St.: *RERG* 4/2/1898; Spruce St.: three-story residence, 46 by 65 feet, *RERG* 3/3/1900; bachelor apartments: *Architects' and Builders' Magazine* 3/25/1899; Lockwood: *RERG* 10/26/1901; Hegeman: *RERG* 4/12/1902; Zollikoffer: *RERG* 6/27/1903.

66   Office for Metropolitan History, 1987, report prepared for Morgans Hotel Group.

67   *AABN* 7/2/1893, *YAL* 1897 #274,275, *RERG* 11/21/1896.

68   *Architects' and Builders' Magazine* 3/1909, pp. 223-4, quoting an unnamed article in the real estate section of the *New York Times*.

69   Russell to Rossiter, letter at Smithsonian's Archives of American Art, Rossiter collection.

70   *RERG* 7/13/1907.

71   The church was sold to a Greek congregation in the 1920s and demolished in 1938 to make way for the 18th precinct police station at 310 West 54th St.

72   *RERG* 12/23/1914.

73   *RERG* 3/12/1910 and *RERG* 2/5/1921.

74   Conversation with the author, 1998.

75   Muller continued the office at 15 West 38th St. until 1940, when he moved to 22 East 40th St. In the 1950s, Muller's son Peter Paul Muller, also a graduate of Columbia's architectural program, joined the firm. Following John Muller's death, the son took on Alfred Ash as a partner in the firm Muller and Ash. Peter Paul Muller opened an independent office in Southampton, on Long Island, in 1975, where he specialized in beach houses and commercial projects.

76   The dates of the libraries were taken from Hepburn's memoir. The Colton library construction began in 1912; the Waddington library was begun in 1919 and completed in 1921; the Edwards library was dedicated in 1921.

77   Mrs. Gibb, the mother of the West Hartford client, was a sister of Clinton Rossiter. Clinton Rossiter was a developer of Belle-Terre, a planned recreational and residential community in Port Jefferson on Long Island, and had been an officer of the Brooklyn Rapid Transit Company; another of her Rossiter brothers was an officer of the New York Central Railroad.

78   Lisa Johnson, director of the Stanley Whitman house in Farmington, Connecticut, reports that the house was published in Edwin Whitefield, *The*

Homes of our Forefathers (Boston: A. Williams, 1879); Norman Isham & Albert Brown, *Early Connecticut Houses* (New York: Dover Publications, 1965; reprint of The Preston and Rounds Company publication of 1900); and J. Frederick Kelly, *Early Domestic Architecture of Connecticut* (New Haven: Yale University Press, 1924). William Sumner Appleton and Wallace Nutting took an interest in the house. J. Frederick Kelly restored the house before it was opened as the Farmington Museum in 1935.

79   Kelly, *Early Domestic Architecture of Connecticut.* The book included an illustration of the drop pendant on the Stanley Whitman house, which was in the center of Farmington, the town just west of West Hartford. In 1935, Kelly, a New Haven architect, restored the Stanley Whitman house, and it has been open to the public ever since. The Gibb house presently has rusticated shingles on the second floor and roughcast on the first floor, and a round-headed dormer window in the center of the roof, which may or may not be part of the original design.

80   For Oscar Houston, a 30-year-old lawyer, whose parents lived with him and his young family, a two and a half-story frame house, 28 by 44 feet, with a garage, valued at $11,000 (1916) *RERG* 7/15/1916; for James Kelly, a 26-year-old real estate clerk, also two and a half stories but built in brick, 30 by 48 feet (1922) *RERG* 5/10/1922; for Angus MacDonald, a manufacturer who built a two-family house in the village of Great Neck (28 Old Mill Rd.); and a house for Charles Andrews, a city employee working in the water department.

81   *YAL* 1921.

82   The interior woodwork of the church was created by Frank Walter, of Long Island, who had recently completed the interiors of St. Bartholomew's Episcopal Church in New York City, where the Townes were members. Walter's grandson Spencer Smith believes that Olga Popoff Muller made clay portrait busts of Muller, his assistant, and herself for Walter to carve and that Walter made the wooden busts of Rossiter and the others in the church interior. Smith's informative website about his grandfather's work includes many color photographs of St. Michael's Church in Litchfield. www.frankwalter-woodsculptor-carver.com/StMichaelsLitchfield/Chapter10-4.html. Mr. Smith writes that the 1924 Episcopal church in Watertown was designed by Rossiter, but that church was designed by Allen & Collum of Boston.

83   Pamela Cunningham Copeland wrote about the church's obligation to build the parish house. The details of the parish house debate are in *St. Michael's Parish, Litchfield, Connecticut* by William Joseph Brewster; both records are in the archives of the Litchfield Historical Society.

84   The project was illustrated and described in *Architectural Record.* Edith Rossiter thought the firm also worked on Fox Meadow School in Scarsdale.

85   Frank Rossiter worked as a stockbroker in New York after graduating from Harvard. In 1907, "he was obliged to give up his business on account of ill health" and spent time in Washington, Connecticut, and Bermuda. He then

turned his hand to the lumber business in Vancouver, Canada. He married a girl from New Jersey and returned to the East Coast, where he became a golfing enthusiast. (Percival) Kensett Rossiter worked for a short time on a newspaper in Maine after graduating from Harvard. He went into the hardware business in Denver, Colorado, and then set up a poultry ranch near Los Angeles, California, where he raised a variety of birds, including ostriches. He wrote adventure stories about outdoor life for magazines, "with a keen feeling for the mystery and romance of the West," according to a reviewer in the *Pacific Monthly* in 1908. Later Kensett lived in White Plains, New York, where Ehrick lived the last years of his life. Edith Rossiter married William Bevan and wrote a number of genealogical and historical essays, particularly about architecture in the mid-Atlantic states. Winthrop was a civilian employee in military intelligence during World War I. Following graduation from Harvard with the class of 1918, Winthrop was admitted to the New York Stock Exchange. He and his wife lived in Washington, Connecticut, buying Edgewood, the home his father designed for Mrs. Baldwin, in 1934.

86 He may have traveled to Italy in 1903, according to The Ridge School newsletter.

87 I am grateful to Robert Rafford for locating this information on Rossiter's travels. Rossiter must have traveled to Europe on other occasions besides these trips, for which official travel records survive. He made a youthful trip after graduating from The Gunnery; he probably went to Europe after his marriage (when he applied for a joint passport with his wife); and he may have been among the family members who accompanied his son Kensett when the young man spent the winter of 1904 in Italy. That trip is noted in the *Ridge Record* class notes.

88 Two of the paintings remain in the museum collections—an Italian Old Master painting *The Triumph of the Cross Over Evil* and Victor Viollet-le-Duc's 1848 painting *Cliffs on the Coast of Normandy*. Thanks to Jonathan Walz, at the Cornell Fine Arts Museum at Rollins College, for this information.

Chapter Four

1 Fiske Kimball, "The American Country Home," *Architectural Record*, 10/1919, pp. 291-349.

2 At the same time, a factory foreman working in Waterbury, Connecticut, could purchase a new row house in the small city near Washington, with three bedrooms and a bathroom, for $1,800.

3 Nelson White, *The Life and Art of Dwight William Tryon* (Cambridge, MA: Riverside Press, 1930), p. 246.

4 Quoted in *Echo,* a booklet published by the Glen Haven Library, NY, 1897.

5 Dr. Safford Perry, who was a Rossiter client in New York City and Washington, CT, was also influential in the Glen Haven community. His wife was a member of the building committee for the Glen Haven library.

6 *Echo,* 1897.

Chapter Five

1 Jan Jennings also quotes Rossiter describing the "so-called Queen Anne, the Modern Queen Anne, or the Free Classic, to distinguish it from the English, as well as the truly grotesque examples in America," in the first edition of Rossiter and Wright, *Modern House Painting*, 1882. See Jennings, *Cheap and Tasteful Dwellings*, p. 140.

2 Rossiter and Wright, *Modern House Painting*, 1883.

3 Aymar Embury II, *One Hundred Country Houses: Modern American Examples* (New York: The Century Company, 1909). Embury listed a variety of styles popular in 1909: the New England Colonial, the Southern Colonial, the Classical Revival, the Dutch Colonial, the Spanish or Mission, the American Farm House, the Elizabethan, the Modern English, the Italian, the Art Nouveau (Craftsman style), and the Japanesque (found in California).

4 *Architects' and Builders' Magazine* 10/1910, p. 29.

5 Vincent Scully, for example, noted that the Cottage style of houses was integrated into the landscape (as published before the Civil War by A.J. Downing). The Gothic Revival was another pre-Civil War style, emphasizing steep pitched roofs, pointed arches, and board-and- batten siding.

6 Rossiter and Wright, *Modern House Painting*, 1883.

7 The drawing was marked Preliminary Study, and it is not certain that Gifford built the studio. A later photo of Gifford's studio appears to be a gabled shingle-covered building with second-floor porches.

8 It's not known whether this house was built; the rendering was published in the *Yearbook* of the Architectural League in 1890. An earlier house for the same client in Dallas was published in *AABN* 3/1/1884. Hughes was a veteran of the Civil War who settled in Dallas, where he founded a bank. He moved to Denver, Colorado, in 1898.

9 The illustration published in the *Yearbook* of the Architectural League looks as if it was inspired by the English Arts and Crafts style, with a roofline sweeping to the top of the first floor and white stucco walls; however, photos of the house as built establish that the massing is still very much in the earlier aesthetic.

10 J. Deming Perkins Collection, library of the Litchfield Historical Society, letters dated 8/5/1887 and 2/7/1888.

11 Rossiter's daughter believed that this house was an original eighteenth-century house that Rossiter & Muller remodeled, adding the two-story porch. The date of the original construction has not been determined.

12 Hepburn was also a big-game hunter, and some of his trophies were mounted in the dining hall of the dormitory, designated by the students the Hepburn Zoo.

13 Rossiter to Buehler, 5/27/1907.

14 Barbour inherited his father's house in Hartford in the 1890s and sold the Washington house to the Seccombs within a decade of its construction. The photos were taken by the new owners. The Seccombs' daughter Grace was married at the house in September 1896, and it's possible that the photos were taken then or following the family's remodeling of the house. Seccomb hired Rossiter to enlarge the house by extending the east wing. The dining room was expanded, and other alterations may have taken place during this time.

15 The interiors of the Carl Stoeckel house in Norfolk also include many of the same kinds of classical finishes, which may have been done during the remodeling of the house at the turn of the twentieth century. However, the details in Norfolk are much more elaborate than those in the other houses known to have been designed by Rossiter. The architect's daughter believed he was responsible for these changes in Norfolk, but no documentation has been located to confirm this, or alternately, to establish that this more elaborate work was done by another architect. The turnings on the stairway newel and balusters, however, are very similar to the ones in Rossiter's 1913 Stedman-Johnson house in Hartford.

Chapter Six

1 One architect who wrote about these principles was A.W. Cobb, in Comstock's 1893 book *Suburban and Country Homes*.

2 Embury, *One Hundred Country Houses*.

3 Ibid.

4 Forbes Morse, a son of friends of Rossiter's family, reported that Rossiter was a collector of Japanese and Chinese art as well as Whistler prints, which were influenced by the keen interest in Oriental aesthetics in the late nineteenth century. Forbes Morse interview, 1971, typescript in the archives of the Gunn Memorial Library, Washington, CT.

5 Siddons Mowbray requested these flowers from Rossiter's daughter for a 1914 charity event in Washington.

6 The contemporary writing on this topic is thoroughly reviewed in Jenning's book *Cheap and Tasteful Dwellings*.

7 We know, for example, that Albert Levi, who owned one of these houses, had two Irish servants living in the household in 1900.

8 Industrial advances in manufacturing and polishing large glass sheets were adopted in Pittsburgh by 1883. By 1895, the Pittsburgh Plate Glass Company was producing 20 million square feet of glass a year. Glass retailers advertised a variety of window glass in the Rossiter and Wright publication *Modern House Painting* in 1883, and in many of the architectural periodicals by the end of the century.

9 Jennings, *Cheap and Tasteful Dwellings*.

10 Embury, *One Hundred Country Houses*. Embury, a highly regarded architect and critic, designed the Litchfield retirement home of Henry Towne in 1915.

11 This house, for Edward D. Page, was published in Frederick Squires, *The Hollow Tile House*, New York: William Comstock Company, 1913, but since the house was credited to Rossiter & Wright, it was designed before the partnership was dissolved in 1910.

Chapter Seven

1 June 1943.

Selected Bibliography

Rossiter & Wright and Rossiter & Muller in Print

E. K. Rossiter and F. A. Wright. *Modern House Painting.* New York: William Comstock, 1882, 1883.

Reprint of the 1883 edition: *Authentic Color Schemes for Victorian Houses. Comstock's Modern House Painting (by) E. K. Rossiter and F. A. Wright.* Mineola, NY: Dover Publications, 2001.

Ehrick Rossiter. "Mr. Gunn as the Citizen," in William Hamilton Gibson. *Master of the Gunnery.* Gunn Memorial Association: The De Vinne Press, 1887.

——. *Washington's Journey through Litchfield County, 1780.* Litchfield County University Club, 1930.

——. *Winter Park Topics,* 3/7/1936; 3/28/1936.

Frank A. Wright. *Architectural Perspective for Beginners.* New York: William T. Comstock, 1882, 1883, 1896, 1904. Also published in six installments in *Building* magazine, beginning October 10, 1882 (vol.1, no.1).

——. *Architectural Studies I.* New York: William T. Comstock, 1885.

——. *Architectural Studies II: Store Fronts and Interior Details.* New York: William T. Comstock, 1885.

——. *Low Cost Houses, Store Fronts and Interior Details, Stables, Sea-Side and Southern Houses, Out-Buildings.* New York: William T. Comstock, 1886.

William T. Comstock. *American Cottages,* 1883; reprinted as *Country Houses and Seaside Cottages of the Victorian Era.* Mineola, NY: Dover Publications, 1989. Illustrations of cottages of several prices and the Baptist Chapel at Long Branch, NJ.

——. *Modern Architectural Designs,* 1881; reprinted as *Victorian Domestic Architectural Plans and Details,* by William T. Comstock. Mineola, NY: Dover Publications, 1987. Illustrations of House at Fairmont, NJ.

——. *Selected Details of Interior and Exterior Finishes,* 1890.

George William Sheldon. *Artistic Country-Seats,* New York: D. Appleton and Co., 1886-87; reprinted as *American Country Houses of the Gilded Age.* Mineola, NY: Dover Publications, 1982. Illustration of Rock Gate.

Frederick Squires. *The Hollow Tile House.* New York: William T. Comstock, 1913.

Architect & Builder, 1/14/1899; 3/25/1899; 6/25/1898; 7/2/1898; 3/1909.

Architecture and Building, 2/2/1889.

Architects' and Builders' Magazine, 3/25/1899; 1/1909; 3/1909; 10/1910.

Architectural Record, 7/10/1907; 10/1919, 1939.

The American Architect, 12/23/1914; 2/9/1916; 5/25/1921.

Architect and Builders Magazine, ill July–Dec., 1889.

American Architect and Building News [AABN]: 7/7/1877; 4/20/1880; 12/4/1880; 8/6/1881; 4/22/1882; 8/5/1882; 6/9/1883; 10/27/1883; 3/1/1884; 4/18/1885; 6/27/1885; 1/11/1885; 11/21/1885; 1/16/1886; 4/10/1886; 1/21/1888; 7/2/1893; 2/24/1894; 7/14/1894; 10/27/1906.

Brickbuilder, 9/1899.

The Builder and Wood-Worker, 6/1881; 8/1882; 6/1884.

Building, 4/1883; 10/1883; 5/1884; 3/3/1888; 7/28/1888.

Echo. Glen Haven, NY: The Glen Haven Library Association, 1897.

House and Garden, 6/1906; 10/1906.

Inland Architect and News Record, vol. 21, no. 5 [6/1893]; vol. 32, no. 5 [1898].

Manufacturer and Builder, 3/1882; 12/1882.

Newburgh Daily News, 3/18/1893.

Real Estate Record and Guide [RERG]: 5/12/1883; 3/15/1884; 4/19/1884; 4/26/1884; 8/16/1890; 5/13/1884; 7/26/1884; 9/20/1884; 11/15/1884; 12/31/1887; 4/22/1889; 6/29/1889; 12/27/1890; 7/7/1894; 10/27/1894; 1/24/1885; 9/21/1895; 10/26/1895; 11/16/1895; 9/19/1896; 10/24/1896; 11/7/1896; 11/21/1896; 4/17/1897; 5/29/1897; 9/11/1897; 9/25/1897; 10/16/1897; 11/23/1897; 2/13/1897; 1/8/1898; 1/29/1898; 4/2/1898; 4/23/1898; 6/25/1898; 7/16/1898; 7/23/1898; 7/30/1898; 8/13/1898; 10/8/1898; 11/12/1898; 1/14/1899; 2/4/1899; 2/18/1899; 6/24/1899; 3/3/1900; 3/21/1900; 4/21/1900; 5/9/1900; 5/16/1900; 7/14/1900; 8/16/1890; 12/1/1900; 12/15/1900; 12/22/1900; 6/15/1901; 7/23/1901; 8/24/1901; 10/26/1901; 11/23/1901; 3/15/1902; 4/12/1902; 10/18/1902/ 1/17/1903; 4/25/1903; 5/2/1903; 6/27/1903; 11/7/1903; 12/9/1903; 8/20/1904; 10/1/1904; 12/17/1904; 7/1/1905; 7/14/1905; 12/9/1905; 2/3/1906; 3/10/1906; 7/6/1907; 7/13/1907; 3/27/1908; 6/13/1908; 1/1/1910; 3/12/1910; 5/21/1910; 7/15/1916; 9/20/1919; 2/5/1921; 5/10/1922.

Scientific American, Building Monthly [SA]: 1/1883; 8/1890; 12/1890; 2/1891; 3/1891; 11/1891; 6/1892; 2/1894; 10/1894; 12/1894; 4/1895; 10/1896; 1/1897; 3/1898; 10/1900; 9/1901; 6/1902; 7/1903; 1/1904; 2/1904; 10/1910.

Yearbook of the Architectural League*[YAL]*: 1886; 1887; 1888; 1889; 1890; 1891; 1892; 1893; 1894; 1895; 1896; 1897; 1898; 1900; 1903; 1912; 1921.

Publications About Rossiter

Alison Gilchrist. *Return to Arcadia, Ehrick Rossiter's Washington; The Architect, His Clients, and Their Houses.* Washington, CT: Gunn Memorial Library and Museum, 1997.

Stephen Ketterer, *Rossiter. Country Houses of Washington, Connecticut.* Washington, CT: Gunn Memorial Library and Museum, 2006.

Scott J. Tilden. "Visions of Summer: Ehrick Rossiter in Washington, Connecticut," *The Magazine Antiques*, August 2007.

Extant Rossiter Architectural Drawings

Row houses, West 81st St., New York City, 1885. Levi Collection, Drawings and Archives, Avery Library, Columbia University

Headmaster's house, The Hotchkiss School, Lakeville, CT

Hepburn Libraries, Colton, NY and Madrid, NY

Stedman-Johnson house, Hartford, CT (fragments)

Norfolk projects, including:
residence for R.B. Stoeckel; bungalow for R.B. Stoeckel; office building for R.B. Stoeckel; sleeping porch for William Moseley; house, stable, and garage for George Case; house (with tea house) for Mrs. Helen Jenkins, 1910-13, second house for Mrs. Jenkins, 1916, gardener's cottage for Mrs. Jenkins, 1916; Norfolk Inn dining room addition; high school building; alterations and additions to residence for Edmund Brown, Norfolk Historical Society, Norfolk, CT; house alteration for Robert Wehner, 1931, Private Collection, Norfolk, CT

Battell Tower at Haystack Mountain, Connecticut State Department of Energy and Environmental Protection

Renovations to the George Lefferts house, Bedford, NY (at the design archives at the University of California, Berkeley, Reed drawings collection no. 63-68)

The Luther Birdsall drawings of Heathcote, Washington, CT are at Columbia University

Archival Collections

Thomas Pritchard Rossiter and Rossiter Family papers, 1840-1957. Archives of American Art, Smithsonian Institution. Collection donated by Edith Rossiter Bevan and Patti Rossiter Ravenscroft.

Avery Library, Columbia University

Alumni Archives, Cornell University, Ithaca, New York

Canterbury School, New Milford, Connecticut

Gunn Memorial Library and Museum, Washington, Connecticut

The Hotchkiss School, Lakeville, Connecticut

Norfolk Historical Society, Norfolk, Connecticut

Building Technology Heritage Library, Association for Preservation Technology International

Sterling Library, Yale University

Other Publications

A. W. Cobb. "Suggestions on House Building." *Suburban and Country Homes*. New York: William T. Comstock, 1893.

Faye E. Dudden. *Serving Women: Household Service in Nineteenth-Century America*. Middletown, CT: Wesleyan University Press, 1983.

Aymar Embury II. *One Hundred Country Houses-Modern American Examples*. New York: The Century Co., 1909.

Ann Havemeyer and Robert Dance. *The Magnificent Battells: An Architectural Legacy*. Norfolk, CT: Norfolk Historical Society, 2005.

Ann Havemeyer, Robert Dance, Barry Webber. *Picturing Norfolk 1758-1958*. Norfolk, CT: Norfolk Historical Society, 2008.

Jan Jennings. *Cheap and Tasteful Dwellings: Design Competitions and the Convenient Interior, 1879-1909*. Knoxville: University of Tennessee Press, 2005.

Lucy Maynard Salmon. *Domestic Service*. New York: MacMillan & Co., 1901.

Donald E. Sutherland. *Americans and Their Servants-Domestic Service in the United States from 1800 to 1920*. Baton Rouge: Louisiana State University Press, 1981.

ACKNOWLEDGMENTS

A number of individuals very kindly assisted in the gathering of information for this far-flung project, ferreting out records and images in town archives that only a local could navigate. I particularly want to thank Joan Baldwin, Joel Finn, Hugh Goodman, Alison Gilchrist, Ann Havemeyer, Mary Jo Kenny, Esther Swift, Chris Woods and David Kensett Rossiter for their shared enthusiasm and kind help on many levels.

A number of librarians, town historians, archivists, and researchers also responded helpfully to my requests, and I am grateful for their speed and courtesy. Gregory Wessner, The Architectural League of New York; Carole Ann Fabian, director, Paula Gabbard, librarian, Erin Schreiner and Jason Escalante, all at the Avery Architectural and Fine Arts Library, Columbia University, New York City; Stephanie Coleman, Ryerson & Burnham Libraries, The Art Institute of Chicago; Evelyn Ryan, director, Bedford Historical Society, Bedford, NY; Christina Rae, assistant to the Bedford Town Historian, Bedford, NY; Bev Mosch, Bethlehem, CT; Esther Munroe Swift, librarian and archivist, and David Miles, Billings Farm & Museum, Woodstock, VT; Mrs. Peter Paul Muller, Bridgehampton, NY; Laura Tosi, Bronx County Historical Society, Bronx, NY; Marc Vanasse, Canterbury School, New Milford, CT; Russell Flinchum, The Century Association, New York City; Nancy McCarthy, Dennis Eickhoff, librarians, Hepburn Library, Colton, NY, and Mary Jane Watson, Hepburn Library, Colton and Raquette River Blueway Corridor Advisory Committee; Alan Levere, Connecticut Department of Energy and the Environment; Nancy Finlay, curator of graphics, Connecticut Historical Society, Hartford; Jan Jennings, Professor of Design and Environmental Analysis, Cornell University, Ithaca, NY; Elaine Engst, University Archivist, Cornell University, Ithaca, NY; Diane Hassan, Danbury Historical Society, Danbury, CT; Joann Schwendemann, Dover Publications; Carolyn Emerson, reference librarian, and Joan Kahnhauser, Emma Clark Memorial Library, Setauket, NY; Margaret Smith, archivist, Episcopal Diocese of Connecticut, Hartford, CT; Bill Fairbairn, Washington, CT; Charlie and Alice Anderson, Charles Jermy, Jr., Lauren Jastremski, and Sue Randolph of the Glen Haven Historical Society, Homer, NY; John Edwards, Grove Street Cemetery, New Haven, CT; Stephen Bartkus, Gunn Memorial Library and Museum, Washington, CT; Paula Krimsky, archivist, The Gunnery School, Washington, CT; Fran Keilty, Hickory Stick Bookshop, Washington, CT; Stephen Doell, head of archives, Historical Society of Western Pennsylvania, Pittsburgh, PA; Caroline Duroselle-Melish, assistant curator, Houghton Reference Library, Harvard University, Cambridge, MA; Debbie Bock, Head of Reference, Johnson Public Library, Hackensack, NJ; Cathy Fields, director, and Linda Hocking, archivist, Litchfield Historical Society, Litchfield, CT; Rachel Carley, architectural historian, Litchfield, CT; Geri Solomon and Victoria Aspinwall, Long Island Studies Institute, Hofstra University, Hempstead, NY; Robert Rafford, genealogist, Middlebury, CT; Randall Gabrielan, Middletown Town Historian, NJ; Nancy Rogers, director, Millbrook Library, NY; John Foreman, Millbrook, NY; Lynne Ranieri, Millburn-Short Hills Historical Society, NJ; Gail Hunton, Principal Historic Preservation Specialist, Monmouth County Park System, Lincroft, NJ; Mark Stewart, Monmouth Hills, NJ;

Diana Waite, president, Mount Ida Press, Albany, NY; Lacy Schutz, Museum of the City of New York; Christine Messing, archivist, National Register of Historic Places and National Historic Landmarks, National Park Service; George Fisher, Nassau County Photo Archives Center, Old Bethpage Village, NY; Mary Jane Blasdale, New Bedford Whaling Museum, New Bedford, MA; Stephen Lasar, New Milford, CT; Terry Karschner, Historic Preservation Office, State of New Jersey, Trenton, NJ; William Krattinger, New York State Office of Parks, Recreation and Historic Preservation; Barry Webber, Norfolk Historical Society, CT; Stephanie Wiles, director, Allen Memorial Art Museum, Oberlin College, Oberlin, OH; Denice Given, museum assistant, Port Jefferson Historical Society, NY; Marcia Rossiter Palmeri; Karen Stone Yannett, Rye, NY; Kay Ables, Town Historian, Ridgefield, CT; Jack Sanders, Ridgefield, CT; Sean O'Kane, Ridgefield, CT; Jonathan Walz, interim director, Cornell Fine Arts Museum and Darla Moore, archival specialist, at Rollins College, Winter Park, FL; Lane Poor and Ward Poor, Shelter Island, NY; Gene Yacobuski, Skytop Lodge, Bucks Hill, PA; David Dempsey, associate director, Louise LaPlante, registrar, Nancy Young, archivist, all at Smith College Museum of Art, Northampton, MA; Robert Mackay, director, Society for the Preservation of Long Island Antiquities, Cold Spring Harbor, NY; Lindita Cani and Michael Pucci, South Orange Public Library, South Orange, NJ; Jean Henry, Charles Henry, and Sylvia Abbate, Southbury, CT; Tod Bryant, Southport, CT; JeanMarie Martello, Archivist, St. Lawrence County Historical Association; Eva Garcelon-Hart, Stewart-Swift Research Center Archivist, Henry Sheldon Museum, Middlebury, VT; Karen Martin, Three Villages Historical Society, East Setauket, NY; Miranda Hambro, assistant curator, Design Archives, University of California at Berkeley, CA; Robert and Virginia Reynolds, Washington, CT; Hans and Louise Van Tartwijk, Washington, CT; Patrick Raftery, librarian, Westchester County Historical Society, Elmsford, NY; Miriam Varian, Local History Librarian, White Plains Public Library, White Plains, NY; Frank Greenagel, Wooden Nail Press; Robyn Christensen, librarian, Worcester History Museum, Worcester, MA; information services staff, Sterling Library, Yale University, New Haven, CT; Joan Jennings, Yonkers Historical Society, Yonkers, NY.

With skill and patience, Louise Johnson and Arthur Foote and their associates at KatArt Graphics enhanced the musty images and challenging page layouts as the book came together. Editor Suzi Arensberg coped gracefully with the densely detailed citations and the lingo of architectural history.

I am grateful to all who helped bring the pieces of this puzzle together. Especially Joel.

INDEX

Barbour, Lucius A., 44, 123, 206. See also *Rock Gate.*

Barnes, Alfred, 31, 42.

Barnes, Richard, 42, 44, 47, 123, 192. See also *Westlawn.*

Billings, Frederick, 28-31.

Billings, Frederick, Jr., 31, 87, 214. See also *Royalton.*

Black, William and Sarah Sanford, 39, 111, 124, 198 n. 36. See also Churches/All Saints Church and Schools/Ingleside School.

Buehler, Huber Gray, 76-78, 106, 108, 176-177, *177*, 184-185, 187. See also Schools/The Hotchkiss School.

Churches: Baptist Church, Atlantic Highlands, 34, 36; Church alterations, Liberty, NY, 84; St. Michael's Church, Litchfield, CT, 99-100, *99-100*, 142, 203 n. 82 and 83; Baptist chapel, Long Branch, NJ, 34, 36; Netherwood, NJ, *34*, 119; All Saints Church, New Milford, CT, 39, *40*, 140, 142, 187; Amity Baptist Church, NYC, 90, *90*; Presbyterian church, Oceanic, NJ, 140; Hillside Presbyterian Church, Orange, NJ, 57; Union Church Society, Ridgewood, NJ, 58; Presbyterian Church, South Orange, NJ, *35*; Presbyterian and Trinity Church, South Orange, NJ, 35, 140; Swedish church, Washington, CT, *46*, 46; St. John's Church, Washington, CT, 99, *99*, 142; Worthington Memorial Chapel, Irvington-on-Hudson, NY, 28, *30*, 126, 140. See also 193 n. 37 for more on the New Jersey churches.

Clubhouses: Orange Mountain Club, Orange, NJ, 57, *58*; Washington Club, Washington, CT, 68, *68*.

Color and architecture: Queen Anne Revival, 19-24, *21-24*, 52; Colonial Revival, 139-140.

Commercial projects: apartment flats and stores, East Orange, NJ, 57; Central Paper mill, Dutch Kills, NY, 83; projects in lower Manhattan, 85-86, *86*, 186; two apartment buildings in Manhattan (by FA Wright, after 1910), 91; commercial building, Rutherford, NJ, 58; commercial building, Scarsdale, NY, 98.

Connecticut: Bridgeport, 80, 94, 98, 176, 200; Danbury, 80, 200; Farmington, 202, 203; Greenwich, 46; Hartford, 96-97, *96*, 111, 140-141, 150-153, *153-154*, 185, 176, 187, 206; Lakeville, 73, 76-78, *77*, 108-112, 132, *132*, 137-139, *138*, 150-154, *151, 153*, 158, 176-177, *177*, 179, 184-185, 187, 199, 205; Litchfield, 46-47, *47*, 73, 78-79, *78-79*, 99-100, 112, 117, 128-130, *129*, 134, 135, 129-130, *130*, 142 n. 45-49, 203, 205, 206 n. 15, 207; New Haven, 97-98, *97*, 141-142, *141*, 176-

177, *177*, 185, 187; New Milford, 38-39, *40*, 66, *66*, 80, 124, *135*, 135, 137, 140, 142, 187, 198; Norfolk, *67*, 73-76, *74-76*, 112, 119, 125-126, 132, 135-136, *136*, 138, 142, *142*, 158, 187, 198 n. 38-39, 199, 205, 206, 219 endpapers; Orange, 98; Ridgefield, 46, 79-80, *80*, 134, 158; Southport, 94-95, *95*, 107, 178, 185; Washington, 38-46, 64-73, *65*, *67-73*, 112, 119, 123-126, 128, 131-134, *130-131*, *134*, 136-139, 142, 146-150, *146*, *148-149*, 150-151, *156-157*, *156-158*, *159*, 167-68, *169*, 181, 185, 188-189, 192, 194 n. 52, 206; West Hartford, 98.

Cooperative apartments: 130 E. 67th St, NYC, 88-89, *88*, 174, *174*, 186; 901 Lexington Ave., NYC, 90, *90*, 128, 133, 186.

Cottage designs, *24-27*, 121-122, 161-165, 181.

Fireproof houses, 57, 95, 178-179, *178-179*.

Floorplans, 160-177; principals of "convenient arrangement", 160-161; cottages, 161-165, *162-165*; Fairmount, NJ, 165-166, *165*; FA Wright house, South Orange, 166, *166*; Fairview, Red Bank, NJ, 166-167, *167*; The Rocks, Washington, CT 167-68, *169*; Van Kirk houses, Pittsburgh, PA, 170-171, *170*; Row houses at 81st St., New York City, 171-172, *171*; Mountain Station, NJ, 172-173, *173*; cooperative apartment buildings, New York City, 174, *174*; Headmaster's house, The Hotchkiss School, Lakeville, CT, 176-177, *177*; Cheney house, New Haven, CT, 176-177, *177*.

Gardens: 156-158, The Rocks, Washington, CT, 156-157, *156-158*, 206 n. 4; The Gables, Washington, CT, *159*.

Goodview, Wright home in Short Hills, NJ, home of Frank A. Wright, 55, 58, 59, 126.

Gunnery School, Washington, CT, 12, 38-39, *39*, 68, *68*, 112, 137, 198 n. 35.

Hepburn, A. Barton, 79-80, *80*, 92-94, 134, 139, 200 n. 50, 205 n. 12. See also Libraries/Hepburn Libraries.

Interiors finishes, 143-154, *144-149*, *151-154*.

Kirby Corner, cover, 71, 72, 133, *134*, *148-149*.

Libraries: Burlington, VT, 28-31, *31*; Hackensack, NJ, 59, *60*, 127, 140; Hepburn Libraries (Colton, Madrid, Edwards, Hermon, Norfolk, Waddington and Lisbon, NY) 92-93, *92-93*, 139, 202 n. 76; Homer, NY, 84, *84*, 107; Setauket, NY, 83, *83*, 126, 128; Washington, CT, 64-65, *65*, 139, 150.

Modern House Painting, 18-24, 143.

Studios: R. Swain Gifford, *27*, 119; Dwight Tryon, 27, 130.

Stoeckel, Carl and Ellen Battell Terry, 74 76, 111-112, 135, 158, 206 n. 15

Texas: Dallas, 124, 205.

Utilities for modern living, 180-185.

Van Ingen, Edward, 44-46, 128, 132, 194 n. 49-51.

Vermont: Burlington, 28-29, *31*, 126; Middlebury, 93-94, *94*, 139, 187, 205; Woodstock, 30-31, 135.

Village Hall, South Orange, NJ, 35, 56, *57*, 126, 128, 187.

Virginia, Jamestown (Exposition), Connecticut State Building, 78-79; *78*, 99, 129-130, 135.

Warner, Ira De Ver, 85, 86, 94-95, 107, 178.

Westlawn, Barnes' home in Washington, CT: 42, *43*; 47, 123, 168-169, *169*, 181, 192 n. 25.

Wright, Frank Ayers, *16*, 28, 31-33, 91, 117, 128, 191 n. 2, 195 n. 2, 196 n. 13; biography, 16, 32-33; education, 16; residence, in NJ, 32, 195, 196, Short Hills: *59*, 205, at South Orange, 35, *35*, 123, 144-145, *145*, 166, *166*, 181, residence at Water Witch, NJ, 55, *61*; family, 33, 192 n. 27.